D0059425

brilliant orange

brilliant orange:

the neurotic genius of dutch soccer
david winner

with a new introduction by
franklin foer

the overlook press
woodstock & new york

For:
Dad, who taught me to love football,
Mum, who taught me to love art
and Hanny, who taught me to love Holland.

This edition first published in paperback in the United States in 2008 by
The Overlook Press, Peter Mayer Publishers, Inc.
Woodstock & New York

WOODSTOCK:
One Overlook Drive
Woodstock, NY 12498
www.overlookpress.com
[for individual orders, bulk and special sales, contact our Woodstock office]

NEW YORK:
141 Wooster Street
New York, NY 10012

Copyright © 2000, 2002, 2008 by David Winner
New introduction copyright © 2008 by Franklin Foer

All rights reserved. No part of this publication may be reproduced or
transmitted in any form or by any means, electronic or mechanical,
including photocopy, recording, or any information storage and
retrieval system now known or to be invented without permission in
writing from the publisher, except by a reviewer who wishes to quote
brief passages in connection with a review written for
inclusion in a magazine, newspaper, or broadcast.

Library of Congress Cataloging-in-Publication Data
Winner, David.
Brilliant orange: the neurotic genius of Dutch soccer / David Winner.
p. cm.
Includes index.
1. Soccer—Netherlands—History. I. Title.
GV944.N4 W57 2002   796.334'09492—dc21   2001055486
Manufactured in the United States of America
1 3 5 7 9 8 6 4 2
ISBN 1-59020-055-1

contents

In the spirit of Total Football, chapter numbers are not sequential – think of them instead as 'squad numbers'.

introduction to the paperback edition

franklin foer

In the United States, we encase the heads of three hundred pound men in plastic and send them to run at one another with the impact of a car crash; in England, one of the national pastimes is interrupted for tea; in Basque country, people recreationally run down narrow streets with enraged bulls in pursuit. How could such bizarre practices possibly be meaningless?

But for many decades, intellectuals considered it just that. They scoffed at the notion that sports could tell you anything about a nation's culture and sociology. Fortunately, that form of academic snobbery has steadily collapsed, beginning with C.L.R. James's great study of cricket in the 1960s. It took a Marxist like James to overcome the Marxist notion that sports sedated the revolutionary masses.

And in this new intellectual environment, it's soccer that has provided intellectuals with the richest subject. That's because soccer is a kind of sporting Galapagos filled with an astonishing array of species. The Italians have catenaccio, their brand of defensive-minded soccer that has yielded some of the most mind-numbing matches known to mankind. Reflecting their stiff-upper lip ethos, the English have historically practiced a style where the ball is booted into the attack from long distance, often with only a slim hope of success, and is chased down by dint of gritty effort. And there's the samba style of the Brazilian game, with its rhythmic passing and capoeira-like dribbling.

Of course, these are cheap, tired clichés. But they are also more than a little true, especially in those moments when the game is on the line and players for some reason resort to atavistic methods. And despite decades of globalization, these styles persist—although the differences between them are, in fact, diminishing.

When writers mine this rich material for broad conclusions about national character, the results are more often than not horrific exercises in pretension. There's a long shelf of dreadful books in this genre. And this brings us to David Winner's *Brilliant Orange*—one of the most thrilling meditations on the meaning of sport that I have read.

Winner, of course, starts with a tremendously appealing subject: Dutch soccer. There's a reason that so many American fans of the game have chosen to support the Dutch, as their second-favorite national squad (or even, in some instances, their first). The Oranje play a charming style, full of dynamism and offense. It's a style that even has a name: Total Football. And, in the 1960s and '70s, it revolutionized soccer, creating an entirely new paradigm and handing the world exhilarating players, the likes of Johan Cruyff, Johan Neeskens, Ruud Gullit, and Marco Van Basten.

Why are Americans so attracted to Holland's national team? I think it's because American soccer fans—who tend to lean liberal— are predisposed to liking the country itself. The reasons for this are manifold: the ubiquity of legal pot, the spirit of tolerance, the output of Rembrandt, Van Gogh, and Mondrian. I've always liked Holland because, in my idealized version, it represents the best that bourgeois society has to offer: a genuine liberal spirit, the epitome of a certain idea of civilization. It was the Dutch who constructed the modern notions of the individual and truly set the enlightenment in motion. (Spinoza came from Amsterdam, not Edinburgh or Paris.)

And the great trick of Winner's book is how it relates the loveable qualities of Dutch soccer to the loveable qualities of Dutch society. Mondrian and Dutch liberalism and Cruyff are of one piece. Reading his book, you find yourself concluding that Total Football is the ultimate product of Dutch Civilization. You'll need to delve into the pages that follow to watch Winner's intellectual high-wire act and to come away convinced by this thesis. But I encourage you: You may have read some of these other books that try to interpret a nation through its sports, and that may prejudice you against Winner. But don't let those biases prevent your enjoyment of *Brilliant Orange*.

Winner isn't a native of Holland, but he has immersed himself in the country. And the result is a penetrating combination of an outsider's detachment and an insider's familiarity. I was reminded of this as I re-read Winner's book along side another important book about Dutch society, Ian Buruma's *Murder in Amsterdam*. Buruma's book is about a much more obviously weighty subject, the murder of the filmmaker Theo Van Gogh. It was a killing, of course, carried out by a radical Muslim, who sought holy retribution against Van Gogh for his hostile film on Islamic attitudes towards women. Buruma tells his tale as a parable for the shock that immigration has caused to the Dutch system. A society that had congratulated itself for its tolerance was suddenly gripped by xenophobia and populist backlash.

It is striking how, in the course of telling his tale, Buruma keeps returning to the soccer stadium. Soccer never directly enters into the tale of the Van Gogh murder. But Buruma, like Winner, believes that soccer proves an indispensable device for understanding Dutch society. In his view, the game has moved beyond metaphor. It has come to represent a kind of religion for the Dutch people. Indeed, it has superseded any faith grounded in God. And what are the qualities of this new religion? According to Buruma, they are not all appealing: racism, kitsch, nostalgia.

You see hints of this in Winner's book, which was first published several years before Buruma's effort. Between the publication of these two books, Europe changed greatly. It has been further integrated into a coherent union; it has undergone a period of simultaneous prosperity and anxiety over its multicultural future. But that so much has changed does nothing to mitigate that power of Winner's account. *Brilliant Orange* elucidates the underpinnings of the society that is in the midst of so much change-you begin to grasp the reason why it might respond with such passion to its new environment.

As soccer has become grist for political and culture analysis, there are new risks. While past generations of intellectuals may have invested soccer with too little meaning, the current generation may invest it with too much. And here, too, Winner's book is a welcome respite. For all its discussions of landscape paintings and Jewry and liberalism, it is, in the end, a book about a game, a game that he explains with clarity, and the Dutch approach, which he renders in all its poetry.

Franklin Foer is Editor of *The New Republic* and the author of *How Soccer Explains the World: An Unlikely Theory of Globalization*. His writing has also appeared in *Slate*, *The New York Times*, *The Wall Street Journal*, *The Atlantic Monthly*, *Foreign Policy*, and *Spin*. He lives in Washington, D.C.

introduction

If this is a book about Dutch football, at some stage you'll probably wonder why it contains pages and pages about art and architects, cows and canals, anarchists, church painters, rabbis and airports, but barely a word, for example, about PSV and Feyenoord. A very fair point. And the reason, I suppose, is that this is not so much a book about Dutch football as a book about the *idea* of Dutch football, which is something slightly different. More than that, it's about *my* idea of the idea of Dutch football, which is something else again.

Ever since I was a small child, I've had the feeling there was something special and great about the Dutch. I was offered one possible reason for this when I went to look at an apartment in the Rivierenbuurt district of Amsterdam last year. My prospective landlady turned out to be a bit of a psychic, and informed me I had had a past life – or lives – there. 'Don't you recognise any of this?' Well, no, actually . . . but she might be right. A more straightforward explanation is that when I was about six my sister and I were looked after by a Dutch au pair called Hanny. She was warm and fun and wonderful and I formed the impression (which I now understand may not be 100 per cent true in every case) that all Dutch people must be warm and fun and wonderful. They certainly all had to be very brave, living as they did below the sea and protected at times only by a small boy with his finger in a dike.

The first time I heard of Ajax was in 1971, when I was fourteen. The team, apparently named after a brand of scouring powder, played

Panathinaikos in the European Cup final at Wembley, and a Greek school friend who went to support the Athens club came back awed. 'We didn't have a chance,' he said. 'That Cruyff! God, he's good.' The next year my club, Arsenal, met Ajax in the European Cup. During the build-up to the first game in Amsterdam, the British press was full of stories about this strange-sounding wonder-team and their star player, who sounded quite a lot better than George Best. Such games weren't televised live, but no pictures could have impressed me more than the BBC's radio commentary by Maurice Edelstone, who marvelled at the billiard-table perfection of the Olympic Stadium pitch and made it clear that Arsenal were up against a team infinitely more sophisticated and skilful than their own. In the return leg, on the mud-patch that was Highbury, Arsenal barely got to touch the ball, and Cruyff and co seemed to be playing a different game entirely.

Ajax's final against Inter Milan in Rotterdam a couple of months later was carried live on TV, and by then I was hooked. Ajax played with a gorgeous, hyper-intelligent swagger. They ran and passed the ball in strange, beguiling ways, and flowed in exquisite, intricate, mesmerising patterns around the pitch. They won 2–0 but it could have been five or six. Ajax were like beings from a quite different, more advanced football civilisation. They were warm and fun to watch. They were clearly wonderful.

A year later I visited Amsterdam for the first time (in this lifetime, anyway), it being the final stop of a month-long InterRail trip round Europe with my best friends, Nick and Trevor. We slept – of course – in the Vondelpark, which was full of bedraggled, dopey hippies and thus deeply cool. (This was 1973, after all.) In a restaurant on the Rokin we employed a favourite scam, involving the three of us ordering a single Coke and then scavenging left-over food from the plates of other tourists as they left. I for one had much more important things to do with my few remaining pounds: I was desperate to buy an Ajax shirt. When I asked a policeman for directions, he sweetly drove us in his patrol car to a sports shop on the other side of the city. I mentioned I was a fan of Arsenal, thinking he might have heard of them. The policeman shook his head and shrugged his shoulders. 'Who?'

At around this time the great Ajax team seemed, for obscure reasons, to break up, but for the 1974 World Cup a year or so later the players got back together and swapped their fancy white and red shirts for orange ones. They were even better now, not least because the slow-moving Feyenoord star Van Hanegem was part of the team. The 'Total Football' the Dutch played that month in Germany was extraordinary. How could anyone have imagined and executed something so dazzling? I adored the Dutch team for both the spectacle they provided on the field and their air of relaxed wisdom and sophistication off it. They apparently stood for some cultural ideal, though what that was I wasn't sure. And they were so smart. When Rinus Michels or Johan Cruyff, Arie Haan or Ruud Krol appeared on English television or in newspaper interviews, they were always fluent and fascinating. They spoke intelligently in several languages, while English players struggled with one. The Dutch all seemed so very . . . what's the word? . . . Dutch.

Somehow Holland lost the final to West Germany. Just as the appeal of *Romeo and Juliet* lies in its lovers not living happily ever after, so I'm sure my obsession with Dutch football would run less deep were it not for that defeat. The Dutch had come close, but missed the great prize. Also my fascination was based mainly on what I saw on TV, which produces its own distortions. Over the years as other Dutch teams came and went – all generally following the model of the great Ajax and the class of '74 – playing their singularly Dutch style and developing a weird habit of blowing important matches, I adopted them in the way football fans do. I came to know the Dutch and their footballers better and love them more. In idle moments I fell to wondering what made the teams tick. What made them the way they were? What was Dutch about them? When they played beautifully, what exactly were they doing? Why did Dutch football look so different from everyone else's football? Why did they so often screw up at the vital moment in the biggest competitions? In the 1990s I started trying to teach myself Dutch in order to find out what the

Netherlanders said to themselves about their football. I saw Holland's football as a mirror to – and the most interesting expression of – its culture. I began to write occasional pieces of journalism about it. The more I researched, the more I understood, but also the more I was confused. With my cousin's Dutch husband, in 1997 I got the chance to translate Frits Barend and Henk van Dorp's collection of interviews with Johan Cruyff. The key personality of the phenomenon of Dutch football, Cruyff spoke not in grand philosophical sweeps but in brilliant details and riddles. 'Every disadvantage has its advantage', 'The game always begins afterwards', 'If I wanted you to understand it, I would have explained it better' . . .

Then, in 1999, I finally got the chance to live in Amsterdam – the city of Ajax, the heart and soul of Total Football – and look at Dutch football and the culture that produced it. I concentrated on the subjects that mystified and fascinated me – the stuff that had always seemed just out of reach. As a teenager, I'd been close enough to the great Ajax and the great Dutch team to become transfixed, but I wasn't close enough to *see* them. Essentially, I'd missed the whole thing because I never saw them in person. When I started talking to former players and coaches, it quickly transpired that they were still out of reach: separated now by time rather than distance. The later generations of players, including that of Gullit, Van Basten and Rijkaard, are much less mysterious to me – thanks to satellite television and the internationalisation of global football culture, I've seen large chunks of their careers. There's relatively little in this book about them. I haven't looked much at the famous Dutch youth system, either, largely because the subject has been well covered by others.

Whereas I had planned to write a conventional history, the book instead evolved into a series of connected obsessional investigations into the things that most appealed to me: why the best Dutch football looks the way it does; its neurotic shortcomings; the key moments of its history . . . I hope that along the way I've managed to convey some of my love for and fascination with both the Dutch and their football.

David Winner, Amsterdam, 2000

5: breakthrough

'Everyone needs to football'
Roel van Duyn, former Provo anarchist

Not so long ago Amsterdam was one of the most frumpy and
tedious capitals in Europe. This takes some imagining: Amsterdam's
present image as a cosmopolitan world city luxuriant with sensuality
and sin, beauty and sophistication is merited. But that most
philosophical of goalkeepers, Albert Camus, spent time in the
Dutch capital during the 1950s and found it hatefully dreary.
'For centuries, pipe smokers have been watching the same rain
falling on the same canal,' he wrote in *The Fall*, published in 1955.
'Have you noticed that Amsterdam's concentric canals resemble the
circles of hell? The middle-class hell, of course, peopled with bad
dreams.' Where the canals are now thronged with Japanese tourists
and pungent with the whiff of marijuana, Camus smelled only 'the
breath of stagnant waters, the smell of dead leaves soaking in the
canals, and the funeral scent rising from the barges loaded with
flowers'. He even found Dutch beds detestable: 'so hard and with
their immaculate sheets – one dies in them as if already wrapped in a
shroud, embalmed in purity.' Camus was a literary tourist, am-
bience-chasing for his next novel. The experience of actually living
in Amsterdam was even less fun, especially for the postwar 'baby
boom' generation coming to maturity at the turn of the decade.
'We were so, so bored,' remembers Max Arian, of the left-wing
weekly *De Groene Amsterdammer*. 'Amsterdam is known now as a
very sexy, good-looking city. But it wasn't at all sexy then. It was
desperately dull. The whole country seemed so limited and old-

fashioned, boring, unimportant and grey, a puritan little country, guilt-ridden, sombre and Calvinist.' Rudi van Dantzig, a dancer who later became director of Holland's national ballet, confirms Arian's assessment: 'Life was terribly boring and heavy. The music and everything in culture was very heavy.'

As it was with society, so it was with football. At the beginning of the 1960s, Dutch football – which within a decade would be considered the most innovative and sophisticated in the world – was startlingly unrefined, amateurish and tactically crude. In 1959 a young physiotherapist called Salo Muller went to Ajax and discovered that the treatment facilities comprised one wooden table and a horse blanket. When he asked Austrian coach Carl Humenberger and the resident Dr Postuma for permission to buy a modern treatment table, they looked at him as if he was mad. 'They said: "Come on, Salo, don't poison the atmosphere. We've been doing it for fifty years on this table",' says Muller. 'Postuma was a general physician and a doctor in the boxing ring. He was from Groningen in the north. Very strong people, hard for themselves and for others. When a player went to him, he'd say: "Come on, it's not broken, so get on with it. Take an aspirin!" He said to me: "When I played, we had to paint the lines on the pitch ourselves. We put up the goals and the flags and everything. So don't talk about luxury." '

Professionalism in football was first permitted in the mid-1950s. Before then, talented Dutch players were mostly obliged to play abroad – and then punished at home for doing so. One of the era's greatest players was Faas Wilkes – the 'Mona Lisa of Rotterdam' – an inscrutably elegant striker and phenomenal dribbler (and the boyhood idol of Johan Cruyff). Along with Abe Lenstra and Kees Rijvers, Wilkes, who had learned his football playing on the streets of Rotterdam, was part of a 'golden trio' of genuine stars. But when he signed in 1950 for Internazionale in Milan, he found himself banned from the Dutch national team for four years. After the disastrous floods in Zeeland and western Holland in 1953, the country's best footballers played a benefit match against the French national team in Paris. This was, however, done in the face of official opposition from the Royal Netherlands Football Association (KNVB). (One of professionalism's fiercest enemies had been the thick-necked patrician Karel Lotsy, trainer of the national team prior to World War II and KNVB chairman between 1942 and 1952. Lotsy was renowned for his thunderous and pompous half-time speeches at important football matches on themes such as duty and patriotism; and in 1979 it was revealed by journalists Frits Barend and Henk van Dorp that during the war Lotsy had collaborated with the Nazis and excluded Jews from Dutch football even before the Germans demanded it.) The Paris match helped force the KNVB's hand, and professionalism was finally permitted in 1954. Yet many clubs remained staffed primarily with amateurs or part-timers and were amateurish in outlook as a result.

Tactically, the Dutch were decades behind the best. The Hungarians had dazzled with a deep-lying centre-forward; the Brazilians had conquered the world with 4–2–4; and the Italians were developing the ultra-defensive *catenaccio* system. Dutch clubs still employed the WM formation (2–3–5), and postwar international results demonstrate its failings. By 1948 coaching dogma in Holland had yet to incorporate the notion of defensive, 'stopper' centre-halves of the kind invented by Herbert Chapman in the 1920s. (Until the early 1960s, in fact, many Dutch teams played with only two defenders.) At Huddersfield in that year Holland were crushed 8–2: England's big centre-forward, Tommy Lawton, was left unmarked to score four goals, and later marvelled that he'd 'never had so much room'. Lawton was not marked because Holland were occasionally able to beat fellow minnows, such as Belgium, Norway and Denmark, and in 1956 beat West Germany on a snowy pitch in Dusseldorf. That in particular was a freak result. In 1957 Holland lost 1–5 to Spain; Turkey beat them 2–1 in Amsterdam in 1958; and the following year West Germany thrashed them 7–0. Hans Kraay, a member of the Feyenoord and Dutch national teams in the 1950s, says: 'We were simply not grown up like the Italians, Spanish or French at that time. We were blue-collar kids, working class, and mentally and psychologically we were not good enough to be good at that moment. We had the talent and the football possibilities, but the personality wasn't strong enough – and the way of life. We were too timid. We were not people of the world yet.'

In the early 1960s everything changed. 'We were the most backward country in all of Europe, except for Ireland. Absolutely backward, especially in the participation of women in the workforce, which was the lowest in Europe,' says Hubert Smeets, a political and cultural commentator for the broadsheet *NRC Handelsblad*. 'Then we experienced a cultural, political and social revolution, with Johan Cruyff as the main representative, and we became one of the most forward, one of the most progressive, countries in Europe.'

With hindsight it is easy to identify some of the contributing factors to Holland's cultural and social upheaval. In wider society the country's infrastructure had been restored after the war, the safety-net of a complex welfare state had been set up and the economy began to boom. As the British class system wilted in the 1960s, so the traditional divisions of Dutch society – Catholic, Reformed, Socialist and so on – rapidly crumbled in the wake of new prosperity. As the prewar generation aged, a generational tension was building. After twenty years of peace, there were unparalleled opportunities for international cultural cross-pollination via the new mediums of television and pop music. For Karel Gabler, a flamboyant and moustachioed former youth-football coach who grew up amid the ruins of Amsterdam's old Jewish district, the 1960s seemed like an eruption of colour into a world of monochrome. In Amsterdam, he says, the first stimulus for change was the movie version of Leonard Bernstein's *West Side Story*. 'We saw it ten or twelve times. You thought, my God there's something else! Then the Beatles came, and all those other groups, and the radio stations – Veronica, Caroline, Radio London, Mi Amigo. And suddenly there were Beat groups around every corner, and the best thing was that the old people didn't like any of it!' Holland's booming economy presented the opportunity to appreciate fully the new world on offer. 'Many youngsters suddenly felt in a kind of paradise. Our eyes were opened; there was more freedom. There were lots of new businesses where you could work on a Saturday, or you could do a paper round so you had money in your pocket. Before, young people had to give their money to the household, but now we could keep it, and we used it to buy records and tickets to football matches, and mopeds when we were sixteen . . .' Televised horrors from America also made an impression. 'The murder of President Kennedy was one thing, but then we saw the killing of Lee Harvey Oswald. With all your family, you saw those things broadcast live from Texas. The old people said only in America. But me and my friends thought it could be happening here, too. It was almost glamorous because it was vivid. Suddenly you saw that life wasn't always as safe as we in Holland thought. There were no guarantees for life and greyness; there was adventure in it. Jack Ruby meant the world was dangerous and interesting.'

In September 1962 there was a national scandal following public revelations about a student corps in Amsterdam. Membership of the corps was obligatory; new students were inducted by older members at what were jokingly called 'Dachau parties'. Initiation rites often involved the new recruits being doused in beer and having their heads shaved. In February 1963 a Nijmegen student called Ton Regtien wrote an article protesting against these practices and attacking the compulsory membership of the corps. A national students' union was launched and became a huge success. By June 1963 Holland's student world was transformed. The old corps was secretive, conservative and reactionary; the new union was leftist, open and alternative. It campaigned for better grants, accommodation, help for poorer students and, later, democracy in the universities. In December 1962 Amsterdam witnessed its first 'happening', poet Simon Vinkenoog's 'Open the Grave' event in which he prophesied that 'the victory over the old ways begins in Magic Centre Amsterdam'.

★   ★   ★

At Ajax, meanwhile, Salo Muller had eventually won his new treatment table; and despite old-fashioned tactics and administration arrangements, by 1965 many of the ingredients for revolutionary Total Football were in place. Although Dutch players were still amateurish, they were also skilled. Ajax in particular had a tradition of intelligent attacking football dating back to World War I and credited to Englishman Jack Reynolds – or *Sjek Rijnols*, as the Dutch refer to him. Reynolds began his undistinguished playing career in 1902 as a Manchester City reserve, and later turned out for Grimsby Town, Sheffield Wednesday and Watford, before coaching Grasshoppers of Zurich and the Swiss national team. In August 1914 he was due to take over as coach of the German national team, but war broke out, so he instead sought safety in Holland. There he coached Ajax for twenty-five years in three spells between 1915 and 1947. The club's tradition of attacking, skilful, quick-passing football played with wingers began with the *gouden ploeg* (golden team) Reynolds built around temperamental genius Jan de Natris. Reynolds's strict discipline, and training that emphasised technique and passing as well as fitness, transformed the then minor East Amsterdam club and propelled it to national importance. According to an unpublished biography of Reynolds by historian Harke Groenevelt, in the 1920s he laid the foundations of the Ajax youth system, working from eight every morning until ten at night coaching teams of every age group in the same style. 'For me, the attack is and remains the best defence,' Reynolds declared in a rare interview in 1946. In the 1930s, the club proclaimed its aesthetic or objectives with a little poem: 'Open game, open game/you can't afford to neglect the wing'. The *Volkskrant* newspaper praised Ajax's 'technically controlled' game, ball skills and tactics: 'Ajax comes close to the English professional game and lacks only the spirit that English teams have.'

Reynolds later had a stand at the Ajax stadium named after him, and his methods and philosophy have set the precedent for all subsequent Ajax trainers. Jany van der Veen, the youth coach who discovered and nurtured the talents of Johan Cruyff, Barry Hulshoff and others, still regards him as the greatest trainer Ajax have ever had. Rinus Michels played under Reynolds in the late 1940s and learned much from him, though he later dismissed his training regime as old-fashioned.

A second Englishman, the late Vic Buckingham (a former Tottenham player), also helped prepare the ground for Ajax's Total Football when he was appointed coach in 1959 for the first of two spells. Later, Buckingham would be the first Ajax man to take over at Barcelona, thus beginning a trend that was followed by Rinus Michels, Cruyff and Louis van Gaal (though Buckingham was the only one to spend six years in the RAF and coach the football blues of Oxford University). The legendary Bobby Haarms, assistant coach at Ajax for thirty-three years, remembers Buckingham as a gentleman, fine tactician and tough disciplinarian, 'but if he smiled at you, you knew you were on the bench'.

'Football is a serious game but an elegant game,' Buckingham told me when I spoke to him in 1993. Unlike most English football men of his and future generations, Buckingham prized thought and skill. 'Possession football is the thing, not kick and rush. Long-ball football is too risky. Most of the time, what pays off is educated skills. If you've got the ball, keep it. The other side can't score. I liked to have people who could dominate other sides playing like that.' He was impressed by Ajax's set-up, philosophy and young talent. 'Dutch football was good. It wasn't a rough-tough, got-to-win-things mentality. They were gentlemen. Ajax was an institution. You had the Ajax stadium and more than twenty football pitches outside it. Every week there were fourteen or fifteen matches going on . . . Johan Cruyff was one of the players I saw out there – I thought, "He's a useful kid".' Compared to English football, Buckingham found the Ajax style refreshing: 'Their skills were different, their intellect was different and they played proper football. They didn't get this from me; it was there waiting to be stirred up – I don't know what they did before me – it was just a case of telling them to keep more possession. I've always thought possession is nine-tenths of the game, and Ajax played possession football. It was lovely. I used to just sit back and relax. After a game I'd think: "Crikey, that was good". It was real stingo stuff. I influenced them, but then they went on and did things above that which delighted me. For instance, two of them would go down the left side of the field passing to each other – just boom-boom-boom – and they'd go thirty yards and two men would have cut out three defenders and created a vast acreage of space. I'd never seen that done before.

'They really were an amazing side. You only had to give them an idea; they added skills, movements and combinations all the time. They'd get into threes and fours without really knowing they were doing it. They were playing "habit football" after a time, and habit football was star football. They could find each other by instinct. They'd have a rhythm; go from the left side of the field to the right side of the field but make progress of thirty or forty or fifty yards as well. Keeping the ball all the time. You have to have a lot of skill to do that, and we trained all the time on it.' Buckingham's thoughtful words may seem familiar – particularly to anyone who's read some of Cruyff's quirky observations on football. He continues: 'To make a good football team, you need a mixture of good players who get on mentally and physically. It's about thought in football. When you see a big fellow going into a tackle, don't go and help him. That's a good player's instinct. If you're good, you know the big fellow will win the ball – and he does. So you've saved that fraction of energy you would have wasted helping him.'

Buckingham's Ajax won the Dutch title in 1960 and scored hattuls of goals in the process – an average of 3.2 per game. Against Feyenoord in the famous championship decider of that year they won 5–1. 'I thought they were the best team in Europe, even then. Ajax were always my favourite club and I think, without being big-headed, I was their favourite manager.' He also later formed a deep bond with the young Johan Cruyff. 'He was one who immediately struck a chord with me, as if he was my son. He was on his own and he showed us how to play. He was so mature. He was such a skinny little kid but he had such immense stamina. He could run all over the field. And he could do everything: set movements up, fly down the wing, run into the penalty area, head the ball in. Left foot, right foot, anything – and such speed. God's gift to mankind, in the football sense. That was Johan. And such a nice kid as well.'

Under Buckingham's supervision, Ajax could play delightfully, but they still used a form of old-style 'WM' and they made no more international impact than previous Dutch sides: in Buckingham's single season in the European Cup, Ajax lost in the first round to Norwegian champions Fredrikstad. On 15 November 1964 the manager gave Cruyff (then aged seventeen) his first-team debut for Ajax in an away game in Groningen. Ajax lost 1–3. A week later, Cruyff made his home debut at De Meer against PSV and scored in a 5–0 win. A week after that, though, Ajax crashed 4–9 away to Feyenoord, a result that put the skids under Buckingham – favourite manager or otherwise. Ajax were perilously close to the relegation zone, and on 21 January 1965, the day after drawing the Amsterdam derby with DWS, Buckingham was sacked.

Across the city a cultural revolution was coming to the boil. Throughout the Western world the relatively affluent and independent-minded youth of the postwar baby boom was generating a mood of cultural, moral and political change. Nowhere, though, was youth rebellion fuelled by so surreal, anarchic and theatrical a sense of playfulness as in Amsterdam. Max Arian's first memory of 'uprising' was on Liberation Day in 1965: 'We heard there would be dancing on the Leidseplein. Thousands more people went than there was space for, so we were stuck in a side street, a huge crowd of us. We started shouting "*Wij willen Bolletjes!*" ["We want our Bolletjes!"] which was an advertsising slogan for a kind of breakfast snack. Thousands of bored young people chanting this absurd phrase! It was our party, our rebellion!' The principal catalyst of the new mood was Robert Jasper Grootveld, a self-styled anti-smoking 'magician' and voodoo showman. In 1964, Grootveld began to attract large audiences to his weekly anti-tobacco 'happenings' at the K-Temple, an old garage behind the Leidseplein. 'K' stood for *kanker* (cancer) and Grootveld (to relieve the general tedium, he later explained) was waging a one-man war against what he saw as modern enslavement to consumer society, as epitomised by tobacco products. He vandalised cigarette ads with a giant letter K and in his temple every Saturday night, dressed as a shaman, he performed weird anti-smoking rituals while the crowd chanted 'Bram bram! Ugga ugga! Bram bram! Ugga ugga!'

Regulars at the K-Temple included a writer called Johnny the Selfkicker, who talked himself into a trance and threw himself from high places, and a 'half doctor' called Bart Huges, who tried to achieve a state of higher consciousness by drilling a hole in his forehead to create a 'third eye'. 'On the streets mysterious graffiti began to appear: "Gnot", "K", "Klaas comes", "Warning". Magic had a magnetic appeal in a city that was so busy with practical matters, building flats and ramming poles into the ground . . . something was blowing in the wind, and the rickety garage-Temple was full every week,' wrote Geert Mak in *Amsterdam*, his history of the city.

The K-Temple was destroyed in late 1964 in a fire lit by Grootveld himself. Later, he moved his weekly Saturday night show to the Lieverdje, a small statue of a street urchin, which had been donated to the city by an American tobacco company in 1960.

This statue (which, incidentally, bears a striking resemblance to the young Johan Cruyff), situated in front of what is now the Athenaeum bookshop on the Spui, became the venue for a weekly ritual that transformed the city. By the summer of 1965 Grootveld's shows were the focus for a new group, the white clad Provos, Amsterdam's archetypal 1960s anarchists, who mixed surreal anti-authoritarian pranks with anti-consumerism and loopy techno-optimism. The Provos looked upon playfulness – *ludiek* in Dutch – as the key to a better world. The Provo writer Constant Nieuwenhuys laid out this much-quoted vision for a 'New Baby-lon': '. . . a world city of leisure and creativity, spreading in all directions, and developing the globe like a net, 50 ft above ground level, leaving the ground for agriculture, nature and highways.

Under New Babylonic circumstances the lust for aggression in mankind will be sublimated into a lust for playfulness . . . This is the only alternative for mankind if it is not to be wiped out by wars . . . The mechanised world of cybernetics and automation will leave much leisure time, and in this free time, a man will establish his own settlement in collective creativity.'

As early ecological activists, the Provos came up with idealistic 'White Plans', the most famous (though never implemented) being Luud Schimmelpeninck's White Bicycle Plan for free bikes all over the city. The White Chicken Plan ('chicken' in Dutch being slang for police) envisaged police in white uniforms handing out chickens to the poor, orange juice to the thirsty and lights to people wanting to smoke a joint. But the Provos were mainly out to have fun by provoking the bourgeois establishment. Their best-known leader, Roel van Duyn, said: 'We are more likely to see the sun rise in the West than the outbreak of a revolution in the Netherlands . . . Here and now we cannot be much more than insurrectionaries. Even as an insurrectionist here you can bash your head to pulp against the granite wall of bourgeois pettiness. The only thing we can resort to is provocation.'

The street around the Lievertje is partly pedestrianised now, but in 1965 it was one of the city's main thoroughfares. Each Saturday night Grootveld, the Provos and crowds of youngsters gathered near the Cruyffish statue and attempted to perform *ludiek* magic on it. Police efforts to break up the gatherings, which technically infringed traffic regulations, were invariably heavy-handed: baffled by a game they didn't understand, they usually resorted to hitting people. In one famous incident a Provo girl called Koosje Coster was arrested and strip-searched, then spent several days in the cells for handing out raisins. 'The police were so helpful because they tried to repress the silliest things,' recalls Max Arian. 'It was a perfect example of how Holland was at that moment.' Geert Mak says the Provos had a 'perfect feeling for images and symbols . . . gratefully recognised by the new medium of television, which only served to multiply the effects of their actions. While they demonstrated, dressed in white and carrying a white banner, the police could be seen in the background waiting to beat them up. The authoritarian and brutal appearance of the police stood in stark contrast to the playful innocence of the Provos. It was a case of the old versus the new, the 1930s versus the 1960s. It was as if these happenings were a last flowering of the resistance, a delayed reaction to the liberation. Twenty years after the war, something really was about to change.'

Ajax were already undergoing a revolution of their own – one that was concerned with football and fuelled by Cruyff's genius and the passionate (and in Holland unprecedented) drive for modernisation and development of their new coach, Rinus Michels.

Vic Buckingham remembered Michels as 'a nice boy, intelligent and well educated'. Over the years he would be called other things, too: 'The Bull', 'The General', 'The Sphinx'. Michels's former team-mate Bobby Haarms, later his assistant, remembers him as an easy-going artist on the pitch with a taste for practical jokes off it. Between his days as a player and joining Ajax as coach in 1965, Michels had studied at the Amsterdam sports academy, taught gymnastics in an Amsterdam school and coached the small amateur club JOS. 'I remember thinking: he's changed,' says Haarms of their reunion. 'He was completely different from when he was a player. The main thing with him was now discipline. Fantastic discipline. Even with the assistant coaches he was like an animal trainer. But he was also like a chess master in football tactics and he had not lost his great sense of humour.' Michels's first job was to save Ajax from relegation. Winger Sjaak Swart recalls: 'In his first game, we played against MVV Maastricht. We won 9–3 and I scored five goals, so I cannot forget Michels's first game as trainer. After that we had a team.' This seems a tad unfair to Buckingham, who had taken over from yet another Englishman, Jack Rowley, with a weakened team at the start of the season. Early results were awful, but the week before the Feyenoord thrashing, Ajax beat PSV 5–0. Of Buckingham's last seven games in charge, Ajax won four, drew one and lost two, scoring twenty-one goals and conceding thirteen (nine of them at Feyenoord). Of Michels's first twelve matches, Ajax won three, drew five, lost four and scored sixteen to thirteen. Yet the MVV match made Michels's early reputation, and Ajax avoided the drop. And the next season they won the Dutch League.

These days the ebullient Michels, at seventy-two, wears a small hearing-aid and his face is noticeably thinner and more concave than it used to be. He suffered a major heart attack during Holland's 1998 World Cup semi-final against Brazil. Nevertheless, he stands ramrod-straight and his pale blue eyes still blaze. In 1965 he was a driven man who wanted victory but who had no precise plan of how to achieve it. 'In starting, you have no exact ideas about the aims you are going to strive after,' he explains. 'The first thing was to get an impression of the material, the quality, and to get an idea about the team spirit, which was very bad at that time. Ajax was in a very bad position, so the first thing I had to strive for was to get in a better position in the League. To do that I especially needed to change the team spirit and I had to change the team tactically, the quality of the team. That meant some essential guidelines, which I developed with the team and executed in the training sessions week after week. That was the first development. The second was to start to find a better balance of the team, to find some key players to improve the performance of the team. Of course, the team-spirit development, the team's tactical development, that just went on. Now I had a few players who were of better quality. At the end of that season we arrived at the aim I posed at the beginning: to become champions.'

Michels tightened the defence and introduced new training methods which, according to Sjaak Swart, were imaginative, intensive and far more intelligently focused than they had been previously. 'As players, we liked it very much,' he says. 'The only thing most trainers at the time were interested in was running ten kilometres every day. [With Michels] there was some running, in the woods every Tuesday, but it was only two kilometres and with

exercises. And we did everything with the ball. At the beginning of
the season we had one week of very hard training: five training
sessions a day. It was like a military camp. Training started at seven
o'clock in the morning. We were not allowed eat or drink anything
yet, and you better not try it because he would see it. He had spies
everywhere – the assistant trainers would be watching for him.
Then at ten-thirty we had an hour and a quarter of a conditional
training. That was good, short work designed specially for football
players. Sprinting, gymnastics – a very good programme. After that
we could eat. And in the afternoon, at half past two, training with
the ball. Because I was outside-right, for example, I would work on
crossing the ball for the centre-forward. And passing, those sorts of
things. But it was also conditional: many sprints to the line. I was
never allowed to just stand and cross it. At five o'clock we played
five-a-side with goalkeepers and man-to-man. If you didn't play
well, you were off. If I was playing against you and you scored two
goals, he'd take me out of the game.'

As a man who had worked under Jack Reynolds, Michels was
instinctively wedded to the Ajax doctrine of relentless attack. With a
forward line including Piet Keizer, Cruyff, Sjaak Swart and Henk
Groot, Ajax could hardly fail to score goals. Michels adopted the
Brazilian 4–2–4 system, and played with the combative Bennie
Muller and the technical, left-sided Klaas Nuninga in midfield.
Off the field he made a more important innovation: at the end of
his second season Michels went to the Ajax board and persuaded club
chairman Jaap van Praag and patron Maup Caransa to guarantee the
players' wages. Until this point, even star players had jobs during the
day and trained at night. Cruyff did odd jobs at the printing works for
Sport World (he even sold the magazine on the street); Piet Keizer was
a tobacconist; Swart had a shop. Now players trained during the day
and had evenings free. Michels noted the motivational potential of
the new set-up. 'I like this new way,' he told Bobby Haarms at the
time. 'The boys know they have to do their best because otherwise
they have to go back to their lousy jobs.' Now, he reiterates the point
of changing tactical balance within the team: 'I was looking within

the organisation and playing style of Ajax. I needed a few better players. One of the most important I found, who had played for Ajax before, was Henk Groot. Sometimes only one or two players who affect the balance mean the big difference between struggling and becoming champions. After that I started to think about reaching international recognition. That meant automatically that we had to go from semi-pro to become professional players, otherwise you cannot compete at that level. That was the third aim I strived for in my first three years.'

Professional recognition was of particular importance to Johan Cruyff, who had by this time become a standard-bearer for a generation of Dutch youth – and not simply because he was instrumental to the new way of playing football. Cruyff was an electrifying presence on the pitch, and even in his first two years he demonstrated an originality and insurrectionary quality to which young Amsterdammers responded. He had also begun to realise his own worth. Karel Gabler explains: 'Cruyff was a kind of model for us, like John Lennon maybe was in England. He talked with a logic our whole generation had. He realised he could make money, but also that his career could finish. He knew he had a lot of talent which people would like to pay for and liked to argue all the time – his famous words were: "When my career ends, I cannot go to the baker and say, I'm Johan Cruyff, give me some bread."'

When playing for the national team was considered an honour, Cruyff insisted on payment. When he discovered that KNVB officials were insured for foreign trips but players were not, he demanded – and eventually forced – a change. In his second international, against Czechoslovakia, he was sent off for allegedly striking the referee. When the KNVB subsequently banned him from Ajax matches but not from internationals, he fought them on that, too, pointing out that it was at Ajax that he earned his money. Gabler: 'Cruyff got into all kinds of conflicts because he started asking the question that the whole generation was also asking: "Why are things organised like this?"'

*   *   *

The high point of Provo influence came in 1966, two years earlier than the *événements* that convulsed Paris in 1968 but similar in impact. In Holland, though, revolution was more cultural than political – and was never followed by a Gaullist, Nixonian or Thatcherite backlash. The pivotal moment came when Princess (now Queen) Beatrix announced plans to marry in Amsterdam a German aristocrat called Claus von Amsberg who had served in the Wehrmacht. Republican-minded Provos and students tapped into popular anti-German sentiment and sowed wild rumours of their plans to disrupt the ceremony. They would put LSD in the water supply or feed it to the horses pulling the royal wedding carriage. Or lion dung would be smeared on the streets to panic the horses. Or laughing gas would be pumped into the church from the organ. On 10 March, the day of the lavish wedding, the TV-watching public saw their screens turn white as Provo smoke bombs went off at the Raadhuisstraat. The police, as was now their custom to do, waded in and started beating people up – much to the shock of the TV audience. While Beatrix and Claus exchanged vows, riots raged.

Three months later the capital once again convulsed as communist workers and Provos momentarily joined forces. When workers took to the streets over holiday pay, the protests led to more fights with police around the Dam. One worker, Jan Weggelaar, died of a heart attack. When *De Telegraaf* claimed the dead man had been hit by stones thrown by his colleagues, new riots erupted outside the newspaper building. The authorities panicked, declared a state of emergency and brought in 1400 national and military police.

British anarchist Charles Radcliffe made a day-trip to Amsterdam just after the riots, and in an article published in a Provo pamphlet captured the mood of the city at this time of change: 'The airport is dull and provincial and it is difficult to believe anything can ever really have happened here . . . The recent riots add a curiously ambiguous touch to Amsterdam's essentially placid, patient nature. The town seems full of kids, police and promenaders. To a

Londoner everything seems to move at half-speed; people have time to walk and talk in the streets . . . For someone increasingly stoned sky-high on possibilities (and no longer sure whether it will all end in social outrage or nervous collapse), Amsterdam is perhaps the most beautiful city in Europe. Not only well planned but, almost overnight, the capital of the youth rebellion. The kids are the most self-assured I have seen anywhere. They have little of the Londoners' sullenness and the rebellion is much more extroverted. They move around in loose gangs or else storm through the streets in twos and threes on bicycles and mopeds. Amsterdam is designed for the guerrilla warfare of provocation . . . The town is full of Beats and the extraordinary decadent Dutch "Mods" decked out in fantastic floral suits. There is a fantastic impression of tranquillity to which the riot police moving around town in small micro-buses add a strange, distorting effect. Kids do not take very much notice. They seem slightly elated by the continuing concern of the authorities as to whether they will explode again.'

Following an inquiry into the summer riots, Amsterdam's mayor, former resistance leader Gijs van Hall, and the Amsterdam chief of police, Van der Molen, were sacked. This was the point at which the Dutch authorities stopped trying to fight the tide and instead began to flow with it. Within a couple of years the Amsterdam police acquired the reputation as the most easygoing in Europe, and the authorities, anxious, as US academic James Kennedy argues, to be seen to be moving with the times, looked on indulgently as hordes of bedraggled foreign hippies turned Dam Square and later the Vondelpark into giant camp-sites. Amsterdam became a city for the artistic, and the sex, drugs and rock'n'roll capital of Europe. In 1969, in a bid for world peace, John and Yoko went to bed for a week at the newly built Amsterdam Hilton.

Without police to hit them, the Provos meanwhile rapidly became irrelevant. (Under the slogan 'Vote Provo – for a laugh!' they won a seat in the Amsterdam City Council 1967 but soon disintegrated.) Hans Righart, professor of modern history at the

University of Utrecht, observes: 'The Dutch élites had learned their
lesson: during the remaining years of that turbulent decade, they
proved to be legitimate heirs of the Dutch tradition of accommodation and pacification. The Dutch had had their May '68 in June
'66, be it in a moderate and therefore typically Dutch way. The rest
was afterplay.'

Ajax achieved their own breakthrough in a foggy Olympic Stadium
in Amsterdam on 7 December 1966, when they played Bill
Shankly's Liverpool in the first leg of the second round of the
European Cup. England had just won the World Cup. Liverpool –
with Ron Yeats, Ian St John, Tommy Lawrence and Peter
Thompson – were imperious; no one in England had heard of
Ajax and the match was considered a pushover for Shankly's men.
Liverpool wore their customary red; Ajax, whose usual change-
colours comprised blue shorts or shirts, played for the only time in
their history all in white. After three minutes, Cees de Wolf tore
down the left wing and crossed for Henk Groot to beat goalkeeper
Lawrence with a header. It was the start of a rout. As Karel Gabler
recalls: 'Everyone respected Liverpool and we were amazed by the
things that happened in that first forty-five minutes. We were
standing at the wrong end of the ground. We didn't see the first four
goals. It was like a mystery. We had to yell to the fellow who was
behind the scoreboard, "Sir! They scored another goal!" He said,
"Come on, boys, don't make up stories!" This fellow couldn't
believe that Ajax had kicked in three goals in fifteen minutes.' After
about forty-five minutes of the first half had been played, Sjaak
Swart heard the referee's whistle, assumed it was for half-time, and
ran straight down the players' tunnel near him by the touchline.
'What are you doing?' asked a steward. 'The game is still going on.'
Swart ran back onto the pitch, received the ball immediately, darted
down the wing and crossed – providing the fourth goal. The match
finished 5–1.

   After the game, an unchastened Shankly predicted a 7–0 Liverpool win at Anfield in the second leg. The Ajax players believed

him. Hulshoff, who played centre-back, recalls: 'We had won five at home but we were still afraid to go to Liverpool. Shankly had said: "Don't worry, we will still beat them." And we were afraid – because of the crowd, because we had never had a good result like that against English teams before. This was the first time we beat a big team. Tactically we were very strong, especially defensively. And we had a very big talent. I played against Ian Callaghan. I had problems for the first fifteen minutes: I didn't see him; he got away from me every time. But after, it was no problem. We played very well.' At Anfield Cruyff scored twice and Ajax held out easily for a 2–2 draw, despite an aggressive crowd and intimidating atmosphere. Michels: 'The Liverpool game was for me an important moment to be acknowledged and recognised internationally. Not only the first game, because that could have been an accident – with the weather conditions etc., etc. No, the performance we achieved in Liverpool under bad circumstances – I've never seen such a hectic situation. We drew that game 2–2 and never really had problems. For me, it was the proof that we were at the international level.' More than that, it paved the way for the creation of Total Football.

Was there a connection between the cultural and football revolutions? Apart from the fact that the football and cultural revolutions happened in the same place at the same time, none at all. Footballers and anarchist revolutionaries alike have always denied any connection whatsoever between each other. Roel van Duyn went on to lead the Kabouters, an ecological party (named after the Dutch word for gnome), which eventually disintegrated over ideological differences in 1971. These days he sits on Amsterdam city council for the Greens. 'Everyone needs to football, but what is Ajax?' he said – gnomically – when I asked him if there might be a connection between the Provos and Total Football. Barry Hulshoff, central defender in the great Ajax team of the late 1960s and early 1970s (and its only progressive rocker), is adamant there's no link. 'The only connection was the music. The boys doing those other things? I didn't care about them. I didn't think about them. I was playing football and I did everything for football. You couldn't do something else. I had my music! Very extreme music, I had. No one in the team liked my music. They preferred pop music like the Beatles . . . [makes face].'

Yet there are those for whom a connection is obvious. Rudi van Dantzig of the Netherlands Ballet draws this parallel: 'Before the sixties, people were interested in theatre and music and literature but not dance. And then all of a sudden came this intense interest in bodily virtuosity: in football and dance. The theatres were suddenly full and there was a fanatical following for dance. The young generation didn't want a grey society any more. You could feel this explosion of being alive and kicking and moving. Of finding our feet, throwing off the old restraints. In a way, we discovered how small Holland was. But we also realised we could make it in the world. Football became international at that time too. We didn't make the connections then, but I think we were all doing the same thing in different ways. Now I realise how similar the goals were. Nureyev came to Holland because things were happening here that were happening nowhere else.'

Psychoanalyst and novelist Anna Enquist sees the period as transitional for everyone: 'People in the sixties were liberating from the fifties – which were so terrible. After the war, everybody had to work so hard. And football was liberated too. It has something to do with playing seriously. Play suddenly becomes a valuable thing, something to talk about, study, take seriously.' Maarten Hajer, professor of public policy at Amsterdam University, adds: 'The connection is a new liberal attitude towards authority. They were revolutionary players, these guys, extremely charismatic. People like Van Hanegem, Cruyff and Ruud Krol, Wim Suurbier. Rinus Michels was obviously an authoritarian figure but even he could not really control them. Cruyff was running the whole thing. He had these bizarre counter-intuitive ideas that were so brilliant that people followed his lead. In their attitudes to the games they were very liberal. When they get the football together, they have a combination of the system and the individual skill with a very high level of individual capacity.' Hubert Smeets says Cruyff was not a Provo but was infinitely more important.

In 'Cruyff gave form to the Netherlands', an essay written for a special edition of the Dutch literary football magazine *Hard gras* marking Cruyff's fiftieth birthday in 1997, Smeets argued that the footballer was far and away the most important rebel, icon and symbol of the 1960s. He explains: 'Johan Cruyff was the first player who understood that he was an artist, and the first who was able and willing to collectivise the art of sports. In that way he was a typical baby boomer. But he did more than only provoking the establishment by having long hair or listening to pop music or drinking too much. He was always a very family man, a religious man. He was never a Provo just willing for fun to provoke the establishment.'

And Cruyff did provoke the establishment – to the limits. He destroyed the hierarchy of the Dutch game. He destroyed the position of the club board. For example, he refused to play in the boots stipulated under the contract the KNVB had signed with Adidas and played instead in Puma. (During the 1974 World Cup he even wore a shirt with only two stripes across the shoulders instead of Adidas's trademark three.) Cruyff was also the first to understand that playing for the Dutch national team was important not only for him but also for the Netherlands. And while his ideals with regard to making money were not entirely altruistic, they can be traced nonetheless to the core values of the 1960s. 'In Cruyff,' Smeets continues, 'you can see both sides of the sixties and both sides of the baby boom. On one side he was against the backwardness of the establishment, and on the other he was rather aware of personal interests. He was not like a yuppie in Thatcher's London. On one side he was altruistic; on the other he was really aware of the new, upcoming neo-liberalism in which money played a role and success was a moral category. In 1971, when everyone was leftist, he said: "I don't want to be a thief of my own pocket. I don't want to steal from myself." He understood both aspects of the sixties. He was not trying to provoke his parents. He was a man in his own right.' Smeets adds that despite his relatively short formal

education, by the age of seventeen Cruyff was 'the most intelligent
player in the team. And he was already able to lead and manage it
without abstract knowledge of the sixties and seventies, without any
political motives. The sayings of Cruyff are strange but sometimes
very beautiful. He said: "Every disadvantage has its advantage." If
you want to be intellectual, you can say that is dialectics in its most
pure form.'

It always struck me that Cruyff is not simply the best-known
Dutch person alive – he's also probably the most important. How
many Dutch politicians can you name? Not many, I'll bet. But
Dutch footballers are known and adored around the world –
Cruyff most of all. Smeets sees him as the main representative of
his generation in the Netherlands. 'All the other guys are of
absolutely no importance. In industry there are no serious baby
boomers; the prewar generation still runs this country. But in sport
he set the tone. He made it clear that to achieve something in
sport you have to combine individualism with collectivism. In a
way, this was the main programme of the sixties. All the others
went too far one way or the other. Collectivism ended in
communism and all that kind of left-wing stuff. Many individu-
alists lost themselves in India or Nepal. Only Johan Cruyff was able
to combine both things and still is trying to combine both things.'
Moreover, Cruyff always understood there had to be a hierarchy
on the field which had to be led by the most important creative
player, as he had been, and as Marco van Basten became in 1988.
'If you read the management theory bullshit from business schools,
you see those kinds of ideas as axiomatic. That is now seen as the
way to manage a company.'

Cruyff was instinctively able to develop further ideas which
were at the core of the postwar economic Dutch miracle. Cruyff
was anti-system but, paradoxically, he had a system: one based on
creative individualism. Of his successors who created their own
rigid football systems – people such as Louis van Gaal – few seem
to have understood this. 'The Dutch are at their best when we
can combine the system with individual creativity. Johan Cruyff is

the main representative of that. He made this country after the war. I think he was the only one who really understood the sixties.'

7: totality

'Michels was the architect of this football. And I helped him the most'

Velibor Vasovic

Before Dutch Total Football there was Dutch total architecture. In the first decades of the twentieth century the wildly expressionist exponents of the Amsterdam school of architecture, responsible for much of the city's extraordinary look as it grew rapidly in the wake of the country's belated industrialisation, came up with the idea of the city as a total work of art. The school's leader, Michel de Klerk, designed strange, fairytale apartment blocks and houses featuring billowing curved brickwork, exotic statuary, soaring towers and oddly angled courtyards. He argued that every separate element of the city – from the carpets, cutlery and furniture in people's homes through to bridges, street lamps and entire buildings – should be seen as part of one unified concept. This sometimes posed problems. Some of the school's most stylish buildings were better at looking good than at keeping out rainwater (an early example of leaky Dutch defences). However, where the Amsterdam school succeeds, the effect is spectacular: carefully calibrated explosions of geometric pattern and art deco extravagance into one grand design. Total City. This architecture also provided the physical context for Ajax's football. A minor member of the school but a prominent member of the Ajax board was Dan Roodenburgh. When the club decided to move in 1934 from their old wooden stadium to a purpose-built brick and concrete home on the Middenweg in the south-east of the city, Roodenburgh designed De Meer in a restrained version of the school style. Anticipating the Ajax school of football by some four decades, the Amsterdam school of architecture found a way to marry collective discipline to individual creativity. This is especially visible in the Old South district of which the centrepiece is Jan Wils's Olympic Stadium, which was originally built for the 1928 games and later became the venue for Ajax's most important home matches. H. P. Berlage, father of modern Dutch architecture, laid out a strict, almost chilly blueprint for the entire district, notable for its large apartment blocks and wide boulevards. Yet space was also allocated for personal invention and free-wheeling artistry. Almost every building is strangely adorned: human and animal faces over doorways; anchors in the walls; Egyptian friezes; monkeys and vultures staring at each other across the pavement; curved walls; nooks for plants in odd places; decorated brickwork on every corner. And in typical Dutch fashion, every wacky detail had to be submitted for approval to a special commission.

As Total Football began to evolve in the 1960s during Rinus Michels's revolution at Ajax, Dutch designers and architects were coming up with Total ideas of their own. In 1963 the doyen of Dutch designers, Wim Crouwel, launched his Total Design studio. At around the same time Holland's most celebrated and original architects, the so-called structuralists, were rebelling against the dreary precepts of functionalism and modernism with open-hearted but efficient, flexible, aesthetically playful buildings that abolished rigid hierarchies. 'All systems should be familiarised, one with the other, in such a way that their combined impact and interaction can be appreciated as a single complex system,' said key structuralist Aldo van Eyck, talking about modern cities but sounding uncannily as though he might be laying down a template for the Ajax football system. Herman Hertzberger, the last of the great structuralists still living, says of the need for flexible buildings, 'Each form must be interpretable in the sense that it must be capable of taking on different roles. And it can only take on those different roles if the different meanings are contained in the essence of the form.'

The ultra-aggressive style of football in which players switched positions and rained attacks from every angle was invented at Ajax in the late 1960s. It was not until 1974 that the word *totaalvoetbal* entered the Dutch language, used as it was to describe the Ajax-style football played by Holland's national team in that year's World Cup. Also in that year J. P. Bakema, colleague of Hertzberger and Van Eyck in the influential Team 10 and *Forum* magazine, passionately advocated a 'Total' approach: 'Total Urbanisation' and 'Total Environment' and 'Total Energy'. 'A man has three life questions: What am I? Who am I? Where am I? In this period of Total use of earth and space, balance between use and care can only be given by Total Architecture.'

In December 1966 Total Football was still some way off. Following their remarkable demolition of Bill Shankly's Liverpool, Ajax's next European Cup match was a quarter-final against the much weaker Dukla Prague. The first leg in Amsterdam was a 1–1 draw. Two weeks later in the Juliska Stadium, with its huge grass terraces, Ajax took the lead through Sjaak Swart before defensive weakness gave the game away. Tonny Pronk conceded a penalty for the equaliser. Then Ajax's captain and centre-half Frits Soetekouw scored an own-goal from a corner just before full-time. The technically superior Ajax had lost and Michels was furious. His first act when he returned to Amsterdam was to place Soutekouw on the transfer list. (Soutekouw never played for Ajax again.) Pronk was moved for a while to midfield. Over the next four years Michels ruthlessly and doggedly pruned, developed and honed a team of winners. The result was Ajax's transformation from talented yet naïve amateurs into a dominant force in Europe.

Contrary to Ajax's mythical status as a team of buccaneering free spirits dedicated only to attack, Michels started by building his defence. His key recruit was Velibor Vasovic, the tough-minded captain of Partizan Belgrade and the Yugoslav national team. In Paris in May 1966 Michels had watched Real Madrid beat Partizan 2–1 in the European Cup final; Vasovic had scored his team's goal. His parents had been wartime partisans and Vasovic was an experienced man whom Michels hoped to use in the way Don Revie had employed Bobby Collins at Leeds United and Louis van Gaal later used Frank Rijkaard at Ajax: a battle-hardened veteran and inspiring competitor who could teach the youngsters a thing or two about winning football matches. Vasovic, now a lawyer in Belgrade, remembers: 'Mr Michels got in touch with me through the Yugoslav wife of a Dutchman called Andres Blankert. I came to Amsterdam in October 1966 to discuss things. They didn't offer me much money – I was not satisfied, but I couldn't go to any other club in Europe because only Holland had a short transfer period in December, so I signed a contract for half of the sum I asked for.' Before putting pen to paper, Vasovic watched Ajax's home game against PSV sitting alongside club president Jaap van Praag. 'I was very surprised. Johan Cruyff played on the left wing but this Yugoslav woman told me I didn't need to watch this young boy because left wing was the position of the club's best player, Piet Keizer. After the game [which Ajax won 3–1] I said to her: "You can tell the president that if they have anyone better than this player, they don't need me".'

Vasovic was important to Ajax both psychologically and tactically. Unburdened by false modesty, he now says: 'I was the best football player of the former Yugoslavia and I came with a lot of experience. I was a winner all my life. I could not understand why we would play a game in which we lose between two and a half and four kilos of our bodyweight for nothing. When you put on your shirt and lace up your boots, you have to win. Otherwise you should stay at home and watch television. With such a character I was very helpful to the Dutch football players because they were not naturally like that.' Following the Prague fiasco, Michels put Vasovic and Barry Hulshoff into the centre of defence, a partnership that lasted four and a half years. 'When I came, I preferred to play a kind of total football,' says Vasovic. 'I played the last man in defence, the *libero*. Michels made this plan to play very offensive football. We discussed it. I was the architect, together with Michels, of the aggressive way of defending. I did small things, like make an

offside or stand in the wall to make a gap for the goals. When you
see examples from other players on the field, you learn a hundred
times better than in training. In that way I was able to make a lot of
changes at Ajax, which was a very young team at that time. Johan
Neeskens was ten years younger than me; Cruyff nine years
younger; Hulshoff eight years. Only Sjaak Swart was older than
me.'

At the beginning of 1967, he says, Ajax were 'two steps behind
the real Ajax team. It was half the team that would go to the top.'
(Goalkeeper Gert Bals was already old, and while Tonny Pronk was
a regular for the Dutch national team on some thirty-five occasions,
he was not a player who could make it at the highest level.) Klaas
Nuninga, Bennie Muller, Soutekouw and Van Duivenbode lacked
the 'quality' to beat the best European teams. 'But when we got
Gerrie Muhren, Barry Hulshoff, Ruud Krol and Johan Neeskens in
the team, and Heinz Stuy in the goal, we changed the quality. Johan
Cruyff was the best player, but he couldn't do it on his own – he
had to have support from both the attack and the defence. Michels
agreed with me about this . . .'

Michels was driven, but he had only books and his own common
sense and insight to guide him. He took the team to Belgium and
Germany to watch how others solved their problems, and learned
by trial and error. (When Ajax first played in Europe, they booked
into central hotels which turned out to be noisy and full of
distractions. Michels used to sit guard through the night to stop
his players going out drinking.) Off the field, every detail was taken
care of. Salo Muller was also important, his job as pysiotherapist
being to keep the players fit and happy. 'Everything changed,' he
recalls. 'In the beginning he got his own office. It's a small thing but
it meant that players, if they wanted to talk to him, went to his
office, not to the dressing room where everyone was listening.'
Unlike his predecessors, Michels discussed the medical and psychological state of the players with Muller in detail every day. The
massage table was moved to a new medical room. The players had

previously taken their kits home to wash themselves; now a man dubbed 'Uncle Jan' collected it, took it home for his wife to wash in her machine and brought it back for match days. Players were provided with towels and shampoo, whereas before they had provided their own.

For some players this new professionalism took some getting used to. Piet Keizer later bitterly complained that while a computer reduces everything to two digits, as far as Michels was concerned all the players were zeroes. Away from football Michels socialised with his team and treated them as equals; at work he was the boss and the players had to follow his instructions to the letter – or rather the number. Hulshoff recalls: 'Michels was psychologically very hard and very strict. He said: "When you come to the stadium, you are a football player with a number on your back. When you leave, you are a person and I can talk to you. When you are in the stadium, I will judge you only by your football capacities." He made a strict distinction – he could do that. We couldn't. On the pitch when we trained he shouted and said some bad things. Or he put you out of the team with no explanation. Sometimes you hated him. You could sit with him in the restaurant and he would be nice and talk with you, and he would go on the pitch and be someone else. It was a learning process. Later we learned to criticise each other, too. Everyone thinks he is weaker when he speaks about things, but later on we talked very openly. For example, everyone knew Johan Cruyff could not defend. I was weak in other things. And we could say these things to each other.' Michels also demanded constant development and improvement. Having disliked heading the ball, Sjaak Swart learned to be one of the most dangerous of Ajax's players in the air.

Ajax soon became the leading power in Holland, winning the Dutch Championship in 1966, 1967, 1968 and 1970. Perhaps more significant was their first European Cup final, against AC Milan in Madrid in 1969. The route there had been dramatic. Fenerbahce were beaten on a sea of mud in Istanbul. Ajax lost the first leg of the quarter-final on a snow-affected pitch in Amsterdam 1–3 to the Benfica of Eusebio, Torres and Coluna, then staged an amazing comeback to win by the same score in Lisbon (a match Dutch TV didn't bother to broadcast because they assumed Ajax could not win). Ajax won the replay in Paris 3–0 and went on to beat Spartak Trnava 5–0 easily on aggregate in the semi-final. Facing the AC Milan of Gianni Rivera, Karl-Heinz Schnellinger and Giovanni Trappatoni was very different. Ajax ran into a red and black brick wall. The Dutch attacks foundered feebly and their defence was ripped apart in a one-sided match which they lost 4–1. All that was still naïve and inexperienced about the team was exposed. Hulshoff remembers: 'We were walking in the shadow of Milan. They counted us out. We were proud to have got to the final, of course. But, you know, a game like this lasts for only ten minutes in your mind. It's so intense, it goes so fast. You don't have time to think. We had such a young team then. They say sometimes you have to lose a final to win a final, and it's true. Later we learned that if it was not going well for us, we could change ourselves in the game – we could change tactics. Against Milan we could change nothing. They were too experienced. We were overwhelmed in every way. In every way they were better.'

The match convinced Michels to clear out the older players and replace them with those who were tougher, more modern and flexible. The technical and gentlemanly Klaas Nuninga had in the early 1960s been considered one of Holland's leading players. Now in Michels's system he was obsolete, his place taken by the hard-running, tactically acute Gerrie Muhren from Volendam. Ruud Krol was brought in at left-back to replace Theo van Duivenbode, who played in that position for the Dutch national team. 'I was in the youth team and I had never played at left-back before except in one friendly match,' says Krol. 'Michels said to me: "Forget Van Duivenbode: you are better." When a coach sells the left-back of the national team and takes you in his place, of course it gives you an explosion of confidence.' Bennie Muller lost his place to Nico

Rijnders. Barry Hulshoff was also dropped, though only for five games. 'Michels wanted me to be harder, meaner, to foul forwards if they beat me. He wanted me to kick a man, just take him out. But I couldn't and didn't do it. Maybe some little holding, but not enough. It wasn't in my character.' Hulshoff later learned to anticipate and read the game so effectively that it was unnecessary for him to foul forwards.

Against Milan Ajax had played a version of 4–2–4. In April 1970, after a 3–3 draw against Feyenoord in which the Ajax midfield was again swamped, Michels amended the formation to 4–3–3. Earlier in the month Ajax had lost 1–3 in the semi-final of the Fairs Cup (precursor to the UEFA Cup) to Arsenal. Arsenal manager Bertie Mee later recalled: 'I formed a peculiar impression. Ajax were very, very effective and played particularly well with very talented individuals. But somehow they didn't quite look the part physically. They weren't a throwback to the Pegasus or Corinthian Casuals days, but they looked very amateurish. From a physical point of view, they didn't look like footballers as we understood them in the English football league. They're a tall race, the Dutch, they looked a bit gangly.'

The following year witnessed two crucial tactical developments at De Meer.

In 1955 Willy Meisl, an Austrian-Jewish football writer in London, published his book *Soccer Revolution*, in which he argued that the future of football lay with defenders who could attack, attackers who could defend and a whirling formation in which players switched positions constantly. His ideas appeared to fall on stony ground. But in the early 1960s Inter Milan's great left-back Giacinto Facchetti began to make a name for himself with his attacking forays up the wing. Within a couple of years, Bayern Munich's stylish young centre-half Franz Beckenbauer started to do something similar, surging forward to create and join attacks when the opportunity presented itself and, in the process, pioneering the notion of the modern attacking *libero*. By 1970 Michels's Ajax were rampaging through Dutch opponents on a regular basis (they scored 122 goals in the 1967–8 League season) and had begun to encounter new problems in the form of massed defences.

Michels encouraged his defenders and midfielders to join in the attacks. Michels: 'In the fourth or fifth year I tried to find guidelines that meant we could surprise a little those walls. I had to let midfield players and defensive players participate in the building up and in the attacking. It's easy to say, but it's a long way to go because the most difficult thing is not to teach a full-back to participate in attacking – because he likes that – but to find someone else who is covering up. In the end, when you see they have the mobility, the positional game of such a team makes everyone think, "I can participate too, it's very easy". And then you have reached the top, the paramount of the development.'

Position-switching looked fluid and chaotic and gave opposing defenders a blizzard of movement and hostility to deal with. Positions rotated strictly down each wing and through the centre. When the full-backs (Krol on the left, Suurbier on the right) advanced, their midfielders (Muhren or Haan) and forwards (Keizer and Swart) dropped back to cover. The same applied through the middle with Cruyff, Neeskens and Vasovic or Blankenburg. With each switch the other players revised their position accordingly, so the personnel changed but the positions remained constant. Barry Hulshoff explains the principle: 'Total Football means that a player in attack can play in defence – only that he can do this, that is all. Everything starts simply. The defender must first think defensively, but he must also think offensively. For an attacker it is the other way around. Somewhere they meet.' Of course, position-switching in this manner meant that players were attempting to fulfil roles within the game that did not necessarily come to them naturally. When a defender attacked and vice versa, it was essential that players resumed their usual positions as quickly as possible. 'The team is stronger when they play from their normal positions, so when the positions change it is only temporary and you switch back as quickly as possible. It never lasts for long. But Total Football is not a fantasy. It is real because the whole team thinks offensively: "We must attack! We must attack!" But the quality of the attack is not so good when the attackers are defenders. It is good, but not *so* good. And the attackers are not such good defenders.'

Constant adjustment was vital to keep only one player in each position at any time. 'It was coming out, going in, coming out, going in . . . You make space, you come into space. And if the ball doesn't come, you leave this place and another player will come into it. This movement flows down the sides of the team and also in the middle.' To begin with, no one took Vasovic's place: 'He was the *libero*, the free man. But when I came out, Vasovic took my place, and later Blankenburg did the same thing. We were so strong it was no longer a risk, we never felt we were taking a risk.'

Sjaak Swart insists position-switching developed naturally. 'When I saw Suurbier [right-back] going forward, I knew I had to go back. I didn't have to be told. And after two years, everybody knew what to do. When Johan went to the left, I knew I had to move to the far post. I was thinking he would cross the ball with the outside of his right foot, so I was coming and could score with my head. When I had the ball, I was looking for Johan. If I could give him a pass, he was away. In four passes we would be in front of the goal. Nowadays they take twenty passes – backwards, sideways, backwards. We didn't play like that. We went for the goal. We could play sixty minutes of pressing . . . I've never seen any other club anywhere who could do that.'

Ajax's other decisive tactical development – 'pressing' and the transformation of the defensive offside trap into an offensive instrument – began with Johan Neeskens's natural aggression and Vasovic's tactical acumen. The ferocious Neeskens, signed from RCH in 1970, usually had the defensive task of marking opponents' playmakers. 'He was like a kamikaze pilot, a forward soldier,' says Bobby Haarms. 'When you said go to the ball, he really went.' Neeskens's prey tended to try to retreat into their own half to try to get away from him. Naturally, Neeskens chased after them, often following them deep into their own half. At first the other Ajax defenders stayed back, but at some point during the 1970 season the rest of the defence began to follow. 'Without studying it, they started to play offside,' says Haarms. 'Vasco took one step forward and suddenly it was there. It was a kind of miracle. Michels saw it and said: "Yes! This is how we have to do it." I don't remember a specific game, but one minute we were playing the old system and the next the new way was there.' Now Ajax hunted in packs. If Neeskens failed to win the ball, the defence would be so far forward that opposition would be caught offside if they tried to attack.

And then there were mind games. Michels developed the 'conflict model': criticising players and provoking arguments in the dressing room. He says now: 'It is an instrument you have to manipulate very carefully because it can have a controversial effect. If you see that something is missing, that you are not up to the level you need in a game, then sometimes at half-time I was looking for a conflict. Mostly I picked the most important player – there is no sense to take someone who is not in a key role. On the pitch something would have happened that I could use. I exaggerated it. I did it to convince the others that we had to change our game mentality. I felt that the end justified the means.' During training sessions he worked to develop aggression. One way of doing this was to play 'sharp' games, in which Haarms acted as a referee from hell. Haarms explains: 'Michels controlled everything. Maybe it was a sunny day and things were too relaxed, so he'd come across and say: "It's dead, Bobby! It's nothing. Make it more vivid, liven things up!" This meant I should give one side an unfair free kick for handball or offside.' Tension and adrenaline levels rose immediately. 'You think this is bad? Wait till you see the referee on Sunday,' Haarms countered if anyone complained. Before important European games a 'cinema committee', headed by Johan Cruyff, picked films for the team to see: if the mood was too relaxed, a war film was chosen; to reduce tension, a comedy.

In 1971 Ajax easily beat Panathinaikos 2–0 at Wembley to win the European Cup for the first time. They repeated the feat twice in the next two years. 'When we played in our own stadium, teams who came here were afraid of us,' Swart recalls. 'In the bus, they were already trembling. Many old players have told me this. Before the game started, it was already 1–0 to us.' He says the secret of the Ajax system was the blend of personalities and talents within the club. 'It came from playing together a long time. Keizer was a fantastic player. When he stood still with the ball, he could give a pass that would take out three men and leave you free on goal. The full-backs, Suurbier and Krol, could easily play one-on-one. They were quick, they were tactically good. In the centre of the defence, Vasovic was fantastic. And when a high ball came, you could move out immediately because you knew Hulshoff would head it because he was so strong in the air. In the midfield Neeskens could play for two. Arie Haan was so good; Gerrie Muhren was technical and always running . . .'

Barry Hulshoff later realised he was part of something extra-ordinary. As a boy he had fallen in love with the Real Madrid of Di Stefano and Puskas he saw on black and white television. After his playing career was over, he worked as a coach in Greece. On one occasion he found himself in a tiny, remote mountain village. 'An old man was standing in front of me. He took my hands and held them and he cried. It went on for four or five minutes. I was very embarrassed, I just didn't know what was going on. Later my translator explained it. He said there was no television in the village, so this old man used to walk for two hours to reach another village to watch Ajax games on television. And in the other village they watched Ajax as I had seen Real Madrid, with many people watching the game on one television set. The man had loved Ajax and now, in front of him, he saw one of the players he used to watch. He couldn't understand it and he became very emotional.'

But he warns against misreading what was created at De Meer

and cites the build-up to Cruyff's first goal in Ajax's second European Cup final triumph, against Inter Milan in 1972. The game is reckoned to be Ajax's peak moment. By this time Rinus Michels had been replaced by Romanian-born coach Stefan Kovacs. The players were sophisticated and irresistible; they attacked cleverly and continuously, relentlessly and fluidly switching positions and appearing to overwhelm the ultra-defensive Italians intellectually and emotionally as well as physically and tactically. Hulshoff insists it was more accidental than it looked. 'The pass I made which led to the first goal was absolutely a mistake.' He draws a diagram. 'I picked up the ball in the midfield – Keizer was here, Cruyff was there, Muhren was over there. I was just moving into midfield, and what did I do? I played the ball without looking to the right. I looked to the left and passed the ball to the right, to where Arie Haan would normally be. Normally, in this situation, Arie Haan would be here. But he wasn't. No one was there.' An Inter defender, baffled by being made a present of the ball, fluffed his control and allowed Swart to pick it up and cross immediately. The Italian goalkeeper then bumped into another defender and the ball fell at Cruyff's feet. Cruyff controlled the ball and lashed it into the unguarded net.

Hulshoff thinks that the Ajax system was subject to over-intellectualisation by those who didn't understand how it functioned. 'You know how it goes. People couldn't see that sometimes we just did things automatically. It comes from playing a long time together. Football is best when it's instinctive, when it comes from the heart. You talk about things after, in the game you just play. This way of playing, we grew into it. We didn't realise the ball was going that fast, that we were changing positions so much. We knew exactly what to do because we'd known and played with each other for five years. We could adapt and fill in for each other whatever we did.'

So who invented Total Football? There are conflicting claims. Some credit Cruyff; others say it was Michels. Others still say it was Michels's relaxed successor, Stefan Kovacs, the coach who gave control to the players. Hulshoff says the players invented Total Football and then 'a lot of other people made theories about it'. Ruud Krol takes the opposite view. 'Michels invented this system, of course. Not the players. Every year he built it. Every year he was looking for the players he could use in creating that system, looking for a new dimension, a better quality. Every year Michels was looking until he found the perfect team and the perfect style.'

Bobby Haarms says the creation of Total Football was a joint effort. 'It was an ideal mix of talents and intelligence and world-class players. Everyone was tactically and technically very strong. In training they were always inventing things, trying tricks on each other. Cruyff was a big influence, especially as he grew older and talked more and more about tactics with the other players. But Michels was the general who pulled it together. You could say it was Michels and Cruyff.' Valibor Vasovic has a different opinion again: 'Everybody is mistaken who says that Total Football started with Kovacs. Kovacs had nothing to do with it. He took over a very good team, the champions of Europe, and just continued this way of playing. No, Michels was the architect of this football. And I helped him the most. Now that we are a little bit older we must tell the truth. Michels is the one who made the big Ajax, but we were the players. You have to separate the roles. He never scored the goals. You know what I mean? He has his part and we have our part. And we don't want to mix those things up.'

Football, like architecture, is a collaborative art form; and it seems that the form for which Dutch football will always be celebrated developed organically and collaboratively. When I ask Rinus Michels who came up with the name *totaalvoetbal*, he floors me by saying: 'The name Total Football is your fault.' My mind races. We've never met before! I was only about thirteen at the time! 'The press. They found this expression, but I must say it covered rather well the development of our game, our style of playing.' And did both Michels and his players contribute to the development of this style? Was it a collaboration? 'Yes.'

9: take an aspirin

Most footballers are superstitious but Ajax were extreme. There was a complicated ritual about the order in which players went to the massage table before a match. 'Every player had his number,' explains Salo Muller. 'If the person at number three, for example, went to the toilet, we all had to wait for him. The number four cannot be number three. The goalkeeper was always last. Sjaakie Swart was number three. Bennie Muller was four. Cruyff was either one or two; I can't remember exactly. And when I'd finished each massage I had to say something special to each player. To Cruyff I had to say: "Yogi twee." I called him Yogi, I don't know why. Not Jopie, Yogi. That means: score two goals. To Henk Groot I had to say: "Henk: a very, VERY good match." Two verys. If I say: "Henk: a very good match," he won't move. "Oh, sorry. A very VERY good match." To the goalkeeper: "Klempie, klempie," because he has to hold the ball. "Klempie, klempie." ' Piet Keizer required a pat on the bottom and the words: 'Piet, do your best.'

Before every European match Muller, the physiotherapist, was required to wear his lucky ski hat – and to supply a special sausage, an *osseworst* from Hergo, the kosher butcher on the Beethovenstraat. Before Ajax's disastrous game against Dukla Prague, Muller's wife forgot to pack the lucky hat. And Hergo was closed, so there was no sausage either. Ajax lost 2–1, and to this day, some of the players blame Muller.

Sjaak Swart made sure his daughter kissed his boots before every match. Johan Cruyff always played in his oldest boots, even if they had a hole in them. 'Johan was very sensitive,' says Muller. 'He would phone me seven times a day: "There's something wrong with my knee. I think there's something wrong with my knee." "Johan, there is nothing wrong with your knee." "Are you sure?" "I'm sure." Later: "But my knee . . ." "Johan, believe me, there is absolutely nothing wrong with your knee. You're fine." "But my neck . . ." "There's nothing wrong with your neck. You're fine. Take an aspirin; go to sleep. Don't worry." "Thank you, Salo. Thank you, Salo. You're so nice." "No problem. You can phone me any time." '

14: dutch space is different

'What is God? God is length, height, width, depth'
St Bernard de Clairvaux (1090–1153)
(from *Interior Light*, a book of photographs
by Dutch artist Jan Dibbets)

Space is the unique defining element of Dutch football. Other nations and football cultures may have produced greater goalscorers, more dazzling individual ball-artists and more dependable and efficient tournament-winning teams. But no one has ever imagined or structured their play as abstractly, as architecturally, in such a measured fashion as the Dutch.

Total Football was built on a new theory of flexible space. Just as Cornelis Lely in the nineteenth century conceived and executed the idea of creating giant new polders and altering the physical dimensions of Holland by dike-building and exploiting the new technology of steam, so Rinus Michels and Johan Cruyff exploited the capacities of a new breed of players to change the dimensions of the football field. Total Football was, among other things, a conceptual revolution based on the idea that the size of any football field was flexible and could be altered by a team playing on it. In possession, Ajax – and later the Dutch national team – aimed to make the pitch as large as possible, spreading play to the wings and seeing every run and movement as a way to increase and exploit the available space. When they lost the ball, the same thinking and techniques were used to destroy the space of their opponents. They pressed deep into the other side's half, hunting for the ball, defended a line ten yards inside their own half, and used the offside trap aggressively to squeeze space further. When he first saw Cruyff play, David Miller of *The Times* marvelled at a 'Pythagoras in boots', yet an acute sense of the fluid structure and dimensions of the pitch was shared by everyone in the team.

This was not abstract, playful exploration of perspective in the style of, say, an M. C. Escher. Partly, it was instinctive. It was also based on mathematical calculations and designed pragmatically to maximise athletic capacity. Ruud Krol recalls: 'We talked always about space in a practical way. When we were defending, the gaps between us had to be very short. When we attacked, we spread out and used the wings. Our system was also a solution to a physical problem. Fitness has to be one hundred per cent, but how can you play for 90 minutes and remain strong? If I, as left-back, run 70 metres up the wing, it's not good if I immediately have to run back 70 metres to my starting position. So, if the left-midfield player takes my place, and the left-winger takes the midfield position, then it shortens the distances. If you have to run ten times seventy metres and the same distance back ten times, that's a total of 1400 metres. If you change it so you only must run 1000 metres, you will be 400 metres fresher. That was the philosophy.' In other words, in some respects it did not matter what 'position' a player was given: the immediate position of play itself determined when and where the players moved within the game. Quick and precise calculations were made by each player in order that every man-oeuvre made the most effective use of pitch-space and player-energy. Krol continues: 'When we defended, we looked to keep the opponent on the halfway line. Our standpoint was that we were not protecting our own goal, we were attacking the halfway line. That's why we played offside. You don't want to run back to defend because you are trying to save energy. Instead of running 80 metres back and eighty forward, it's better to run only ten in each direction. That's 20 metres instead of 160. When we got better and the system became more perfect, we would often score one or two goals in the first five minutes, and after that we could play our own game because the position was demoralised. They gave us space.'

. In the 1970s, this approach was startling to the outside world. Dave Sexton, the English former Chelsea and Manchester United manager who studied with Rinus Michels and tried to emulate Total Football with his QPR team in the mid-1970s, recalls: 'With their pressing and rotation, the Dutch created space where there wasn't any before. Everyone else still played in a rigid way, in straight lines and fixed positions. The Dutch approach was quite different. Michels never talked to me about it in theoretical terms, but he didn't have to because if you were in football, you understood immediately what it meant. Instead of straight lines, his concept was people changing positions. By itself, that freed up huge amounts of space and gave defenders a problem: if the Dutch left-winger moves infield, what should the right-back do? Go with him, or stay put? If he goes, he leaves a hole where immediately the Dutch left-back will pop up. But if he doesn't go, the winger gets the ball to his feet in midfield and turns and runs at you through the centre.'

Artist Jeroen Henneman argues that the genesis of this spatial awareness was the spoken word: 'Football was always unconsciously about space. The good players were always the ones who instinctively found positions to receive the ball in space. But the big change in Dutch football happened when these ideas became words, when Cruyff and Michels started talking about space. No one ever looked at it in that way before. Because they drew attention to it and talked about it, something came into existence which had always been there but no one had ever noticed before. That was their big invention: to analyse certain aspects of football. Before, people had always talked about formations: 2–3–5 or 4–2–4 or whatever. But suddenly Cruyff was saying, "If there is an attack and this person runs to the side of the field, he will attract a defender who goes with him, so there is room for a midfielder to run in and score." And because they talked about it, it opened a whole vista of seeing football totally differently.'

'We discussed space all the time,' says Barry Hulshoff. 'Cruyff always talked about where people should run, where they should stand, when they should not be moving. It was all about making space and coming into space. It is a kind of architecture on the field. It is about movement but still it is about space, about organising space. You have to know why building up from the right side or from the left side is a different movement from when you build up from the centre. In defence, if you play against three strikers, you play "out of defence" with the centre two. If you play against two forwards, you build up from the side, and so on.' A similar though more high-speed version of this approach was at the heart of Louis van Gaal's Ajax in the mid-1990s. Gerard van der Lem, Van Gaal's former right-hand man, explains: 'We talked always about speed of ball, space and time. Where is the most space? Where is the player who has the most time? That is where we have to play the ball. Every player had to understand the whole geometry of the whole pitch and the system as a whole.'

The football pitch is the same size and shape everywhere in the world, yet no one else thought about football this way. So why did the Dutch? The answer may be that the Dutch think innovatively, creatively and abstractly about space in their football because for centuries they have had to think innovatively about space in every other area of their lives. Because of their strange landscape, the Dutch are a nation of spatial neurotics. On the one hand they don't have nearly enough of the stuff. Holland is one of the most crowded and most intensively planned landscapes on Earth. Space is an inordinately precious commodity, and for centuries the use of every square centimetre of every Dutch city, field and polder has been carefully considered and argued over. The land is controlled because as a matter of national survival it must be. The Dutch water system has to be regulated tightly because more than fifty per cent of the country is below sea level. In the west of the country, the entire landscape is man-made — from the astounding network of canals, dikes and waterways to the awesome sea defences in Zeeland, to the great port of Rotterdam, the giant airport at Schiphol and the remarkably complex ancient compactness of the cities. Large parts of the country were literally dragged out of the sea and dried using centuries-old techniques of dike-building and drainage systems. As the old boast-cum-joke puts it: 'God made the world, but the Dutch made Holland.'

The land the Dutch made for themselves is extremely odd. 'We live in a complete knot of artificialness,' says influential landscape architect Dirk Sijmons. 'What is nature and what is artificial? You can't say. The landscape is an abstraction in the sense that it is only points, lines and surfaces, like a painting by Mondrian. We live in a kind of inhabited mega-structure below sea level. It is a form of degenerated nature, but at the same time it is a beautiful landscape.'

Experiencing this landscape for the first time from the window of a train or car can be hypnotic: an endless procession of orderly, rectangular fields and drainage ditches, dead-straight waterways, neat lines of trees. In his 1977 book *Planned Landscapes*, photographer Ger Dekkers noted the underlying structures of 'perspective, accumulation, isolation, rhythm, seriality' in this countryside. British anthropologist Mark Turin has written of the startling contrast between Britain and Holland from the air. 'Over the fens of East Anglia, in the part of the British Isles that most closely resembles Holland when on the ground, you see nothing but unordered chaos, the countryside divided and re-divided over centuries into increasingly illogical portions.' Holland, however, seems 'a world of order and peace, sense and judgement, where shapes tessellate and the pieces join together neatly. A land in which roads go around landholdings and farms, not through them . . . a nether-land, whose constant struggle against the encroaching water is somehow intertwined with its Protestant ethic of order and control.'

The giant domed skies and limitless stretches of flat, geometrically ordered land have also turned the Dutch into agoraphobes. In the absence of natural mountains – or even hillocks worthy of the name – the Dutch have made their own in the form of tall houses with terrifyingly steep and narrow staircases. Dutch staircases are a shock to a non-native. Among the most extreme examples are those in the Edwardian-era tenements of west Amsterdam. In the Tweede

Helmersstraat there are staircases that make the prospect of climbing the north face of the Eiger seem attractive: sheer stairfaces rising almost vertically for five storeys with barely enough room for a toehold on each rung, and tiny landings all the way up. The traditional explanation for these extraordinary structures is that their lack of large stairwells or lifts saves valuable living-space. Yet old Dutch farmhouses also have steep stairs, and even in the Amsterdam Arena, the stairways are noticeably steeper and narrower-stepped than their Continental or British equivalents. Turin, who divides his time between a canal house in Amsterdam and the Nepalese Himalayas, senses the 'trauma of Dutch space' in this and in the oddly narrow city trams and trains and planes, which provide barely enough leg-room for those who are statistically the tallest people on Earth. 'The sheer abundance of the horizontal plane in everyday rural life leaves people lusting for something more vertical,' he says. 'It is as if the Dutch compensate for the over-whelming vastness of their sky and horizon by manufacturing uncomfortably small spaces for themselves to squeeze into.' By contrast, he notes that amid the mountains of the Himalayas people compensate for the 'oppressive verticality' by building houses as low and flat as they possibly can.

Since World War II, the Dutch have put their faith in a series of national plans, the Ruimtelijke Ordeningen, or National Spatial Planning Acts. These are a little like the old Soviet Five-Year Plans, except that they are concerned solely with the use of space and they lay down a blueprint to be followed by every local and municipal authority in the Netherlands. Maarten Hajer, professor of public policy at Amsterdam University, explains that the Dutch have been developing their planning doctrines since the twelfth century. 'We tend to think we invented the idea of land-use planning. Our problems with water meant we had to take collective political action in order to be able to build dikes. You can't do that on your own. We always say that the origin of Dutch democracy lies in this co-operative dike-building.'

The Dutch were also among the first to plan and enforce a rigid separation between compact, crowded cities and their open rural areas. This first developed for strategic military reasons during the war for independence with Spain in the sixteenth century. Anticipating by nearly 400 years the Total Football concept of squeezing space in defence, the Dutch (literally) made their land as small as possible by flooding the farm lands between their walled cities when the Spaniards attacked. Even after their military and political victory, the Dutch continued to develop the Netherlands as a country of compact cities surrounded by spacious green countryside. Definitive images of this Dutch ideal can be seen in the pages of the classic children's picture book *The Cow Who Fell in the Canal* by the Americans Phyllis Krasilovsky and Peter Spier. The book first appeared in 1957, around the time the planners were developing the idea of 'concentrated deconcentration' (moving people from the crowded big cities to crowded new towns built on land newly squeezed from the inland sea, the IJsselmeer). The book tells the enchanting story of Hendrika, a north-Holland dairy cow who is 'bored with life on the farm and longs to see the city she has heard so much about'. One day, her wish comes true when she stumbles from her sweet-grass meadow and falls into the canal beside it. She finds a raft and floats far away, past the barns and houses and windmills and tulips of the tranquil, pancake-flat Dutch countryside, and arrives in the bustling city. Amid strange, tall buildings, Hendrika's appearance (a cow! in the canal! on a raft!) causes a sensation. Followed by excited crowds and mooing with happiness, she prances through cobblestoned streets, looks in windows and naughtily eats a straw hat at the Alkmaar Cheese Market (quite close, in fact, to AZ Alkmaar's pretty Alkmaarderhout Stadium, a detail mysteriously omitted from the story). Eventually, Hendrika's owner, Mr Hofstra, restores order (and the balance between city and country) by taking her home to her pasture and giving her a pretty straw hat with a red ribbon on it. 'A hat is not to eat; a hat is to wear', he tells her. (Rules, rules . . . The Dutch have rules for everything.)

*　　*　　*

If the planners have always known how to compress – and defend – space, what of the reverse? How good have the Dutch been, in Dave Sexton's phrase, at creating space where there wasn't any before? The short answer is: pretty nifty. As well as draining their seas, lakes, swamps and such, the Dutch also pride themselves on their ability to make less tangible forms of space. The Dutch pavilion at Expo 2000 is called 'Holland Schept Ruimte' – 'Holland Makes Space'. At the exhibition site in Hanover, the flattest nation in Europe has the highest pavilion: a dazzlingly clever forty-metre-high structure designed by Rotterdam architects MVRDV, which plays with some of the most familiar Dutch clichés. The country's position partly under sea level is represented by a large artificial lake on the roof; below this, huge trees grow through the middle of the open-sided structure. In the basement there are sand-dunes. The building aims to show off Holland's talent 'for making space for new environments, for new solutions, for new land and nature, and for new lifestyles and ideas'. The concept's author, Dr Michiel Schwartz, explains that the Netherlands is a 'country by design' which thrives by creating cultural and personal 'freedom by design':

'How can a small country like Holland, one of the most crowded nations on Earth, offer space?' he asks. 'The answer lies in the Dutch ability to create new space – not only literally, in the form of new land reclaimed from the sea, but in the form of new political structures, new social compacts and new relationships between society, technology and nature. This ability to make space gives rise to a host of surprising hybrids: what seems natural – the land, for instance – is in fact artificial, and often what is man-made has become intertwined with nature. This is the heart of the Dutch notion of *maakbaarheid*, the ability to shape, form and control every aspect of the social and physical environment . . . the belief that a country can be planned and made, from its physical environment to its social and cultural life.' The land has been reclaimed and the water channelled, he says, and the Dutch have also created 'cultural spaces for new lifestyles and freedom of expression which are unique in the world. The man-made character of Holland is reflected in all areas of life, from the way the Dutch deal with nature and the environment to the design of its cultural institutions and a concern for democratic consensus building. In Holland the open sky and the open mind go hand in hand.' With sixteen million people crowded into a physically small space, the Dutch opted for a policy of openness, hospitality and multiculturalism. 'The open character of the Netherlander has a rich tradition,' says Schwartz. He cites the 'Dutch history of providing space and shelter for minorities and oppressed communities. The way the Dutch see their personal social relationships appears to mirror the openness of their traditional landscape. In Holland there is space for freedom, to a degree unthinkable in some other democratic countries – think of gay marriage, or the liberal drugs policies, or the way people can make a personal choice for euthanasia.' The Dutch also 'make ample space for cultural expression – witness the high level of government support for the arts, the high number of artists in the Netherlands. But there is also space for fun and *gezelligheid*, recreational activities, special and im-material concerns.' Han van der Horst, author of *The Low Sky*, a popular book that seeks to explain Holland to foreigners, says that 'tolerance became second nature' to the Dutch. In terms of its approach to authority and order, the Dutch culture is also unique: 'Society too has its *uiterwaarden*, water meadows outside the dikes, where administrators find it impossible to impose any clear order.'

The Dutch landscape has also shaped the Dutch way of seeing the world – and, of course, the way they view their football. Rudi Fuchs, director of the Stedelijk Modern Art Museum in Amsterdam and also one of the country's most influential art critics and historians, argues that every country and culture has its own way of seeing. 'The psychologists deny these differences exist, but it's there in the [Dutch] art and culture. Ask any Dutch person to draw the horizon and they will draw a straight line. If you ask someone from Yorkshire or Tuscany or anywhere else, it will have bumps and hills. A Scandinavian blue is cold and steely, completely unlike a blue in Italy. Italian painting is rich in warm reds, but when red appears in the work of a northern artist like Munch, it's blood in the snow.' Furthermore, these climatic and geographically shaped aesthetic differences are inevitably reflected in football. 'Catenaccio is like a Titian painting – soft, seductive and languid. The Italians welcome and lull you and seduce you into their soft embrace, and score a goal like the thrust of a dagger. The Dutch make their geometric patterns. In a Vermeer, the pearl twinkles. You can say, in fact, that the twinkling of the pearl is the whole point of Vermeer. The whole painting is leading to this moment, the way the whole of football leads to the overhead goal of Van Basten. The English like to run and fight. When Gullit tried to transplant this Dutch art to Newcastle, he was trying to do something impossible. He was bound to fail.'

To make sense of the vast flatness of their land, Fuchs says, the Dutch developed a way of calibrating distances from the horizon, calculating space and paying meticulous attention to every object within that space. Dutch art thus developed an extraordinarily precise and reverent approach to this reality. The nineteenth-century French writer Eugène Fromentin wrote about this in his *Masters of Time Past*, his study of Dutch art in the Golden Age: 'Every object, thanks to the interest it offers, ought to be examined in its form and drawn before it is painted. In this way nothing is secondary. A landscape with its distances, a cloud with its movements, a piece of architecture with its laws of perspective, a face with its physiognomy, its distinctive traits, its passing expressions, a hand with its gesture, a garment in its natural folds, an animal with its carriage, its frame, the inmost characteristics of its kind.' Fuchs develops the idea: 'To measure distance is a natural inclination, an instinct for Dutch people. We measure space quietly, very precisely and then order it in detail. That is the Dutch way of seeing, the Dutch approach to space: selective detail. It's a natural, instinctive thing for us to do. You see it in our paintings, our architecture and our football too. Dutch football also is all about measuring space very precisely.'

Fuchs suggests that all Dutch painting from the time of Van Eyck to that of Mondrian is both a meticulous rendering of things observed and a form of landscape. In relation to seventeenth-century landscape painting, he notes their 'architecture' and 'the careful disposition of objects in space . . . the clear logic of their organisation and of the measured progression into a deep and ordered space'. Objects, the spatial relations between them and their surroundings are explored in minute and reverent detail. Fuchs suggests that this all helps to explain why 'the Dutch instinctively revere the "architect" on the pitch, the one who has a grasp of the overall picture and every detail in it. We want to have an overview, a command of every detail. A Johan Cruyff or a Danny Blind, who has that conception of the overall picture of the football game. There is a Dutch way of seeing space, the landscape. Cruyff sees in that Dutch way and he is admired for his innate understanding of the geometry and order on the pitch.'

Jeroen Henneman also sees a link between this art and Dutch football: 'Historically, Dutch painters always wanted a special quality in their work which looks easy to do but is very hard to achieve. When you see a painting by Mondrian or Vermeer, it feels very silent and fresh and quiet and "roomy". When you space things, it becomes very quiet. No noise. If you translate that to football, it means it's easier to play because there is more room to receive the ball. In the time of Cruyff, the footballers at Ajax began to want the same thing as the painters. Suddenly football was not about kicking each other's legs any more. You went to matches at Ajax and came away with the feeling that you had seen something very special and that only you could see it. But then you talked to other people and you realised everyone felt the same thing. There was something spiritual going on, though exactly what would be hard to discover. Perhaps it is to do with the sense of beauty that goes with the football in Holland. The beauty is in the space and in the pitch. It is in the grass, but also in the air above it, where balls can curl and curve and drop and move like the planets in heaven. Not only on the field. The folding of the air above it also counts. The Dutch prefer to work out how to beat someone with intelligence and beauty rather than power.'

Henneman knows a bit about football, and is probably the only post-modernist sculptor to influence the outcome of a major international. In February 1977 he travelled to London with his friend Jan Mulder, once a great centre-forward for Anderlecht and Ajax, to see Holland play England at Wembley. Before the match, he and Mulder went to see national coach Jan Zwartkruis and team captain Johan Cruyff to discuss a proposal. 'I was an admirer of Jan Peters, an unusual player who at that time played like a pinch-hitter for AZ '67. He played only twenty minutes, but in every game he scored one or two goals. I said: "Jan Peters is in incredible form. The English have never heard of him. Put him in the team, from the start, not as a substitute, and see what happens." We talked about it for a long time and finally Cruyff and Zwartkruis said: "OK, we'll play with Peters in from the start."' Holland won the game 2–0, though it could easily have been by five. Don Revie's England, which included Kevin Keegan and Trevor Brooking, were humiliated. And Jan Peters scored both goals.

Slender, thoughtful and original, Henneman lives and works in a house five minutes' walk from the Leidseplein in the centre of Amsterdam. Like Vermeer and Mondrian before him, he is exploring space and light. Inside his remarkably calm studio from where he can look down on the fluid army of cyclists, joggers and rollerbladers pouring perpetually through the Vondelpark, he shows me some of his experiments with a type of painting he has just invented. He has been producing a series of canvases with an almost identical pattern: a flight of three thick, dark lines surrounded by various shades of grey. I stare at one. I don't get it. The painting seems purely abstract. It's quite nice but it still looks like three thick lines on a grey background. Then I get it. Extraordinary! The top line is a light, the middle one a solid object, and the bottom one is the shadow caused by the interaction of the other two. Clever and mysterious; a holy trinity of optical effects. The illusion is so strong that I find myself trying to peer under the rim of the top line to see the electric light which must surely be hidden there. But there is none. It's just paint. 'Interesting, huh?' he says, delighted by my evident rapture. 'I started doing these six months ago. I don't know how it happens but it happens.' In his other works he plays with scale. Above a desk is a sculpture of an anglepoise lamp, prototype for a giant twenty-metre-high version that will adorn the top of an office building. By day it will be a witty black silhouette. At night it will light up like a Christmas tree and be visible for miles.

He takes a sheet of paper to illustrate an example of particular Dutch spatial awareness on the pitch. 'If you've played football, you know that moment where you are in a situation and the ball comes and you hit the ball and somehow every millimetre is perfect. When it happens to you, it's a wonder and you are amazed by your luck because usually you will fail. And when you see it done on the pitch, you see a miracle. I love it when the defenders are in a line to prevent the forward breaking through, to keep him on side. And a player plays a curved ball across the back of the defence. The defenders start to run back, but the forward, who was behind the line, gets the ball because it curls back to him. That's a miracle. Cruyff used to make passes like that, and it is even nicer the way Dennis Bergkamp does it.' He starts drawing. His precise, elegant lines and curves on the creamy paper are the neatest and clearest I've seen in a month of tactical diagrams. 'When Bergkamp was playing with Nicolas Anelka, Anelka would be covered, like this, by two men. So Bergkamp would give a very beautiful curved pass forward and a little to the side. Anelka would start to run as the pass was hit and his defenders would go with him. But because the pass was curved, Anelka is closer to the ball. Before the pass, Anelka was out of the game, marked by two defenders. Now he is completely free and heading to the goal where he will score. It's a miracle. One moment the pitch is crowded and narrow. Suddenly it is huge and

wide and Anelka can show his speed and skill. He cannot be
touched any more. A pass like this is not hit very hard, but it must be
very precise. In Holland everybody wants to do it like this, not to
score the goal. It's beautiful thing, a beautiful curved ball, and it is
effective. It is also quiet, modest. No one dances and takes their shirt
off after a pass like this. It's not even physically demanding. A little
player can play it but it is in how you kick the ball. And you take a
risk. A pass like this can go totally wrong.

'Cruyff, Bergkamp, Van Basten, Muhren, Van Hanegem, Jonk
. . . they all like to play passes like this. At RKC Waalwijk, they
now have two brothers and one of them can also do this. He can
open the pitch by crossing the ball with a curve: a simple pass to the
other side and suddenly the team have all the room in the world.
This idea is quite Dutch, I think. I was so disappointed when I went
to Brazil. I'd thought: finally I will see the great Brazilian football! I
expected to see a very "roomy" football. But they play in the most
boring way, on technique, only to show off. A personal beauty is of
course also valid. But the passing was very short all the time and the
game was slow. Not slow in a Dutch way. The progress was slow,
like gridiron football. So slow! They go forward, they go back.
Some do little tricks, nice little things. But it is not football.'

Watching the great Ajax, Henneman was beguiled by the
extraordinary shapes unfolding on the pitch, patterns of movement
and passing that had never been seen in football before. 'In a lot of
football going on at Ajax in the late sixties and early seventies, there
was no direct line to goal. The normal way of playing is that you
want to score a goal, and everything you do is for that purpose. But
at Ajax you saw them just playing football, making patterns. The
movements existed simply for the sake of playing football. They
played with the ball. Suddenly they might have an urge to score a
goal. But sometimes they wouldn't. That's a very artistic thing to
do. If there was an opportunity to score, they would score, of
course, but not before. This was also the time when the play began
not only to move forwards but also backwards. They liked to pass
back to the goalkeeper. They would actually give up terrain they

had gained and play it back to keep the ball, and then they would start again and again. Goalscoring was the possibility, but the real aim was the beauty of the football itself. Johan Cruyff seemed to see football as a total movement of the whole field, not as individual actions in only one part of it. Everyone runs to find space. That is an aspect of the horizon; the pitch is finite. But I think maybe Cruyff would be satisfied with a pitch two kilometres long with these beautiful waves of abstract movement going up and down.'

The Dutch footballers' appreciation for abstract movement on the field echoes a wider Dutch taste. In 1995 two New York-based Russian artists, Vitaly Komar and Alex Melamid, conducted an international poll on the Internet to discover the world's favourite types of art. The project, in which people on four continents were asked questions to find out what kind of pictures they would like in their homes, was a playfully subversive look at the world art market. Lighthearted as the experiment was, it produced at least one intriguing finding. All over the world people seemed to want exactly the same things: pictures of Arcadian idylls with some nationalistic symbols. The least-wanted images were abstract modern paintings. Only in Holland were the results the other way around: there the most wanted paintings were abstracts. 'There is a link between the landscape,' says Dirk Sijmons. 'This must have something to do with the liking of abstract paintings and abstract football: you could call it "spatial football".'

The ultimate space-measurer in Dutch football is, of course, Johan Cruyff. He was only seventeen when he first played at Ajax, yet even then he delivered running commentaries on the use of space to the rest of the team, telling them where to run, where not to run. Players did what the tiny, skinny teenager told them to do because he was right. Cruyff didn't talk about abstract space but about specific, detailed spatial relations on the field. Indeed, the most abiding image of him as a player is not of him scoring or running or tackling. It is of Cruyff pointing. 'No, not there, back a little . . .

forward two metres . . . four metres more to the left.' He seemed
like a conductor directing a symphony orchestra. It was as if Cruyff
was helping his colleagues to realise an approximate rendering on
the field to match the sublime vision in his mind of how the space
ought to be ordered. Dirk Sijmons marvels: 'There was something
spiritual about it. To me, he seemed like a grandmaster of chess
playing twenty games in his head simultaneously. And there was
almost a kind of telekinesis. He seemed to know where everybody
would be in the next three seconds. Not only was he kicking a ball
in a certain direction, he was also making sure his player would
appear in that place at exactly the right time.' A beautiful little poem
(later made into a song) by the veteran cabaretier Toon Hermans
captures the feeling that there was something sublime about Cruyff
in this respect:

> En Vincent zag het koren
> En Einstein het getal
> En Zeppelin de Zeppelin
> En Johan zag de bal

> (And Vincent saw the corn
> And Einstein the number
> And Zeppelin the Zeppelin
> And Johan saw the ball)

Cruyff's conception of the football field seems so utterly original
and deep – and so essentially Dutch – that it is tempting to say that
Cruyff sees the pitch the way Saenredam saw Holland's churches.
Who? Pieter Jansz Saenredam, a contemporary of Rembrandt and
Vermeer, who devoted himself almost entirely to painting the
interiors of Dutch churches, mainly in his native Haarlem. Almost
unknown in Britain outside academic circles, he is perhaps the most
mysterious and deep of all Dutch artists of space. (Dirk Sijmons
ranks him just below Vermeer but above Rembrandt.) Saenredam is
a J. S. Bach of the visual arts. His austere, oddly shadowless images of

Gothic arches, pillars and organs capture far more than the fabric of the buildings he recorded; they seem also to be visions of divine spatial harmony and order. Humanist connoisseur Constantijn Huyghens, one of the most powerful politicians in the Dutch Republic, said that looking at the depiction of space in Saenredam's paintings was 'like looking at a portrait of God'.

It is only a coincidence, of course, but just as Dutch football has flourished in the last thirty years, so interest in Saenredam has been somewhat revived. It is also only coincidence that during Euro 2000, as the Dutch footballers attempt to dazzle Europe with their passing and spatial organisation on the pitch, a major Saenredam retrospective is to be staged at the Central Museum in Utrecht.

By the banks of the Herengracht, I consult former mathematician Dr Rob Ruurs of the University of Amsterdam's art history institute, author of *Saenredam: The Art of Perspective*, the definitive study of Saenredam's methods and exploration of space. Ruurs's taste in football is austere, electric and unmistakably Netherlandish: Cruyff, Van Basten and Bergkamp are the kind of players he admires most. 'Among most of my colleagues there is a view that someone like Dennis Bergkamp . . .' he pauses, weighing his words carefully, '. . . is certainly a great artist. It is to do with his use of space.' His taste in art is similar. He loves Saenredam and Vermeer for their 'calm, quiet spaces' and regards the infinitely more flamboyant Rubens with distaste. 'I wouldn't say Rubens is loud-mouthed, but he is opulent, cluttered.'

If Dr Ruurs is not entirely convinced by my theory that Cruyff and Saenredam may be connected in some deep way, he does observe some similarities in approach. 'In the same way players like Van Basten and Cruyff cared about, utilised and considered precious every single square inch they had on the field, you could say that Saenredam was obsessed with details of space. When he painted a church hundreds of feet deep, he would still be obsessed by fractions of an inch at the top of a pillar, even though in the painting you wouldn't be able to see the difference.' Saenredam's working methods were far more obsessive than those of any football coach,

and his paintings often took years to finish. First, he would visit a
church, pick a vantage point and sketch what he saw. 'The point of
view and the perspective always seems a little odd,' Ruurs explains.
'He chose strange and surprising angles. It's as if Saenredam used a
fish-eye lens, but then shows us only half the image. The vanishing
point is never where you expect it to be. It does something odd to
the architecture. It's not straightforward.' Saenredam would later
return to the church to check the physical measurements of its every
element, climbing ladders to check the precise height of arches,
going on hands and knees to measure objects at ground level. Years
later, in his studio, he would use these measurements and his
original sketch to create a precisely accurate architectural drawing
of the church. He would then blacken the back of this drawing, nail
it to a white wooden panel, and trace the key lines of the drawing
on to the panel with a sharp object, using the drawing as carbon
paper. Only then would he start to paint. Having evolved from such
mechanical methods, the finished paintings generate an intense
spiritual and emotional charge. One of the most haunting and
mysterious is *Interior of the Church of St Odolphus in Assendelft* (1649),
a rapture of cool cream and white, stone-grey and light wood. The
building is so luminous it appears almost floodlit. A tomb in the
foreground on the right of the picture is the grave of Saenredam's
father, but the living human figures – a sparse congregation listening
to a preacher in a high pulpit – have the shape and vitality of turds,
appearing as shapeless, dull, dark blobs in the pews or slumped on
the floor.

'Saenredam was obviously not very interested in the human
figure; only in notating space,' Ruurs explains. 'The people in his
paintings were painted on later, either by himself or by other
painters. They are not blobs, exactly, but they are certainly very
small, sometimes smaller than they should be. In his system, Rinus
Michels talked of players as numbers to fit a system rather than as
individuals. In Van Gaal's system, the individual player is far less
important than the shape of the team and the structure of the passing
and running movements. In South America the individual players,

as human beings, are much more important than the overall system. But in Holland we are more concerned with overall systems. Saenredam is magnificent but, unlike in Mediterranean art, there is no place for opulence or personal magnificence. He is profoundly Dutch. He simply could not have existed in Italy because there, no matter how interested they were in perspective, they were always much more interested in the human figure.'

Whether or not there is a connection between Cruyff, Van Basten and Bergkamp and the Dutch master of space, football certainly merges with three centuries of Dutch landscape painting in the work of photographer Hans van der Meer.

In 1995, Van der Meer, previously best known for a book of Cartier Bresson-like pictures from Budapest, took his aluminium stepladder and set off on a three-year journey to the heart of Dutchness to photograph amateur and village teams playing on some of the country's oldest football pitches. Dirk Sijmons called the resulting book, *Hollandse Velden* (*Dutch Fields*), 'the best collection of photographs about the Dutch landscape I have ever seen'. They are also among the most beautiful photographs of football to be found anywhere. 'We wanted to make a book that was as far away as possible from professional football,' explains Van der Meer. 'At first I started with top amateur clubs, which have a lot of spectators and are a lot like professional clubs. Then I thought: no. I wanted to go back to how it started a hundred years ago. Just the field, twenty-two players and a horse in the background. Like the original form of football. That's how I ended up far away from pitches with spectators around them.' The adorably bathetic action on the field is only half the story. His photographs show middle-aged footballers falling over in front of goal, mistiming tackles, getting injured and taking throw-ins under huge domed skies in immense flat landscapes dominated by the distant horizon.

The pictures are funny, moving and touchingly human. In one, a player stands on a plank of wood laid over a small canal, contemplating the mirror-like water and wondering how to retrieve the ball that has fallen into it. In another, as a bald, skinny striker with his socks round his ankles prepares to take a corner, he stops to bend down and remove a blade of grass from the perfect white ball at his feet. The orange-flagged corner-stick sways in the wind beside him, but he inhabits a world of straight lines – the edge of the pitch, the side of the canal, the silver-grey of the water, a line of trees, a pasture on the far bank, the dead-straight horizon and more domed sky. One of the strangest images – a huge version of which hangs on the main wall in Van der Meer's apartment in the centre of Amsterdam – is of a goalkeeper's clearance during a game in Gouda. The picture has a flattened, luminous quality. It's a perfect example of how photography can mummify a moment in time, rendering a forgotten split-second of action simultaneously dead and eternal. A line of leafless poplars, fences, a thin strip of canal and low, white, ochre-roofed storehouses are visible, as is most of the middle of the pitch. Of the sixteen featured outfield players wearing yellow or blue-and-white striped shirts, only one appears to be running. Two others jog. Everyone else is walking or standing completely still, including both linesmen and the referee, who even holds his hands behind his back. The ball, presumably hoofed by the goalkeeper, is far overhead in the right corner, several metres above the trees, looking like a small, new moon in the pale-blue and puffy white-clouded sky. No game of football has ever looked so much like a still life.

'Not that I studied it, but I know the rules those guys in the seventeenth century had about horizons, perspective, the landscape and all that', says Van der Meer. 'I never think of those things when I'm working, but when I see the pictures later I see there is something of that in there. The pictures are not chaotic; there are straight lines all the time. I try to make it simple. The corner-flag is interesting. When I first went to these amateur matches, the play always seemed to be on the other side of the field. For half an hour no one would be near me. I made the mistake of changing my position to be closer to the action. Then I understood I simply had to wait for it to come to me. Often, my picture would be ready and I only had to wait for the players.'

Van der Meer has taken memorable photographs of Ajax matches, too – but never from the traditional photographers' vantage point at ground level behind the goal or on the sidelines. He prefers to work high in the stands, usually near the halfway line, from where he aims to capture what he calls 'the moment of tension'. His deep-focus, pin-sharp images freeze the game, the crowd, and the trees and clouds beyond the stadium. Although his pictures are taken from a similar angle to that of TV cameras, they capture something quite different. 'Football is a game of space. So why should you leave the space out?' he says. 'Every Monday in the newspapers you see the same stupid, boring close-ups taken from behind the goals with long telephoto lenses which distort the space. Those pictures show you football situations but you have no idea what they mean. Two players fight for the ball. So what? Where on the pitch are they? In the 1950s, we had different pictures, more interesting photographs of the crowd, wide-angle pictures of the game. The close-ups tell you so little. When the sports photography archives are opened in a hundred years, there will be a whole part of the history of the game missing because all the interesting little things around the pitch were simply not photographed.'

Also on Van der Meer's wall is a large photograph taken at the old De Meer stadium in 1995, the year Van Gaal's Ajax was the best team in the world. The image captures the tactics and the system at its peak. Tearing forward, the Ajax 'shadow striker' Jari Litmanen has the ball at his feet near the centre-circle. Ten metres ahead of him, centre-forward Patrick Kluivert is a ball of coiled energy, surrounded by defenders, but poised to make his move. Left-winger Marc Overmars and right-winger Finidi George are already running into space. Behind Litmanen, the three other members of the midfield diamond that day, Edgard Davids on the left, Arnold Scholten on the right and Winston Bogarde behind, are advancing with cool menace. (A copy of the photograph also hangs on the walls of the café at Ajax's school, De Toekomst (The Future).

'There are one or two moments when a situation develops and you understand something will happen. This is the moment of tension, of possibility. This is what I look for. You see the possibilities. The next moment they are over – the game moves to something else. Everyone in the crowd shares this tension. The pleasure of going to a football game is that you all feel this together. It's like chess. When newspapers report a chess game, they don't show you the final move. They show you the position ten moves from the end because that is the most dramatic situation. The midfield is often more dramatic than the penalty area. The moment of the goal is not particularly interesting. What happens just before the goal: that is much more interesting.'

He shows me another picture, taken two years later – in the Arena – on the night of the first leg of Ajax's Champions' League semi-final against Juventus. The tactical pattern of the game – and the moment when the world understood that Van Gaal's Bosman-ravaged Ajax was finished – is captured in a single image. Four black-and-white-shirted Juventus players – Lombardo, Zidane (who has the ball at his feet), Inzaghi and Vieri – are attacking in a neat curved line five metres from the Ajax penalty area. Facing them are just two Ajax defenders, Bogarde and Mario Melchiot. Goalkeeper Van der Sar is on his line. Juventus won the match 2–1 and later crushed Ajax 4–1 in the second leg in Turin. 'Newspaper picture editors always say it's much more dramatic to have a close-up. That is bullshit. The problem is basically they don't understand football, they don't know what they're looking at. Of course, yes, it is nice also to have close-ups, to see footballers looking like heroes. But you need both kinds of picture. What can be more dramatic than this? Four Italian attackers converging on two Dutch defenders. It's a terrifying image.'

Even though Van der Meer's pictures are drenched in Dutch sensibilities, something about the hyper-measured Dutch landscape makes him uncomfortable. 'We shouldn't be too proud of our landscape. When you see Holland from the air, it is so precise and mathematical that it's scary. You look at the old straight canals, all perfectly the same distance from each other. It's too much. It's like we are living in the paintings of Mondrian. I wouldn't necessarily like to be in a room with Mondrian, with him as my father. It would drive me crazy. You go to the new towns. The architects have made little playful curved roofs, which is nice. Not every damned thing is straight. But they forgot that every little house is still precisely ten metres apart and they are all in completely straight lines.'

10: curves

'It's simple mathematics, pure mathematics . . .' Barry Hulshoff, amiable part-time philosopher, is drawing a series of complex diagrams on a tablecloth in a café near the railway station in Breda. Hulshoff now coaches Belgian First Division side Eendracht Aalst, but to save me a trip into darkest Flanders he has sweetly agreed to meet me in this Dutch town near the Holland–Belgium border. The old rock of the Ajax defence, once known for his long hair, shaggy beard and love of heavy-metal music, is now demonstrating as simply as possible how, in a hypothetical position, two mobile and intelligent defenders can neutralise four attackers simply by standing in the right place and moving smartly. 'You see? In this position, you can cover this player . . .' – a swirl of neat lines, arrows and blobs appears on the paper – 'OK, maybe. But if you stand here, it is twice as good.' More lines and a swirl of movement ending with a flourish of the pen. 'You see? This is better; it's very simple. Why? Because in this position, you have ninety degrees to play. If I stand here, I have 180 degrees. Pure mathematics, simple mathematics. And the only reason players don't do this is that they don't know. Everyone does it the bad way, the stupid way. To do it better means they have to move. They have to go this side or this side. They have to run a little. This man must go a little nearer to the ball, the other one a little further away. But you can do it with two defenders. Ninety degrees or 180 degrees. Simple mathematics. Only mathematics.'

*   *   *

One of the most striking exponents of modern, fluid Dutch architecture is the witty and inventive Rotterdam architect Lars Spuybroek. He's widely thought of as one of Holland's most original young architects, and I'd love him to show me a clear link between Dutch football and Dutch architecture. But he's playing hard to get, insisting there is no connection of any kind between football and architecture. 'Architecture has to do with lots of rules, many hierarchies of rules and organisation. It is materialised. A football match is a constant recharging of space. It's pure affect. There are rules but the rules aren't materialised. It's dynamic. When there are transformations within a game, there are transformations within your body and in the emotions. It's a very emotional space. It's a space of affects. A building also is an emotional space but it tries to transpose it into architecture.' He insists there is only one architectural structure in the game: the defensive wall – and that should have been rendered obsolete when Platini found a way to curl free kicks around and over it.

At school, Spuybroek was a 'Feyenoord freak' and a style-obsessed goalkeeper. 'If I made one beautiful save, I was happy. It didn't matter after that if I let in five.' Instead of wearing the traditional No. 1 on his goalkeeping jersey, he wore a No. 10 in honour of his hero, Wim van Hanegem, who was nicknamed 'De Kromme' – 'The Crooked' – in part because of his bandy legs but mainly because he hit sensational curves. From his childhood on, Van Hanegem preferred to kick the ball with the outside of his left foot. As a child neither he nor his opponents knew what the ball would do when it bounced or where it would end up. By the time he was a star in the Feyenoord and Dutch national teams, however, his technique was perfected. Not only did he produce some of world football's most peculiar curved balls, he also had become extraordinarily accurate with his passing, shooting and free kicks. It is of course pure coincidence that Spuybroek grew up to design buildings with nothing but curves in them. Curves in steel, in concrete, rubber, wood . . . anything, so long as it curls and swoops and bubbles in space. 'A curve is the most natural, the strongest way between A and B, between two points in space. The straight line is always warped by effects.'

In the past, architects dealt primarily in flat surfaces because curves were difficult to make. Architects such as Gaudi or the leader of the Amsterdam school, Michel de Klerk, who wanted curved walls or billowing brickwork, had to rely on dedicated artists and craftsmen to make their visions a reality. These days computers, quantum mathematics and new manufacturing processes mean curved surfaces in a variety of materials can be designed and produced both economically and efficiently and then easily incorporated into buildings. The shapes Spuybroek produces are radical, bewildering and strangely beautiful. He won an award for a vaguely sinister, bright yellow vase that looks like a melted instrument of discomfort you might see in a David Cronenberg movie.

Rinus Michels and his Ajax team may have invented the idea of defenders who attack and attackers who defend, but Spuybroek has taken the notion of position-switching in an entirely new direction. His design for a traffic-noise barrier near Eindhoven allowed drivers and people in their homes to switch roles. While the homes were shielded by earthworks from the noises of the road, drivers could tune in to hear what was going on in the houses as they drove by. Household sounds – people watching TV, shouting at their children, vacuuming, running showers, having sex – were picked up by microphones and broadcast to the cars via a local radio network.

Lars believes in intelligent, flexible systems – like flocks of birds (and Dutch football teams) – rather than inflexible phalanxes (and old-style English football teams). He talks fluently, passionately and playfully about vectors, tangents, splines, tectonics . . . I'm having trouble keeping up. He loathes the 'Bill Gates idea that every behaviour can be analysed and replaced with a copy of machines. Gates would build a "smart house" which replicates and anticipates your behaviour. It would run your bath for you to the right temperature. You could have a holiday in your own house because the house lives your life for you. I think technology is perfect. But you shouldn't use it to pacify or change reality, but to motorise it, speed it up.'

He shows me on his computer an animated model of his latest project, a scheme for more than one hundred houses near Eindhoven. The houses will not have flat walls or designated kitchens, bathrooms, bedrooms or many of the standard paraphernalia of 'tectonically Euclidean' architects. Instead they will have curves like voluptuous women and they will have 'radii of action': fluid spaces that will give people the freedom to construct their own living arrangements, their own places to cook and bathe, park their cars or throw wild parties. The twisting, multi-coloured, almost alive 3-D image on the screen pulses and blobs like the pod that explodes into John Hurt's face in *Alien*. 'Generally an architect says: we have functions – a toilet, a corridor, a study, a living room, and so on. Architecture is tectonically Euclidean because it sees the user's behaviour as mechanised, something you can reduce to a type. So cooking is cooking and every point in the space that is the kitchen is to do with cooking. The building isn't interested in whether you kill your wife or make love or whatever. It's just cooking.'

In Lars's buildings, as the critic Bart Lootsma observed, 'Architecture becomes one constant metamorphosis.' There remains no connection between football and architecture but Lars does love his football. He talks me through his favourite goal, Van Basten's greatest, the extraordinary dipping volley from an impossible angle in the 1988 European Championship final in 1988. A goal, he says, that was made by a system. 'It is sort of obvious that this goal was not an invention by an individual. Muhren already hit the ball too far before Van Basten touched it. So Muhren had the idea, but this idea was not morpho-genetically transposed into the brain or foot of Van Basten. It was the system which moved forward, which found a way through the Russian players. The system is larger than the individual. Poor Dassayev! Every night he wakes up in a cold sweat as he sees this incredible ball moving like a baseball over his head! You can't rationalise it. It's like driving a car. That is also about being part of a system larger than you . . . the car becomes you. You can only drive it when you don't know the rules any more, when you forget everything they taught you. Every time you turn a corner, you don't get out of the car to measure the curves and then get back into the car. You do everything blind because of the system, the road and the other cars, which are part of the system too . . . And that's the moment when you are 'in form' in both senses. It feels good and there's this whole hectic feeling of extension into the world that is being "informed".'

Spuybroek's most famous building is his 'water pavilion' in Zeeland, a museum built for the water ministry. Here not only have the tyrannies of wall, ceiling, floor and furniture been abolished completely, but the distinction between solid and fluid is hazy as well. Water cascades, spurts and drifts everywhere; mists float through the strange, cavelike structures. 'It's space, experience, electronics, concrete, light, sound, flashing. One integrated thing. It's not like seeing a painting and looking at the horizon in a frame. There is no horizon. It is the watering of space.' The rubber floor, which is controlled by high-powered computers and an array of sensors, is programmed to behave like water. Mesmerised, delighted children run up and down, and the floor responds with a medley of ripples and flows. 'It's like a heartbeat,' he explains. 'A programme calculates the splash of the virtual-water. The computer makes 800,000 calculations a second, which is as quick as water molecules. The sensors can even make waves which interfere with each other. It's a simple algorithm,' he says, 'just simple mathematics. Pure mathematics.'

1: democracy

In the hot summer of 1975 Wim van Hanegem was offered the chance to leave his beloved Feyenoord and join the French club Olympique Marseille for a very large amount of money. He couldn't decide what to do, so he went to an island in Zeeland to talk it over with his wife, Truus, his best friend (and fellow midfielder) Wim Jansen, and Jansen's wife. The four of them took a picnic to the beach and mulled over the pros and cons for hours. Finally, Van Hanegem called for a show of hands: two votes to go; two to stay. So he turned to his dog: 'We can't decide. It's up to you now. If you want to go to Marseille, bark or show me.' For several minutes the dog and Van Hanegem stared at each other. The dog didn't move. 'OK,' said Wim, 'he doesn't want to go. We're staying.'

6: who's in charge?

'We would have been champions of Europe for eight years if we'd stayed together'

Gerrie Muhren

Ajax seemed majestic and invincible in their golden age. But by July 1973 discipline, team-spirit and the righteous harmony essential for continued success had waned. Rinus Michels had gone to Barcelona after Ajax's first European Cup victory in 1971, and there were rumours Johan Cruyff wanted to join him there for the 1974–5 season. Some of the lesser-known Ajax players were said to resent Cruyff's star status and earning capacity. When Michels's successor, Stefan Kovacs, also departed following the club's third European Cup triumph, a new coach, George Knobel from MVV Maastricht, had been appointed in his place. The genial Kovacs had presided over a prodigious flowering of talent at Ajax largely by taking a back seat. He enjoyed the sense of freedom he found in Amsterdam and encouraged it in his players; he made astute tactical observations and set the mood. But he let assistant coach Bobby Haarms organise training sessions and gave the players, especially the most dominant personalities, Johan Cruyff and Piet Keizer, a remarkable degree of authority on the pitch. The freedom the players enjoyed is probably without parallel at the highest level of the modern game. Even in the post-Bosman era in which power has shifted sharply from clubs to players, there has been nothing to compare with this giddy, unintentional experiment in football democracy. It was probably as close as anyone has ever come to running a major football team like a workers' co-operative: not only did the team practically pick itself, but the players also determined most of their own tactics and decided which friendly matches they wanted to play.

They had fallen into the habit of choosing their own captain, too.

In three years Ajax had won three European Cups, and each time a different leader had received the trophy at the presentation ceremony. In 1971, at Wembley, it was the tough-minded Yugoslav Velibor Vasovic, Rinus Michels's appointee. At De Kuip in Rotterdam the following year, when Ajax beat Inter, it was Piet Keizer. After Ajax's defeat of Juventus in Belgrade in May 1973, Johan Cruyff, who had taken over without a hint of dissent after Keizer relinquished the job, was the man given the honour of hoisting the trophy. Cruyff was still captain at the start of the 1973–4 season when Ajax gathered, as had become their pre-season ritual, for training camp at De Lutte, a small, quiet hotel near the German border. On the first day George Knobel assembled the players and gave an unremarkable team talk. The meeting was winding to its dull conclusion when Knobel remembered something. 'There's one last thing. The captaincy. We'll have to decide who's the captain.'

If there was a single instant when Ajax's golden age ended, this was probably it.

To this day Knobel insists he was simply abiding by a club tradition. 'Every year the captain of Ajax was chosen by the players without the presence of the coach,' he says. 'It was the custom for many years. The assistant coach, Bobby Haarms, told me that every year it was the same system. I wasn't even in the room when they voted. When the meeting was finished I heard the results and that was it.' The names of the three candidates were written on the blackboard: Johan Cruyff, Piet Keizer, Barry Hulshoff. There were no speeches or arguments – the players simply wrote one of the names on a piece of paper and put it into a plant pot on the table. The whole process took only a few minutes – and, nearly thirty years after the event, it seems no one can remember the precise result. Indeed, rather in the spirit of the event itself, accounts of the meeting and its background flatly contradict each other and it's impossible to determine whether it *was* traditional for such a vote to be held.

No one voted for Hulshoff. Most people present reckon Keizer received about twelve votes. Cruyff got between three and seven. The precise figures were probably irrelevant. Jan Mulder remembers Cruyff's expression when Knobel uttered his fatal words. 'I saw it in his face. He didn't know this was coming. It was like a coup — that was the terrible thing. Johan Cruyff was the captain of Ajax and suddenly, with a new coach, the players wanted to have a new election. He was shocked, his confidence in them was shattered. He didn't understand it. He was furious. To undermine his authority like that, it was a deep insult. I saw it in his eyes. As soon as the question was put, he wanted to leave Ajax. It was over for him in that moment. Maybe he even voted for Keizer himself. It's possible, he's a strange man. Perhaps he thought: "Just throw it all away".' After the meeting Cruyff went upstairs. Mulder continues: 'Cruyff at that time had a room together with the goalkeeper, Heinz Stuy. Heinz and myself went upstairs and Johan was there. He said, 'No, it's OK.' But there was a phone hanging on the wall and we saw him go to the phone. He called his father-in-law; he was open about it. We heard him say: 'You have to call Barcelona immediately. I'm leaving here.'' '

Cruyff played two more League games for Ajax, the last a decidedly bitter-sweet 6–1 victory over FC Amsterdam on 19 August, and left for the Camp Nou two weeks later for a record transfer fee of $1 million. He was so determined to leave quickly that he joined FC Barcelona despite being ineligible to play competitive matches for them until the end of the year. Neither he nor the players he left behind ever achieved quite the same level in club football again. In Catalonia, Cruyff's impact was so extraordinary that he was known as '*El Salvador*', 'The Saviour'. When he arrived, Barcelona were bottom of the Spanish League; by the end of the season, they were champions for the first time since 1960. But he was unable to repeat the trick and the furthest he took Barcelona as a player in the European Cup was the semi-final of 1975, when they were beaten by Leeds. The great Ajax played one last great match – a 6–0 thrashing of AC Milan in the Super Cup in January 1974. But they had already lost their European Champions' crown, having been knocked out in the first round by CSKA Sofia two months previously. The team disintegrated rapidly. Sjaak Swart had already retired, in August 1973. Knobel fell out with his stars, not least because of a newspaper interview in which he accused some of them of drinking and womanising, and he was sacked in April 1974. Johan Neeskens stayed until the end of the season, then followed Cruyff to Barcelona. Keizer fell out with Knobel's replacement, Hans Kraay, in a dispute in October 1974 over tactics and walked out not just on Ajax but on football itself as well. For nearly three decades Keizer refused even to kick a ball again, on one occasion famously stepping away from the ball as it rolled towards him on the touchline while he stood watching his son playing in a boys' game. Arie Haan went to Anderlecht in March 1975. A month later Horst Blankenburg headed home to Germany. A month after that, Johnny Rep was off to Valencia. Heinz Stuy left in January 1976; Gerrie Muhren went to Seville five months later. The defenders stayed a little longer. Barry Hulshoff and Wim Suurbier both departed in 1977. Ruud Krol stayed until 1980 – and came to regret staying for so long.

Knobel argues, as do some of the players, that the 1973 captaincy election was largely inconsequential: Cruyff was going to leave anyway because he could earn more money in Spain, and the team was bound to break up. 'When I signed for Ajax, I expected to work with the best professionals who ever played football in the world,' says Knobel. 'But the players were thinking they could go to the clouds. "No problem", "We are the best in the world", "We can beat every club". They were arrogant. Getting to the top in the world is very difficult, but staying in that position is more difficult. I was not surprised when Cruyff left because I already knew for a long time that he would not stay at Ajax. Everyone knew it. And I think the whole incident of the captaincy is blown up without any normal proportions. It was nice for the media to say Johan Cruyff is no longer captain and now he is leaving Ajax. [The election] had nothing to do with it. Cruyff had the impression that the other players didn't like him any more, and that's right. The players *didn't* like him any more because everybody was jealous. All the publicity was for Cruyff, and some of the players were thinking: "We are as good as Cruyff".'

Jan Mulder says Knobel was unwise to announce the election, but that no one could have stopped the ultimate break-up of the team. 'The election was a mistake, but Knobel didn't screw it up. The team fell apart – it's normal. It would have been the same with anybody. It was natural. Three great years and then, yes, players like Arie Haan and Krol wanted to earn as much money as Cruyff did. And it was possible in Spain and Italy. So they began to manoeuvre too. There was a little bit of jealousy but that's human.'

Gerrie Muhren, on the other hand, does lay much of the blame at Knobel's door. 'It was not a question of tradition. It was the trainer [Knobel] who said we'd have an election. It had never happened before, this was the first time. That's why it was so strange. I'd played nine years for Ajax and we only had an election one time. It was not a decision for the players. This was a decision the trainer had to make. The trainer was new. He thought it was a good idea to ask the players to pick a captain. It was a shock to all the players. But no one discussed it beforehand. If Johan Cruyff was the captain, why have an election? It can only make problems. All I remember is that I voted for Johan because I knew that if we didn't vote for him, he would go to Barcelona and then we would all have a problem. Some players said, "We can play without Johan" – there was a little bit of jealousy in it. The vote was the last drop for Johan. He had already been offered a lot of money. But if there had been no election he might have stayed a couple more years with Ajax.'

Muhren likens the disintegration of the great team – alongside Di Stefano's Real Madrid quite possibly the most gifted club-side ever – to the break-up of the Beatles. 'The Beatles are a good example.

In the beginning, like them, we had enthusiasm together. But later the pleasure was gone, we didn't want to play together any more. We still had the same qualities, and when we were on the field we were the same players. But after the game, everyone was starting to go their own way. If you don't have pleasure in soccer, then it goes wrong.' Muhren says there was already some degree of competitiveness between the players, but that the disintegration of the team began with Stefan Kovacs's term as coach. 'He was a very good trainer but he was too nice. Rinus Michels was more professional. He was for total discipline; very strict; everyone at the same level. In the beginning, in the first year, we played even better with Kovacs because we were good players and now we were free to make our own fantasies on the field. But after that, the discipline went and it was over.' Everything – including winning – had become too easy for the Ajax players. They were regularly Dutch Champions; they'd won the Super Cup; the Dutch Cup; and the European Cup three years in a row. 'We were all stars, a little bit. In the last year [1973] we still won everything, but not with the same spirit as before. It's a pity. If we could have kept the team together, we could have been champions for eight years running. It was a very young team; only Sjaak Swart was old, but we had Johnny Rep to take over.'

Johnny Rep, who broke into the first team in the 1972–3 season, voted for Keizer and remembers the election as a low-key affair. 'We just wanted to take someone else, but, yes, I think it broke something for Johan. That was it for him.' According to Rep there were no arguments from anyone concerned; Cruyff was a leader but Keizer was more easygoing and better suited to the captaincy. 'We went further with Johan as a player. But the talking, it was terrible! It was not easy, not all the time. He said you must do this in a game, or you must do that. It was not easy for me to shut my mouth. He was always saying: more to the right, or to the left, or the centre. Always! If he gave a bad ball, it was never his fault. And he is always right! He is the best and all the time he is right. That was the problem with him for me; but only at the beginning [Playing together in the national team for the World Cup] in 1974 it was fine. I don't remember everything but I think Johan only got two or three votes.'

Barry Hulshoff also voted for Keizer and says Cruyff misunderstood the vote. 'On the field there was no problem with Johan. But off the field, in dealing with the board and so on, Keizer thought more about the team. Johan put himself in a more exceptional position; so when things had to be done for the team, Piet Keizer was better.' Hulshoff insists Cruyff was always the star of the team, was treated as such by the other players on the field and should never have worried about the captain's armband. 'Johan was clearly the star – he didn't need the captaincy for that. Johan always said: "You didn't vote for me because you didn't like me." But it had nothing to do with that. He was very important for the team. But I felt he needed this captaincy to expose himself more and more to the world as the star. We thought he already was that; and for the team it was more important to have Keizer. It had nothing to do with Johan's ability.'

Another Keizer vote came from Ruud Krol, who says that with hindsight perhaps things would have been different. 'After the election we spoke with each other; we spoke with Johan and he spoke with the team and everything, and he promised to stay. But then, two weeks later, he went. I think it was a matter of money. That was the main reason all the players left.' There were other factors, too. 'In the time of the super-team at Ajax, we played in front of crowds of 12,000 people. We talked about that all the time. If we had been in Italy or Spain, each week there would have been 100,000 people watching. We were a little frustrated by that. For European Cup games, OK, it was better. There were 60- or 70,000 people. But they weren't really Amsterdam people. About half the crowds for those games came from outside the city. They couldn't come to every League game.'

In less than a year, Cruyff and his Ajax colleagues – Haan, Krol, Suurbier, Rep, Neeskens, Keizer – had all more or less made their peace, and played together in the 1974 World Cup. Ajax, though, entered a long, bleak period that lasted through Cruyff's Indian summer until he returned as coach in 1985. (This time the motive was clearly financial: in 1979 Cruyff lost everything he owned when an unscrupulous business partner persuaded him to invest all his money – some $2.4 million – in a disastrous pig-breeding venture in Spain.)

The plant-pot election may have been rooted in the personalities of the players, but it was also influenced by wider Dutch political culture. It particularly has some of the flavour of the intense participatory democracy that developed in Amsterdam in the 1960 and early 1970s, spawned by the success of anarchist and counter-culture groups, such as the Provos and Kabouters.

Playwright Johan Timmers, co-author of the tragi-comedy *De Reunie*, which explored the painful legacy of the lost 1974 World Cup final, observes: 'There was a strange tension in that team between the individual and the collective. Being together in the group made the best team, allowed everyone to do their best work. The group was everything. The group, the group. This was very important in the seventies. There were theatre groups, collectives of all kinds. Here we had a collective with an extraordinary leader inside the collective – Cruyff – who always talked about the collective as the most important thing. Yet he was the only one not doing what the collective did! He went his own way within it. It's a contradiction in one person. He was always telling the other players: "We must play as a group". But the moment he got the ball, he was allowed to run everywhere with it and at the same time he would criticise the others for doing the same thing. And at a certain point, the collective stands up and attacks its leader.'

The behaviour of the Ajax players certainly reflected deeper traditions in this respect. For centuries, the Dutch have rejected strong leaders. Indeed, the notion of leadership itself is problematic in a country where Calvin taught that every individual should read the Bible and decide its meaning for himself. In Holland, the ideal decision is a unanimous one agreed by a group. No decision in business or politics is ever taken without endless rounds of discussions and meetings to reach consensus. A tradition going back to the *regenten* – the cabals of wealthy men who ran the Dutch Republic – decrees that Dutch leaders shun the limelight and act in the name of the collective. The usual explanation for Dutch democracy is one of hydraulics: because of their watery landscape, the Dutch have always had to co-operate with each other to keep their land dry. 'Co-operation and making agreements with each other was the only way to survive,' says Dirk Sijmons. 'Our very earliest traces of something you would call government had to do with building dikes together and maintaining them. The late twentieth-century expression of it might be the Polder Model, which means there is co-operation between antagonists, between, say, the labour part of the spectrum and the capitalist industrialist part. So we have a really strange political system with far too many parties – about twenty. We have far too much co-operation, too much consultation. As a comedian said, every Dutch man is his own political party. So when you ask: "So, who's in charge here?", everyone shouts out: "Well, no one!" No one is really in charge. Maybe this egalitarianism and co-operation is why the Dutch see football as a form of co-operation: everybody has to be in the service of the system.' The Chinese curse 'May you live in interesting times' is never liable to apply to Dutch politics, which are almost certainly the dullest of any nation in Europe. Dutch politics are based on an elegant, slow-moving system of consultation, discussion, checks and balances that slowly drains away all traces of drama or sudden changes of direction. Writer Michiel Schwartz jokes: 'The political system is designed to be dull. If anything exciting, interesting or dramatic ever happens in Dutch politics, it means that something's gone horribly wrong.'

How does anything ever get done? Jan Benthem, one of the country's most effective and influential architects, has a reputation for being able to manoeuvre his giant projects – such as the re-design of Schiphol Airport and Amsterdam's Central Station – through the morass of Dutch bureaucracy and consultation. 'Part of the trick is not talking about it. Never discuss your method. I especially don't discuss it with journalists or in public. You do things somewhere in the background and let someone else enjoy the success. When your head is above the level of the grass, it will be cut off in the Netherlands. We have a lot of grass here and we always have to cut it. It is very Dutch not to like people who really excel in something. That's why people here don't like Ruud Gullit. That's why we don't have architects like Lord Norman Foster or Sir Richard Rogers. They simply don't exist in the Netherlands. They can't exist here because if they did, someone would try to bring them down. Rem Koolhaas is definitely the best, biggest and most influential Dutch architect, but he doesn't get the biggest jobs. Why isn't he asked to build a large government building, or an airport or a railway station? It's part of the tradition. The Dutch like things level, to keep the country flat, to keep the landscape flat, to keep the cultural landscape flat. We don't like high peaks.

'Maybe in football you have the same thing. Teamwork in Dutch football is based on the equality of all the players. It cannot be built, say, only around Johan Cruyff. Even with Cruyff it was not built around Cruyff. When it worked well, it was a team of equals with everyone expecting each other to be equal. For the team to work, the team has to be the star, not the players. This is quite different from Italian football, which is constructed around key figures.' To get things done at Schiphol, Benthem says, he rarely deals with the airport's top executive. 'I never see the president more than once a year. If I wanted to, I could go every week, but if I did that it would be impossible for me to work with all the other people. Responsibilities are delegated to a low level in the organisation. There is no president who says: "We do it like this". He has to have agreement with all of his management. And if I don't work on a daily basis with this level, much lower to the floor, nothing will happen.'

Unlike in England, rank alone confers very little natural respect in Holland. It's natural for British footballers to defer to 'the gaffer' and call him 'boss'. In Holland respect has to be earned. 'Knobel was a really nice person but he was not so respected by the players. I think he had too much respect for us,' says Johnny Rep disimissively. Players always accepted orders from Rinus Michels and from Johan Cruyff as coach. But even Ernst Happel, the brilliant and enigmatic Austrian who led Feyenoord to the European Cup in 1970, was initially regarded with some disdain by the former Ajax stars when he took over as coach of the national team before the 1978 World Cup. He solved the problem without a word in a training session by lining up balls on the eighteen-yard line and then striking each one precisely against the crossbar. The players listened to him after that.

The famous Dutch sense of democracy and equality is based less on ideology than on the country's habitual reliance on contractual rights and agreements. The most controversial current Dutch coach, Louis van Gaal, often refers to such things after matches when discussing his players' performances: 'We lost control over the game because some of us did not keep the agreement.' Frank Rijkaard, who played his last two seasons under Van Gaal, uses similar language now that he is the national coach. The most commonly heard complaint about Van Gaal is that he is a 'fanatic', a 'dictator', a man who treats his players like children (a consequence, it is said, of his being a schoolteacher for twelve years). Most Dutch journalists can't stand the man, and his uncharming image hasn't been helped by his constant aggressive confrontations – sometimes actually shouting at members of the press who criticise him. This is interpreted as bullying. If he *is* a dictator, though, Van Gaal is a very Dutch one. He is neither a once-corrupt autocrat and martinet like George Graham nor a capricious eccentric like Brian Clough, who made a career out of hectoring young men and really did treat his players like children. (Lee Chapman, a father of two when he played at Nottingham Forest, recalls Clough challenging him as he came out of the toilet: 'Have you washed your hands, son?') Van Gaal may be a devout disciplinarian but while the press loathe him, most of the people who have worked closely with him speak of his integrity and honesty. It is striking that so many of his former Ajax players (Reiziger, Bogarde, Litmanen, Kluivert, Frank and Ronald de Boer) were keen to rejoin him at Barcelona. Van Gaal believes in constant communication and improving the team through constructive criticism. He encourages his staff and players to criticise each other and themselves. Van Gaal's former deputy, Gerard van der Lem, has a picture on his wall of himself and Van Gaal. The picture was taken the night Ajax won the UEFA Cup in May 1992. Van der Lem is holding the cup aloft and Van Gaal is holding Van der Lem aloft – carrying his friend on his shoulders. Van Gaal's usually unsmiling face is a beacon of ecstasy and radiance; he doesn't look very dictatorial.

Van Gaal does have quite definite ideas about how processes of consultation and leadership will be resolved in his team. He is willing to consult, he has said, but he makes the decisions and does not tolerate public dissent. 'The media frequently portray me as an authoritarian figure who thinks he knows it all; the people who work with me daily know better. I learn something new every day from the people around me. I ask everyone to say what he feels. I talk to players every day. It is then my task as the leader of that team – and I very definitely count players as part of it – to make a selection from all the information available and to decide on the course to be taken. But then I expect everyone to support this course in public, because to do otherwise is simply asking for problems.'

Nearly three decades after the 1973 captaincy election, Barry Hulshoff is clear what the experiment in player power proved: 'When you are all equal, at the same level, you have to make decisions together.' But that's in part what broke up the great team. 'It's better that one man is outside the group, controlling everything. Then you can talk together as equals. But there must be someone outside who is above, who makes decisions and controls, takes sanctions and so on. And therefore you need a trainer. A team on its own can't do it. The team can't make the rules.'

13: Football Is Not War

"Football is war"

Rinus Michels

The events of Munich, July 7, 1974 are burnt into the Dutch soul the way Dallas, November 22, 1963 haunts America. It may be obscene to suggest any precise equivalence between the horrific murder of President Kennedy and the losing of a mere football match; yet all over Holland grown men wept the day the Dutch lost the World Cup final to their neighbours. A TV poll conducted on the twentieth anniversary of the episode revealed that every sentient Dutch person recalled precisely where they were and what they were doing. Playwright Johan Timmers studied the calamity and its aftermath and concluded: "The defeat of 1974 is the biggest trauma that happened to Holland in the twentieth century, apart from the floods of 1953 and World War Two."

The Lost Final is still the subject to which every conversation about Dutch football eventually turns. Why did Holland's greatest team ever – Cruyff, Van Hanegem, Neeskens, Krol, et al. – fail at the final hurdle? The Total Footballers scored in the first minute of the match, played dominating, superior possession football for twenty-five minutes and then spent the whole second half attacking relentlessly. And they lost. The most talented group of footballers their country – almost any country – ever produced blew it. How? Why? It's a riddle wrapped in a mystery inside an enigma.

Holland's defeat by West Germany marked not only the demise of a footballing ideal but also the end of an era of cultural and political optimism. "It should have been the epiphany of the sixties. Instead it turned out to be its requiem," says historian Bastiaan

Bommeljé. "The team was a product of an age that had put all its money on youth and the promise of youth and the idea that good times will be here when a new generation takes over." Much more problematically, the game also became a vehicle for complex feelings about the Nazi occupation and post-war Germany.

It is startling to recall that until the 1970s Holland had an international football record almost on par with Luxembourg. Holland was a third-rate nation which had failed to qualify for any World Cup since 1938. In 1974, they were lucky to be going to the World Cup in West Germany at all. In qualifying matches Holland had walloped lowly Norway and Cyprus, scoring twenty-four goals to two. But they had drawn with their much more dangerous rivals, Belgium. In the hard-fought and decisive second match in Amsterdam in November 1973, Belgian striker Jan Verheyen scored in the last seconds. The goal should have knocked Holland out, but Russian referee Khazakov ruled it offside. TV replays showed he was wrong.

The finals of a modern tournament were thus a new experience for the Dutch, and it was fortunate that the KNVB for once appointed the best man as national coach. Three months before the World Cup finals began, Rinus Michels replaced Frantisek Fadhronc, who had been in charge for the qualification period. Michels had a remarkably seasoned and talented group of players at his disposal with Feyenoord (who won the European Cup in 1970 and the Uefa Cup in 1974) and Ajax (winners of three successive European Cups between 1971 and 1973) supplying the bulk. Johan Cruyff came home from Barcelona; Rob Rensenbrink, the winger who had become a legend in Belgium, arrived from Anderlecht.

Michels planned to replicate the system that he and the players, and later Stefan Kovacs, had brought to perfection at Ajax. Not all the Ajax – or Ajax-trained – players were available, however. Sophisticated stopper Barry Hulshoff was injured and Horst Blankenburg was German. Left midfielder Gerrie Muhren refused to join the squad because his son was ill. Winger Piet Keizer was

in the squad but at thirty-four was past his best. (Also, Keizer and
Michels had never got on personally; Keizer would play in only
the second game of the tournament, Rensenbrink taking his place
for all the other matches.) The presence of talented Feyenoord
players added guile and strength to the squad. The midfield was
covered by the canny and thoughtful midfielder Wim Jansen, who
took Arie Haan's place on the right side, and the tough-tackling,
visionary passing genius Wim van Hanegem in Muhren's place on
the left.

The biggest problem for Michels was his defence. Ajax's great
attacking full backs Krol and Suurbier would play; but what to do
without the normal central defenders Barry Hulshoff and 'Iron'
Rinus Israel, whose father died before the finals? Michels adopted a radical solution. The hard and mobile (though uncapped)
Feyenoord defender Wim Rijsbergen and Arie Haan, who had
never before played in defence, would be the central pairing.
Haan's fine passing meant he would operate as sweeper in front
of the last man. Michels intended to make attack the best form
of defence. Even more bold was his choice of goalkeeper. The
man generally considered Holland's best, Jan van Beveren, was
slightly injured and perennially in conflict with Cruyff. Another
obvious candidate was Piet Schrijvers of Twente. But, at Cruyff's
prompting, Michels opted instead for the veteran Jan Jongbloed
of FC Amsterdam. It seemed a bizarre choice. Jongbloed was 34
years old and had played just one international match before, a
1-4 defeat by Denmark way back in 1962. Jongbloed remains the
only World Cup goalkeeper ever selected for his outfield qualities. He was a talented shot-stopper, but he could also play with
his feet. In the final stages of a game, if his club was losing – and
usually they were – he loved to race out of his goal to join the
attack. In Germany, Michels wanted a goalkeeper who could
function as a sweeper rather than an old-fashioned type who
would stay on his line.

The Ajax-trained players were already thoroughly familiar with
Michels's doctrines of permanent attack, 'pressing' deep inside the

opponents' half and constantly switching positions. The Feyenoord stars and Renesenbrink had only three weeks to get to grips with these ideas during the hard pre-tournament training at the KNVB's headquarters at Zeist. That they adapted so smoothly was a testament to their intelligence. Ruud Krol: "Everyone had to go into the system. Michels had his strong hand and his strong training. It was very hard. But we had the feeling, even when we were very tired, and although we played very badly at the beginning, that we could do something. Two weeks before the tournament, we lost a friendly match 2-0 to a Second Division German team. But Michels had only one thing in mind: the first match in the World Cup. Everything was fixed on that. One week before the first match we played a friendly against Argentina in Amsterdam and we beat them 4-1. That gave us so much confidence. We thought we could win if we started well. We had the feeling that if we clicked, we could come far. . . ."

Although this was to be Holland's first major tournament of the modern era, the Dutch did have one precedent for success: a friendly match in Düsseldorf in March 1956. Kees Jansma, now press chief for the KNVB, was nine at the time and vividly recalls the excitement of going to the match with his father. "My mother waved us good-bye at the station in Amsterdam. To go to Germany was quite a trip in those days." Back home, most people followed the match on radio and a handful watched on the fledgling Dutch TV service. Jansma: "It was very colourful. It was very cold and the pitch was very bad because of snow. The game itself was very bad. Germany's goal was an own goal by Cor van der Hart. Abe Lenstra scored two goals for Holland, not very magnificent goals – just reflex shots from five yards – but the emotion was enormous. When we won 2-1, I saw my father jumping and crying because we'd beaten the world champions. There must have been between six and eight thousand Dutchmen there, and they invaded the pitch and carried the players on their shoulders. In the train going back, everybody was celebrating wildly. I'd never seen my father like that – he'd gone mad, singing and

dancing. Later I realised it was because of the war, because of the
feeling about the Germans. It was a very strong feeling for all the
people there, that we had some kind of revenge for everything
they had done to us. Nowadays my father says I understood it
wrongly: that it was just about soccer. But it was more than soccer alone. We have to admit that one of our weak points is that we
always have to start talking about the war and about revenge when
we play against the Germans, no matter what the sport is. I wrote
after 1974 that for me it was over; we don't have to talk about
those things anymore. But in 1956, it was understandable. My
father had been in the war – he had been put in prison for a short
while. The game made him so happy. There was light in his eyes."
Jansma was neither the first nor the last Dutchman to wrestle with
and be troubled by the fusion of feelings about football and the
war he describes.

The Dutch were the last squad to arrive in Germany. They
installed themselves at their headquarters in Wald Hotel in Hiltrup
and 'clicked' almost immediately.

In Hanover, in their opening match, Holland dominated a
cravenly-defensive Uruguay and won with two Johnny Rep
goals, the first a header, the second arrogantly stroked with the
outside of his foot after sweet passing between Van Hanegem and
Rensenbrink. The game against Sweden in Dortmund is best-
remembered for the 'Cruyff turn', but Holland failed to score
from their many chances and the Swedes escaped with a draw.
(One of Holland's weaknesses, it became apparent, was profligate
shooting, a consequence of defenders and midfielders so often
arriving in front of goal. The ratio of chances to goals was sometimes as high as ten to one.) Only in the third match against
Bulgaria, on a blazing Saturday afternoon in Dortmund, did
Holland truly catch fire. The 4-1 win was more than joyful and
exhilarating. It was one of those very rare moments when football touched the sublime. Thirty years later, Simon Barnes, the
great sports writer for *The Times*, recalled that of all his footballing memories this ("the moment when Total Football was

born") was his favourite match. "I have never loved a side so much: it combined wit and brilliance with ferocity. It was the best I have seen." By now the stadiums where Holland played were full of Dutchmen wearing orange T-shirts and singing themselves hoarse. Back at home, in a country which had been largely indifferent to the national team when the competition started, the Dutch had become a nation of passionate armchair fans. As *totaalvoetbal* overwhelmed one opponent after another, sales of colour televisions rocketed. This was, among other things, the first TV world cup in Holland.

The sheer beauty of Dutch play was a revelation. Cruyff was the star, of course, a graceful human whiplash dancing away from tackles, ripping defences with his speed, guiding sumptuous passes around the field, exhorting and instructing teammates. Then again, every Dutch player looked a virtuoso as they swirled around and through opponents. The Scottish journalist Hugh McIlvanney likened the Dutch style, at once so spirited and so cuttingly precise, to "a cavalry charge of surgeons." The bright orange of their shirts overwhelmed the early colour TV cameras too; to the worldwide TV audience, the entire team sometimes seemed a shimmering blur.

Into the second round now, and Holland were rapidly becoming irresistible. In heavy rain in Gelsenkirchen came the most electrifying display so far: a 4-0 demolition of Argentina. Cruyff scored first and last, Krol and Rep providing the other goals. Long before the end, dishevelled, bewildered Argentinian defenders were reduced to making rugby tackles on Cruyff just to keep the score down. Four days later, in the same stadium, East Germany were comfortably dispatched 2-0. Now came what was in effect the semifinal against an enemy the Dutch feared: reigning champions Brazil. It was an epic and ferocious collision in Dortmund and, for the first 20 minutes, the Dutch were in trouble. Paulo Cesar and Jairzinho missed easy chances though and, after a bad foul by Suurbier broke the Brazilian rhythm, Brazil turned nasty. Unrecognisable from the sublime team of Pele, Gerson and Tostao in Mexico in 1970, their attempt to physically intimidate the Dutch backfired. Ruud Krol remembers: "That was the best game, the hardest game. It had everything. There was nice football in it – nice combinations, dirty football. It was a game on the limits and I like that, where both teams go to the limits, when both teams do everything to win the game. We played the game that was necessary to beat Brazil." The goals came in the second half: Neeskens stuck out a leg to lob the goalkeeper, then Cruyff at full stretch swept in a breathtaking volley after position-switching between Krol and Rensenbrink had sheared away the right side of Brazil's defence.

As the tournament progressed, the Dutch headquarters in Hiltrup become a symbol of sophistication. Unlike the old-fashioned training camps of other nations, the Dutch were friendly, open, multilingual and grown-up enough in sexual matters to allow visits from wives and girlfriends. A leading Brazilian journalist declared the Dutchmen "100 years ahead of us culturally." Off camera, though, things were not quite running so smoothly. On Tuesday, July 2, before the game against Brazil and five days before the final, *Bild Zeitung* published a story on an inside page claiming there had been a 'naked party' in the hotel swimming pool involving several unnamed Dutch players and local girls. The paper claimed to have photographs of naked footballers and naked girls, but no such photos were published and *Bild* illustrated the report instead with a picture of the pool. Rinus Michels held a press conference and denounced the story as a fabrication and part of a German media hate campaign against his team. This was surprising, as the German press and public had been friendly and full of admiration for the Dutch. Michels angrily refused to speak German at press conferences, and his denunciations of *Bild* were backed by Cruyff, the other players and the entire Dutch press corps. Contradictorily, the Dutch would later claim the *Bild* story was either exaggerated or had been a set-up involving payments to the girls. If Holland had won the final, the entire incident would no doubt have been forgotten. Instead, the Pool Story became a key component in the Dutch narrative of defeat.

Meanwhile, as the Dutch entranced the football world, the West Germans had charmed no one. The pre-tournament favourites were dismal against Chile and Australia, inspiring only boos from their own fans. Embarrassingly they then fell to Jürgen Sparwasser's goal against the DDR. In the second round, though, Franz Beckenbauer led a marked improvement. Yugoslavia were beaten 2-0 in Düsseldorf, then Sweden fell 4-2 in a thrilling match in the same stadium. The semifinal match, on a rain-soaked pitch in Frankfurt, saw off the excellent Poles thanks to a late Gerd Müller strike.

As the final in Munich approached, the Dutch should have had every reason to be wary. West Germany were reigning European Champions and the team was heavy with Bayern stars, who, two months earlier, had assumed Ajax's fallen mantle as European Cup holders. Moreover, in Beckenbauer and Müller they possessed the world's most remarkable defender and its deadliest striker. Yet form and recent club history suggested Holland should win. Six of the team (Cruyff, Haan, Krol, Neeskens, Rep, Suurbier) had played for Ajax, the same number for Bayern (Beckenbauer, Breitner, Höness, Maier, Müller, Schwarzenbeck), and in recent club matches, Ajax had comprehensively outclassed the Bavarians. In 1972, in pre-season friendlies, Ajax had won 5-0 in Munich and 2-1 in Amsterdam. In a European Cup quarter final in Amsterdam in March 1973, Ajax ran riot in the first leg, winning 4-0 in one of the decade's great displays of attacking football. Bayern were angry with themselves for having played poorly. Goalkeeper Sepp Maier was so disgusted by his own performance that he threw his clothes from his hotel window. Less well-remembered in Holland was what happened two weeks later in the largely academic second leg in Munich: Cruyff did not play and the Germans won 2-1.

German preparations for the final were exemplary. The most intriguing incident was a secret practice game organised to help

Berti Vogts prepare for the impossible-seeming task of marking Johan Cruyff. The job of impersonating the Dutch captain was handed to fit-again Günter Netzer who, over German media protest, had been replaced by the more reliable Wolfgang Overrath. Netzer-as-Cruyff played so brilliantly that he ran Vogts ragged; after 20 minutes a halt was called and adjustments made. In the final, Vogts rendered Cruyff a shadow of his normal self. But a more intriguing question remains: in the week of the final, if the Germans had a player who was as good as or better than the best player in the world, why wasn't he on the team? (In the years to come, German football would come to regret turning away from the kind of free-spirited creativity Netzer represented.)

In the wider world, memories of the war clearly played a part in shaping perceptions. Hugh McIlvanney caught the mood in *The Observer* on the morning of the match, arguing that the game would inevitably evoke "atavistic prejudices that go as deep as the marrow" and that many neutrals were "tense as they talked of their hunger to see Holland win." He feared history was about to stage a "callous repetition" of Germany's shock victory over the brilliant Hungarians in 1954. Germans fondly remember that match as the heart-warming "Miracle of Bern," but not many others enjoyed it and there are Hungarians born decades after the event who still feel the pain. Parallels between Cruyff's orange outfit and the Golden Team of Puskas were striking. Both teams had perfected a style of attacking football of revolutionary brilliance; both were universally admired and seemingly unstoppable; both had survived a draining battle with a thuggish Brazil team a few days before the final. McIlvanney was full of foreboding for Holland: "The Germans wait again, and the shadow they cast is broadened and darkened by the fact that they are on their own soil and have the fierce commitment of their own people pressing at their backs like a forest fire."

Yet even the Germans expected to lose. "[The Dutch] were a better team," confessed Uli Höness later. Winger Bernd Hölzenbein recalled the intimidating demeanour of the Dutch players in the tunnel: "We planned to look them in the eye, to show we were as big as they were. The Dutch players had the feeling they were invincible. You could see it in their eyes. Their attitude to us was: 'how many goals do you want to lose by today, boys?' While we waited to go onto the pitch, I tried to look them in the eye, but I couldn't do it. They made us feel small."

The game started with preposterous drama. Holland kicked off and began insolently moving the ball backwards, forwards and sideways, with the Germans unable to make an effective challenge . . . Van Hanegem to Neeskens . . . Krol . . . Rijsbergen . . . Haan . . . Rijsbergen again. . . . It was an arrogant exhibition of precision and control, and the Munich crowd howled their annoyance. After 17 passes, Cruyff dropped deep, collected the ball in the centre circle and began a sinuous run. A sudden swerve and burst of acceleration took him past his marker Berti Vogts and to the edge of the German penalty area. Uli Höness, lunging desperately, tripped him and English referee Jack Taylor pointed to the spot. As Neeskens prepared to take the kick, a camera in the stands caught the wives and girlfriends of the Dutch players. The footage is still affecting. Truus van Hanegem cannot bear to watch and turns away, sobbing, almost hyperventilating. Off camera, as Neeskens blasts home the penalty, the women scream with relief and joy. 120 seconds into the match, the first German player to touch the ball is Sepp Maier as he picks it out of his net. No team has ever made so perfect a start to a major final. Johnny Rep shudders at the memory: "It would have been much better if Germany had scored in the first minute."

The next twenty or so minutes determined the match – and helped shape post-war Dutch history. The Germans were on the ropes, but instead of going for a second goal, the Dutch began to play taunting possession football, weaving exotic patterns and demonstrating their technical superiority but making little attempt to score. None of the Dutch players can now explain why this happened. Rep: "We wanted to make fun of the Germans. We didn't think about it but we did it, passing the ball around and around. We forgot to score the second goal. When you see the film of the game, you can see that the Germans get more and more angry. It was our fault." Van Hanegem is more candid: "I didn't mind if we only won 1-0, as long as we humiliated them." Had Aristotle been watching, he would have spotted the danger immediately. "As for the pleasure in hubris," he wrote, "its cause is this: men think that by ill-treating others they make their own superiority the greater."

Nemesis followed swiftly. In the twenty-third minute, Overrath played a raking pass to the left wing where Hölzenbein controlled the ball and cut inside. It was a simple enough move, but it exposed Holland's defensive frailties. Arie Haan was the only Dutchman nearby. Inexplicably, instead of moving to stymie the run, Haan backed off, covering a non-existent overlap and unwittingly allowing Hölzenbein a free run into the box. As he exploited the opening with swiftness, Wim Jansen raced forty metres to cover. At the last moment Jansen swerved aside to leave Hölzenbein to Rijsbergen. But the blond defender hesitated. Hölzenbein darted past and, too late now, Jansen lunged in, missing the ball and apparently catching Hölzenbein's left foot. Hölzenbein flung himself down theatrically, and Taylor pointed to the spot. Up stepped Paul Breitner, the Maoist defender with a Zapata moustache, to drive the penalty low into the corner. In Dutch eyes, Hölzenbein's fall was a despicable *schwalbe* – a dive.

Legitimate penalty or not, the game was suddenly transformed. Now West Germany rampaged and, for the first time in the tournament, the Dutch were rattled. Cruyff, playing too deep, virtually disappeared for long periods as a creative force, dominated by Berti Vogts. At one point Vogts even danced forward to make a marvellous chance for himself, Jongbloed saving well. Höness surged past Haan only for Jongbloed to scramble the ball away. Then the goalkeeper leapt acrobatically to push away a chipped free kick by Beckenbauer. The Dutch had one last chance to save themselves, Cruyff darting away, drawing Beckenbauer and slipping the ball to Rep . . . who shot straight at Maier.

And thus it came: the moment of Der Bomber. Two minutes before half-time, Bonhof ran clear on the right. In Dutch memory, the moments that followed still have the slow-motion quality of a nightmare. Bonhof crosses low to Gerd Müller, but the great man's contact is odd: he knocks the ball behind himself, *away* from goal. Momentarily, the chance seems lost, yet Müller springs backwards, and in one impossible-seeming movement, wraps his right leg around the ball and drives it softly towards the far corner. The shot evades Krol's attempted block and Jongbloed, anticipating a strike to the near post, stands frozen as the ball glides gently past him into the net.

On Dutch TV, horrified commentator Herman Kuiphof uttered the line destined to become as famous in Holland as Herbert Zimmermann's "*Aus! Aus! Aus! Aus! Das spiel ist aus!*" was in Germany after 1954. "*Zijn we er toch ingetuind!*" said Kuiphof: "They tricked us again!" This was widely interpreted as a reference to Holland's wartime trauma: In 1940 the sleepy Dutch imagined the Germans would never attack because they had promised not to. In the first phase of the final the Germans also somehow gave the impression they would not attack, so the Dutch went to sleep ... and while they were asleep were indeed attacked ... again! But Kuiphof insists he has always been misinterpreted: "I wasn't thinking about the war. I just thought how stupid the Dutch were. They had everything in hand and under control and they didn't use that for scoring another goal and maybe deciding the whole match. They were trying to humiliate the Germans. And that's stupid against the German national team in their own country ... playing in the final you cannot underestimate them. The Dutch did that. That's what I meant."

In the second half, the Dutch at last played something closer to their normal game and generated a string of chances. "I kept looking at the clock," said Müller later. "It moved so slowly. I was certain the Dutch must score." Sepp Maier makes one mistake, flapping weakly at a cross that Paul Breitner heads away as the ball dips under the crossbar. Rep, clear on the right, shoots narrowly wide when the better-placed Van Hanegem is unmarked and

screaming for the ball; Maier saves at Rep's feet. Van Hanegem
launches a diving header five yards from goal but directs the ball
into the turf from where it bounces softly into the grounded
Maier's grateful gloves. Van de Kerkhof's long cross from the left
reaches Neeskens at a narrow angle on the far post. Neeskens's
volley is hit with such power at point-blank range it seems certain
to take both ball and goalkeeper into the net. Somehow, Maier
blocks and turns it away for a corner. The Germans defend desperately. Rep hits the post. Both teams play like men possessed.
When a goal eventually comes, it is at the other end. Müller again
– on this occasion with a run timed perfectly to beat the offside
trap and drill the ball past Jongbloed. Incredibly, when Taylor mis-
takenly rules it out for offside, neither Müller nor any other
German players offer a murmur of protest. In the ninetieth
minute, Taylor blows the final whistle and Müller sinks to his
knees, arms raised in triumph.

Ruud Krol's handsome, intelligent face darkens and floods with
feeling at the memory of the game, which still distresses him. "If
. . . it is always if. It never happens. But if we had played Germany
in the game before the final it would have been better for us. Brazil
were the world champions – we beat the world champions. The
Dutch were the Dutch. We didn't say it, but maybe inside we were
already satisfied. Against Germany we were not as *sharp* as we were
against Brazil. We had the confidence but not the right form. We
had no luck in the final. In the first half, after the early goal, we
forgot to continue. I don't know why. We wanted to demonstrate
how good we were. Maybe it was because Ajax had beaten Bayern
so easily [4-0 in 1973]; maybe that was in our minds. But it was
something that came from us, we wanted to show off. And the
Germans fought very hard. . . ." He maintains that the German
penalty should have been disallowed. "It still makes me angry.
Hölzenbein did it very cleverly [mimes dive] and the referee is
tricked. And we cannot change it. With Müller, I blocked the first
ball. Then the ball came back by him, and he turned and I . . .
Normally, if he was shooting straight, I would block the ball. He

didn't hit it well – you can see it on the television. The ball goes slowly, slowly to the corner; through the legs. But even in that moment you can see our defence is not organised like before."

Looking back, Krol says that the Dutch players didn't realise how good they were at the time. "I played with Gerrie Muhren and for a long time with Van Hanegem, and even though we played from different clubs and other systems, we understood each other so easily. It was football intelligence, which has nothing to do with normal intelligence. But it was so easy. It looks as if it was normal; but it was not. . . . In every position we were like this – we were the best, we had the best way. But it sometimes happens in football that the best team doesn't win."

Jan Mulder offers a more psychological explanation: "Why didn't Holland win? Because the players used to listen to the radio like me when the Dutch national team always lost. And now here they were in the final of the World Cup. You know, winning is frightening. When you are 1-0 after one minute, the future is suddenly frightening. You *have* to win now. Isn't it possible to lose, sir? It's much more comfortable to lose. You have to win, but you know you can't do it because you are Dutchmen and the Dutch always lose against the Germans. It's in our veins. The Germans are harder. They are accustomed to winning." His explanation of the Dutch attempt to humiliate the Germans in the first 25 minutes is intriguing: "It's to show their superiority but in reality it's an inferiority complex. Because we are a small country. It's normal. And you have the memories of the World Cup finals you've seen on television. And now you are yourselves in that position. It's horrible! The Dutch got vertigo. They were very nervous. They played well in the second half because they were losing."

After the match, all the Dutch players attended the official banquet, except one, Wim van Hanegem. Years later, he told me: "I don't like the Germans. Every time I played against German players I had a problem because of the war. Eighty percent of my family died in this war; my daddy, my sister, two brothers. And every game against players from Germany makes me angry. The Germans were good players but arrogant." Van Hanegem says that his feelings have subsided somewhat since 1974, but at the time losing the final affected him deeply. "I hated that after the game there was a big party. I was in my hotel room. I was so angry about losing. If we had lost in the final to England or Brazil then, OK, sorry, but not more than this. But to lose to the Germans. . . ."

I watched the game with my family as a 17-year-old in London. We all fervently wanted Holland to win. I had already fallen in love with the Dutchmen's marvellous football. Now I was enchanted by their apparently gracious reaction to defeat. After the game we went to a pub in Hampstead and met a Dutch couple. When I attempted to commiserate, the husband waved me away: "Oh, we don't mind too much. It's only a game." This, I now realise, could not possibly have been what he truly felt: Dutch pain was raw but hidden. Foppe de Haan, for example, politely asked his wife and children to leave the house – then sat down and bawled. The young Bastiaan Bommeljé was struck by the depth of feeling everywhere. "It made an immense impression on me to see grown men cry because we had lost to Germany, but then no one spoke about this game for a decade." All across Holland there was a gulf between private anguish and public expressions of disinterest or pride that a small nation had played so well and reached the final. Michels and his players were treated as heroes when they arrived at Schiphol. Later, together with Prime Minister Joop den Uyl, they congaed around the garden of the Royal Palace while Queen Juliana looked on beaming. The team even appeared on the balcony of the Stadschouwburg in Amsterdam, the traditional location for Ajax's European Cup celebrations, to receive the cheers and thanks of an orange-clad crowd.

In the years that followed, the anguish did not fade and the match gradually entered the realm of myth and legend. As the novelist and psychoanalyst Anna Enquist put it in the nineties: "It's a very living pain, like an unpunished crime. We can't admit to ourselves that something can be so important. But it matters very much. There is still deep, unresolved trauma about 1974." By the end of the decade, the defeat by Germany had come to be seen as marking the end of a political era. Just as the hubristic dream that the Dutch would teach the world to play beautiful football crumbled in Munich, so the country's unrealistic *nederland gidsland* foreign policy fell to dust. The literal meaning of the term is: 'Netherlands Guiding Land' and its aim was to spread justice and peace by showing other nations how to live as the Dutch lived. The fall of the Dutch footballers also prefigured the fall of Joop den Uyl's Socialist government, the political high-watermark for the sixties idealists. Simultaneously, the defeat marked the arrival of the 'baby boomers' who took cultural power in the late 1970s. Bastiaan Bommeljé: "Ajax's European Cups and the World Cup of 1974 somehow blended together with the rise of this generation. In reality there was no connection, but every group and nation has its own myth of origin. You see it all through ancient history: Rome, Athens and Sparta all invented their origins in complex myths explaining why they were in power, why they were the best, the brightest and the most beautiful. That's what happened with this generation. . . . The Lost Final was their binding, defining moment."

In the absence of clear-headed analysis of what had gone wrong – a process which might perhaps have stopped the final from becoming the template for future Dutch football disappointments – whispers and rumours flourished. The Dutch found defeat so hard to accept and were so unwilling to examine their own failings that they came to believe Kuiphof's line that they had somehow been tricked or cheated. Hölzenbein's *schwalbe* was seen as decisive. Everything Michels had said about a German media conspiracy was believed. Indeed, the story about the *Bild* article became a legend in its own right, the Dutch equivalent of the Grassy Knoll in Dallas. It was believed that *Bild* had printed the story on the front page and on the day before the final. The paper was also said to have triggered a catastrophic intervention by Danny Cruyff, wife of Johan. She allegedly called Johan the night before the final and kept him on the phone all night. This call was ludicrously reputed to be the most influential in the history of football, and is said to have determined the outcome of two World Cups: Danny is said not only to have put Johan off his game against the Germans but *also* to have prevented him from travelling to the next World Cup, in Argentina. (Cruyff announced this decision shortly after the Munich final and never went back on it, despite intense pressure. With a weaker team, Holland still reached the final.) Jan Mulder, for one, treats this version of events with derision: "Why didn't Johan Cruyff go to Argentina? I don't know. Because of Danny? It's part of Dutch history. Why didn't we become world champions? Because Danny wanted to stay home? It's unbelievable that Danny Cruyff could forbid Johan to play the world cup in Argentina because he swam 40 metres in a swimming pool! It's rubbish! One has to conclude Cruyff didn't have the ambition otherwise he would have been in Argentina. Pele and Maradona had the ambition. They wanted to be world champions."

When I first started researching this book and asked Dutch journalists about the Lost Final, they all wanted first to tell me about the Pool, but no one was willing to tell the full story. Instead, I got off-the-record hints seasoned with innuendo and contradictions. 'It's all true' . . . 'none of it is true' . . . 'Cruyff was definitely there' . . . 'Cruyff was never there' . . . 'Trust me: it was nothing' . . . 'I know everything, but it's still a dangerous story'. . . "If you write about this Cruyff will never talk to you again.' For thirty years, the Dutch press followed the example set by *De Telegraaf* on the day of the final: the paper had the story on the front page but pulled it at the last minute.

At first, the legacy of the final did not spill over into bitterness on the field. Van Hanegem apart, none of the Dutch players of '74 had particular animus towards their German rivals. Cruyff and Beckenbauer hugely respected and admired each other, and lingering bad feeling about Munich failed to express itself with any force on the pitch when Holland and Germany met again over the next few years, even in the tense, drawn second-round group match in Argentina. By the time West Germany beat Holland easily at Euro '80 the age of the Total Footballers was coming to an end. During the eighties, the German economy boomed while that of Holland stumbled, and prosaic German teams reached successive World Cup finals while Holland failed even to qualify for three major tournaments in a row.

Only in 1988, with the coming to maturity of a new generation of Dutch players including Ruud Gullit, Marco van Basten, Frank Rijkard and Ronald Koeman, did it become possible for the two nations to face each other again as equals. By then, however, Dutch attitudes had changed. Freud coined the term 'return of the repressed' to describe the way unresolved traumas resurface in odd forms many years after the original event. The Dutch attitude to German football in the late 80s and early 90s seems a textbook case. Before 1974, Belgium's national team – The Red Devils – had always been Holland's natural football rivals. Now it was the Germans who appeared as demons. Why?

The wartime occupation obviously plays a large part in this. But the Dutch suffered less and collaborated more than many other occupied European nations. So why were they more willing to view post-war soccer matches as symbolic re-runs of 1940-45? Dutch suffering, for example, was dwarfed by the horrors inflicted by Nazism on the Soviet Union and Poland. Yet major World Cup defeats by West Germany of Poland (in 1974) and the Soviet Union (in 1966) failed to produce national trauma in those countries. For decades, the English viewed football clashes with West Germany through the prism of 'two world wars and one World Cup,' yet English anti-German feeling was mild compared to that of the Dutch. The French view is even more revealing. France's wartime experience was similar to that of the Netherlands. And a magnificent French team playing beautiful football suffered a genuine football atrocity at German hands in the 1982 World Cup semi- final. Yet Schumacher's brutal assault on Battiston in that match (a crime unpunished by the Dutch referee) never became a vehicle for anti-German feelings. The French mostly contented themselves with hating Schumacher as an individual.

What made the Dutch – reputedly so placid in other areas of their lives – different in all this? One of the leading historians of Dutch-German post-war relations is Hermann von der Dunk, retired professor of modern and contemporary history at the University of Utrecht. He argues that more than a century of Dutch peace, neutrality, and warm relations with Germany, meant the Nazi invasion and occupation came as more of a shock to the Dutch than it did to other countries with more experience of war, turmoil and revolution. "Holland didn't experience the first World War, which was an enormous experience for all other European countries. The Netherlands had been neutral since the wars of Napoleon. It was a very quiet society. The Dutch saw themselves as spectators of great politics. So the very severe German occupation was a greater shock than for the Belgians, French, or the East European countries."

In the years immediately after 1945, the Dutch tended to repress memories of the occupation and looked mainly to the future. By the sixties, Holland was rebuilt and had become a prosperous and close ally of West Germany in NATO and the European Community. Yet now the past resurfaced with a vengeance. Holland was flooded with memoirs and other books about the war, including the works of two historians, Lou de Jong, who wrote an encyclopaedic study of the war in the Netherlands, and Jacques Presser, who told the story of the Dutch Holocaust in detail for the first time. (About 105,000 Dutch Jews were murdered – 80 percent of the pre-war total – double the proportion of Belgian Jews killed and nearly three times the proportion in France.) There was also huge interest in a wave of war crimes trials, beginning with that of Adolf Eichmann in Israel. In Holland, the 'Breda Three', three SS officers who had sent thousands of Jews to death camps and been responsible for mass terror in the Netherlands, were kept in jail because of a wave of protests by the young. In 1966, the high-point of Provo agitation in Amsterdam was the disruption of the unpopular royal wedding between Princess (now Queen) Beatrix and Claus von Amsberg, a German who, during the war, had been a very junior member of the Wehrmacht.

By the 1980s, Holland's defeat and occupation was taught intensively in schools and had become a constant theme in the media. This helped shape a new generation of self-righteously and openly anti-German Dutch youngsters. In Amsterdam, the game of giving false directions to young German tourists was played with relish by kids born long after 1945. In the popular Dutch view, Holland had been a nation of heroic resisters. The truth was rather different. Only a small number had resisted, about the same number had actively collaborated, and most of the population cynically accommodated to the occupation. Holland had had the highest proportion of citizens to join the Waffen SS of any occupied country and the Dutch economy assisted the Nazi war effort. Von der Dunk: "There was a lot of Dutch collaboration, but after the war nobody would speak about that. They spoke only about the resistance. It was exactly like in France. The resistance was a minority and the fascists and Nazis were also a minority. The majority of the population, as elsewhere, were anti-German in their hearts but they didn't do much about it."

In the symbolic realm of football, an almost unspoken extra twist was added: the Germans now dominated football through "ugly" methods somehow analogous with German methods of the 1940s. Whereas the Dutch were beautiful and creative in football, the German game was informed by *kampfgeist*. The Dutch were idealistic and free-spirited; the Germans were ugly, pitiless, indus-trial and martial. Indeed, German players and teams were routine-ly described as "panzer-like" and players deemed to epitomise such values – Hans-Pieter Briegel, for example, or Lothar Matthäus – were particularly despised in Holland.

This was the atmosphere in which Dutch football's second generation of great players came to maturity. When Holland qualified for Euro '88, to be staged in the Federal Republic, links to 1974 were still strong. Most of the new players were protégés of Cruyff, either in his last years as a player or his first period as a coach. Rinus Michels – "The Sphinx", "The Bull" "The General" – now aged 60, came out of retirement to lead the team. A new generation of boisterous Dutch fans, now dubbed the *oranje legioen,* poured across the border to support the team.

Initially, Holland's players displayed little of the magic of their predecessors. Instead of mesmerisingly fluid attacking football, the new *oranje* played 4-4-2 with players mostly sticking to their positions and the defence notably rugged. In Hans van Breukelen they even had a good goalkeeper. Holland started unfortunately, playing well but losing 1-0 to the Soviets in Köln. In Dusseldorf, Holland were fortunate indeed as England more than matched them and hit the post twice before Marco van Basten exploded into form to score a famous hat-trick, securing a 3-1 win and setting both the team and the nation alight. (If Van Basten had listened to Cruyff, none of this would have happened. Van Basten had spent most of his first season at AC Milan injured. When Michels initially left him out of the team, Cruyff advised the striker to deem this an insult and refuse to play at all. Happily, Van Basten ignored him and went on to score five goals, one of them among the greatest ever seen.) In their final group match the Dutch had to beat Ireland, who needed only a draw to reach the semi-final. Holland laboured pitiably but were saved, seven minutes from the end, by a truly bizarre goal. When Wim Kieft was struck on the ear by a miscued shot by Koeman, the ball spun wildly, changed direction completely and looped around the Irish goalkeeper. It was Total Fluke rather than Total Football, but the Dutch had made it. The semifinal in Hamburg would be against West Germany.

The German coach was a tall, imperious-looking man with a high forehead, greyer than before, wearing a suit and spectacles, 14 years older but still, unmistakeably . . . Franz Beckenbauer. Dutch

fans – kept to a minimum in Munich 14 years earlier – were allocated some 6,000 tickets, but crammed into the Volkspark in huge
numbers. It was invasion in reverse, journalists gleefully noted in
Holland. These fans were decked in orange, their mood edgy and
ebullient. Many of their banners blatantly and bitterly referred to
the war. "Give us back our bicycles," they chanted, a reference to the
German's mass confiscation of the Dutch *fietsen* in the war, remembered as one of the most humiliating acts of the occupation. "*Ein
Reich, Ein Volk, ein Gullit,*" mocked one banner. But, for once, the
Dutch seemed driven rather than blocked by history. As the Dutch
fans taunted their hosts, their team played with rare focussed aggression and skill. Probably never before or since has an historic game
developed into so haunting a mirror image of its predecessor. A
night of dark memories and seeming redemption unfolded with the
intensity of a duel in a Sergio Leone western. When the decisive
moments came, it was as if Morricone music swirled and dangerous
men reached for their guns in extreme close-up. Yet no film ever
produced so dramatic a reaction in a mass audience.

Hamburg '88 seemed Munich '74 replayed in reverse. In
Munich, the goals came in the first half; now they arrived in the
second. Like '74, there were two penalties, the second questionable.
Like '74, the winning goal was scored by the greatest centre-forward in the game. Early in the half Rijkaard fouled Völler in the
box. Lothar Matthäus took the penalty: 1-0. Twenty minutes later,
the Dutch were awarded a penalty when Marco van Basten
brushed against his marker Jurgen Kohler and simply fell. It was
hard to see the foul, but the Rumanian referee pointed to the spot.
Up stepped defender Ronald Koeman to coolly place the ball – as
Breitner had done – low to the goalkeeper's right. 1-1. Now the
Germans were rattled and could do little to stem the tide of terrific Dutch attacks. Two minutes from the end a pass reached the
deadliest forward of his generation on the edge of the penalty area.
Marco van Basten, playing the Gerd Müller role, hared after the
ball, extended his long leg in an impossible-seeming movement,
and contrived to pull the ball back softly towards the far corner.

The shot evaded Kohler's attempted block and goalkeeper Immel's despairing dive . . . and glided gently into the net.

Van Basten, soon to have Amsterdam's Leidseplein temporarily renamed in his honour, peeled away with one arm raised in triumph and was engulfed by teammates as the Dutch fans erupted in astonished ecstasy. That was as nothing compared to what happened back home when the final whistle blew a few seconds later. The men in orange had beaten the hated Germans 2-1 and the Dutch — the sober, sensible, calm and careful Dutch — went completely, totally, utterly, entirely out of their minds with joy. In the minutes after the game more than half the Dutch population (nine million out of a population of fifteen) surged into their tidy streets, drinking, singing, throwing bicycles into the air, setting off fireworks, cavorting in anything orange they could lay their hands on. It was the biggest party the country had seen since the Liberation and the celebrations went on for days. In the euphoria, the Dutch persuaded themselves that the country had been liberated for the second time, not by Canadian and British soldiers this time but by their own righteous footballers. As the Dutch-raised writer Simon Kuper put it: "Hamburg was not only the Resistance we never quite offered [during the war] but also the battle we never quite won." Political scientist and journalist Paul Scheffer was caught up in the party: "To beat the Germans was already fantastic, but to do it in the *German* way, fighting back and winning with a goal in the last minute! My wife, who doesn't even like football and would never normally do such a thing, found an orange dress and we went out into the street where everyone was jumping and singing and we started moving towards the Leidseplein with everyone else. It seemed just the right thing to do."

"REVENGE!" exulted the banner headline in *De Telegraaf* the next morning, summing up what everyone in the country felt. Yet as the Dutch expressed their righteous contempt, the German reaction could hardly have been more generous. Franz Beckenbauer went to the Dutch team's bus after the game to offer his congratulations and wish his conquerors luck in the final. A headline in *Bild* – the newspaper the Dutch most liked to hate – read: "Holland Super." The Dutch went on to beat the Russians in the final, in Munich, and that was nice too. For the first and only time, the Dutch had won a major international tournament. The party after the final was the Dutch equivalent of a New York tickertape parade – the team rode on boats through the canals of Amsterdam while the city, decked completely in orange, feted and adored them. But even that was a muted affair compared to the ecstasy of beating the now openly-hated Germans.

In the next few years, these war-related football feelings became ever darker. Ronald Koeman had notoriously admitted using as toilet paper the German shirt he had swapped with Olaf Thon in Hamburg. When Holland and Germany met in Rotterdam in 1989, a Dutch banner compared Lothar Matthäus to Adolf Hitler. A year later, in the World Cup, Frank Rijkaard expressed Dutch contempt (and helped ensure his team's defeat) by getting himself sent off for spitting at Rudi Voller, another hate-figure for the Dutch. After Germany's 2-1 victory came fighting on the Dutch-German border. When the sides met again in Gothenburg in Euro 92, German and Dutch hooligans battled in the Swedish streets. By the early nineties, the overriding nature of Dutch obsession with Germans had become all-too evident. In a group match of Euro '92 in Sweden, the Dutch produced a great performance to win with Van Basten, Gullit and Rijkaard all at their peak and the young Dennis Bergkamp chipping in with a goal. As Holland scored their second, radio commentator Jack van Gelder screamed: "We should go down on our knees and give thanks to God!" The game finished 3-1, prompting yet more wild, righteous partying in Holland. When Holland lost in the semifinal to Denmark, Dutch disappointment was compounded by thought that Germany would beat the Danes in the final. When Denmark confounded everyone and won 2-0, the Dutch threw almost as big a party as if they had won themselves.

By now, border clashes between Dutch and German hooligans were commonplace. In 1993, fire-bombings against Turkish *gastar-*

beiters by German neo-Nazis triggered a wave of protests in Holland. More than a million Dutch men and women, who had signally failed to mobilise in such numbers to protest evidence of Dutch racism, signed the "I am Angry" petition delivered to Chancellor Kohl. "I am Angry Too" would have been more like it: in German cities, hundreds of thousands of horrified Germans also turned out to protest the bombings. In the same year, a study by the Clingendael Institute for International Relations in The Hague made worrying reading. It showed that large numbers of Dutch youngsters believed young Germans thought like Nazis and wanted to start another war. By now the Dutch authorities were working hard to repair the damage. In her Christmas TV address to the nation in 1995, Queen Beatrix felt obliged to remind the Dutch that the Second World War had been a dark time in which dark things happened, including collaboration as well as resistance. In the same year, she also apologised in Israel's Knesset for Holland's behaviour towards Jews during the Holocaust.

By the late 90s, many Dutch intellectuals had come to feel distinctly queasy about anti-German attitudes. The Frisian playwright Bouke Oldenhof put it particularly strongly: "People use the war as a moral legitimation of a very emotional thing; maybe the same emotion as the Germans had about the Jews, to say it in a very sharp way. This football hatred against the Germans has existed only for 10 or 20 years, and it has nothing whatever to do with the war. They say that it has. But that's rubbish. It is more than 50 years after the war. The Germans have far more problems with the war than we have. I was born 20 years after the war, so why should I be against the Germans? You always hate your big brother. Frisians, in a way, hate Amsterdammers. And people in the west of Holland relate in the same way to the Germans. Did you ever go to Auschwitz? It is very interesting. Every country has its own barracks where it tells its own history. If you want to hear all the lies a nation has about itself you should go to Auschwitz. Holland is the country of the most tolerant. We have a long history of tolerance. Austria was the first victim of the Nazis. Yugoslavia liberated itself. Poland won the Second World War. And only the Germans are honest . . . all lies!"

"You really can't make it a moral issue or a war issue," said the late, great football-loving German-born rabbi, Dr. Albert Friedlander. "The Dutch were the finer, nobler team. Cruyff and the others were geniuses. They deserved to win." Friedlander wrote weighty books about the Holocaust such as *Ein Streifen Gold – Auf Wegen zur Versöhnung* and *Riders Towards The Dawn: From Ultimate Suffering To Tempered Hope* and worked mightily for post-Holocaust reconciliation. He knew both his history and his football. "I was rooting for the Dutch rather than the Germans because they were a great team and one had the feeling they should win. Football should be like the Olympics were in ancient Greece: when you took part in the games you moved into an area of peace. Bitter adversaries could compete without bloodshed. Even if they were at war, there was no fighting. Enemies could engage in sport with all hostilities suspended. In terms of guilt, Holland was no shining hero against the dark villain, Germany. After the war, we visited Holland and we were careful, when people didn't speak English, to speak very poor German so no one mistook us for Germans. There was a great deal of anti-German feeling at the time but a lot of it was guilt. They knew there had been a lot of collaboration so they were keen to show how much they hated the Germans. For a long time we used to think that Holland tried to protect the Jews, protected Anne Frank. But Anne Frank was betrayed by a Dutch thief. The Jewish tradition says guilt cannot pass down the generations. The children of criminals are not criminals, they are children. Beckenbauer and most of the German players were not old even enough to have been alive in the war, let alone fight in it."

Jan Mulder, whose son Youri's career with Schalke in the 1990s helped to change Dutch attitudes, said: "No one speaks about the final against Argentina. I despise it actually, this talking always about the war. The Germans who play in their national team were born long after the war. It's stupid, a cliché to think we have something against the Germans. We have nothing! Many Dutch were collaborators. The Jews were betrayed in Holland by the Dutch. And it's a cliché about German football being ugly. Germany had a great team. I always loved the short passing game of the Germans. And Beckenbauer was this great 'Latin' player at the back. Beckenbauer would have been a great Dutchman."

By the turn of the century, much of the poison had drained away. In both economic matters and football, the Dutch now saw an ailing Germany with condescension rather than fear and hostility. The inept *mannschaft* of Euro 2000 was a pitiful sight by comparison with the great German teams of the past, though when Holland failed to qualify for the 2002 World Cup it was the turn of Germans to mock the Dutch, something that had not happened before. Dutch popular attitudes to Germany were changing and the simplistic, false image of Dutch heroism during the Nazi occupation had been dismantled. Indicative of the change were two movies by Holland's best-known film director. In 1977 Paul Verhoeven made his name with *Soldier of Orange*, a patriotic wartime romp featuring dashing and noble Dutch Resistance heroes and a particularly sadistic Gestapo torturer called Breitner. By the time Verhoeven returned to the subject in *Black Book*, released in 2006, his vision of wartime Holland had become bitter. Members of the Resistance were now anti-Semitic, the film's most glamorous Resistance fighter turns out to be a treacherous murderer, the post-liberation treatment of supposed collaborators is depicted as being almost as nasty as Nazism – and the moral centre of the movie is a sympathetic SS officer. In the seventies, such a film would have been unthinkable, yet *Black Book* was received warmly in the Netherlands. According to Verhoeven: "There have been enough books about the war in Holland for people to realise that what the resistance did was not all great and what the Nazis did was not all bad."

In this new climate, the football-related hatred of Germany of the late eighties and early nineties became simply untenable. A few months before Germany and Holland faced each other at Euro

2004 a book was published that further altered the Dutch view of the game. Auke Kok's ironically-entitled *1974: Wij Waren de besten* (*1974: We Were the Best*) revealed that the Dutch had only themselves to blame. The Germans had thoroughly deserved their win and later anti-German prejudice was based entirely on Dutch "lies" about the game. Kok made it clear that defeat in Munich was rooted in overconfidence: the Dutch players had been arrogant and unprofessional, and Rinus Michels had behaved badly. Kok's conclusions were also backed by a collection of essays by a special edition of the Dutch football journal *Hard Gras*, published simultaneously in German and Dutch in both countries. The Dutch title: "They Were Better." Kok's book became a surprise best-seller in the Netherlands and was voted the best sports book of the year.

"Our myth was that we were so brilliant and perfect, and the Germans were such poor labourers they could only have beaten us through dirty tricks," he says. "Later Dutch hostility towards Germany was based on our myth about 1974, and that was all based on lies. The title of my book is double-edged. Holland were the best team in the tournament, but the best team doesn't always win, and in the final, the Germans deserved their victory." Kok also revealed the truth about the Swimming Pool. He tracked down key witnesses and demonstrated conclusively that there had indeed been a conspiracy – but it was a Dutch one. "*Bild*'s story was essentially true, but Michels gathered the players and said: 'Our strategy is that we deny everything and we blame the German press.' The players stuck to that line, and so did the Dutch press. But it was a lie, and an absolute failure of Dutch journalism." Moreover, contrary to later Dutch myth, most of the German press and public were notably warm towards the Dutch team throughout the tournament – even before the final – and the *Bild* story was published (without fanfare and on page 5) on that Tuesday. In other words, it appeared a full five days before the final, and before it was known whether Holland or Germany would even be *in* the final. "It's incredible that not one Dutch journalist at the time ever thought: 'might this story be true?'" Kok revealed that on the night in question, Cruyff, Rensenbrink and two reserve players had indeed been naked in the pool with local girls, though there was no sex and the incident was "rather innocent". Such parties, though, had become something of a regular occurrence at the hotel where the Dutch players were living rather like rock stars. "I'm not talking about orgies. But they received a lot of German girls, and there was a lot of drinking, and a lot of cigarette smoking, and a lot of playing cards behind closed doors at night. The players had the idea that Michels did not want to know all these things." Indeed, contrary to his reputation as a strict disciplinarian, Michels had abdicated much of his power to the players and had become an almost part-time coach, flying three times during the tournament to Spain to coach his club Barcelona in the Spanish Cup. "Michels really let things go."

With the aid of photographs and video, Kok also demolished cherished Dutch views of the game itself: "If the referee had had a perfect match, like a robot, it would have been at least 3-0 to the Germans." Holland's penalty in the first minute was wrongly awarded: the foul on Cruyff was outside the box. The German penalty, however, was justified. "When you look at the tape, you see Hölzenbein falls easily but Jansen's challenge on him is late. As a referee, you don't have to give the penalty, but you may give it. In the second half, Gerd Müller scored a goal wrongly disallowed for offside and Germany should have had a second penalty, when Jansen fouled Hölzenbein again. For 30 years, we looked at this tournament, especially the final, with closed eyes. We never looked at the facts. What have the Germans done to us since 1945? Nothing. Nothing! You look at the later incidents with Koeman and Rijkaard and think: 'What sort of a country *is* this?'" Indeed, where for decades the Germans had paid little attention to Holland, Dutch denigration of German football as 'ugly' had final-ly provoked a perfectly understandable response. "On the internet, the Germans speak to us as we have spoken to them. Younger Germans laugh at us when we lose. When we didn't qualify for the 2002 World Cup, the Germans put up hate sites against the Dutch.

And it's our own fault because they are reacting to our misbehav-
iour." Henk Spaan, Dutch co-editor of the Hard Gras special,
agreed: "Everybody realises now that our defeat in the final in '74
was merited. The Dutch preparations were so poor they didn't
even scout the semi-final game between Germany and Poland.
The Germans had prepared very well. We had better stop talking
about '74 and the war and all these things because they don't matter any more."

And yet. . . . And yet. . . . There is something unduly self-
lacerating about this new Dutch thinking. For the Lost Final
remains a genuine tragedy. On the very day they were to fulfil
their dreams, the beautiful team died. History then denied them
redemption or healing. Four years later, in Buenos Aires, some of
the Total Footballers played their second – and last – World Cup
final against three opponents: Argentina, a dubious referee and a
hysterically belligerent crowd. The match turned into the equivalent of Bobby Kennedy's encounter with Sirhan Sirhan. As the
years passed it also became clear 1988 was only a very partial
recompense for 1974.

Knowing that the Dutch defeat in Munich was a case of accidental self-destruction rather than murder does nothing to dimin-
ish the sense of loss. Indeed, it makes the story more compelling.
The self-destructive demise of the brilliant and beautiful always
exerts a special fascination: think of Jim Morrison, Marilyn
Monroe, Kurt Cobain or Rainer Werner Fassbinder. And while
football may tell us interesting things about politics, history and
culture, it works much more powerfully as a pure narrative ritual.
On that level, the Dutch joined the ranks of great fictional characters destroyed by the weight of their own gifts and a single fatal
flaw, like Achilles, Othello, King Lear and Oedipus. Paradoxically,
the reputation of the Dutch team that lost now far exceeds that of
the Germans who became world champions. Like Keats or Byron,
the Total Footballers became authentic, tragic Romantic heroes.
Burnished by nostalgia, their status and appeal is growing still.
They are routinely described, alongside Brazil 1970 and the

Mighty Magyars, as the best ever. The *Times* of London recently voted Rinus Michels the greatest manager of all time. As Jan Mulder puts it: "We are still talking about the great team that lost *because* they lost. If they had won, it would be less interesting, much less romantic. So we are in the same room as Puskas and the great Hungarians. We are together with the best team in the history of football. Second but imperial! Unforgettable seconds! Better seconds!"

2: brothers

'In Seville they treat me like a king. I don't like it. It's better
to be modest'

Gerrie Muhren

'It's strange, all those people who are related to each other who you
never realised were related to each other,' muses Michael Angelis in
Alan Bleasdale's *GBH*. 'There's Douglas Hurd and Thora Hird,
Paul Gascoigne and Bamber Gascoigne, Julie Christie and Linford
Christie . . .'

When people with the same name appear in Dutch football teams,
though, it's usually the case that they really are brothers – often
identical twins. If soccer theory ever merges with genetics, someone
is going to have to do some pretty serious research into why Dutch
football produces so many brilliant brothers. They've had loads of
bros. An embarrassment of siblings. Consider: Holland and Barcelona's current pair of identical twins, Frank and Ronald de Boer,
grew up together, played together went on strike together at Ajax
and were even dropped from the Barça side simultaneously. Erwin
and Ronald Koeman both played for their hometown club, Gronin
gen, and, at different times, for PSV, before helping Holland win
Euro '88. A decade earlier the 1978 Dutch World Cup final team
featured winger Rene van de Kerkhof alongside his older (by thirty
minutes) brother Willy, a clever and combative midfielder. Rob and
Richard Witschge played side by side for Ajax in the late 1980s and
both played for the national team, but – oddly – never together. In
the 1950s and early 1960s Ajax had the Feldmanns (Wim and
Donald) and the Groots (Henk and Cees). The De Nooijer twins

(Dennis and Gerald) now turn out for Heerenveen. Between 1908 and 1926 the famous four (count 'em!) Pelser brothers (Adriaan, Fons, Jan and Joop) all played at Ajax, though never all at the same time, either. Probably the most sublime Dutch footballing brothers, however, were Ajax's fabulous Muhren boys, Gerrie and Arnold, from Volendam.

Only twenty kilometres but a world away from Amsterdam, Volendam is a drop-dead gorgeous tourist trap nestling tidily beside a shimmering inland sea. It's a famous fishing village with virtually no resident fishermen, a Catholic enclave in an ocean of Calvinism, a town of Dutchmen who think of themselves as Spanish, a place fervid with invention and brimming with workaholics. The village has a reputation for creativity and craftsmanship. Holland's greatest guitarist, Jan Akkerman, lives there, and two of the country's most popular bands – Band Zonder Naam (Band Without a Name) and The Cats – come from Volendam. (So, incidentally, does Sheffield Wednesday's favourite Dutchman, Wim Jonk.) And almost every-one seems to be related. The founder and leading member of The Cats (house musicians for Ajax and the Dutch national team in the 1970s) is another Arnold Muhren, the footballers' cousin. Their fathers, Jan and Pé Muhren, were twins in a family of twelve children. Pé (the musical Arnold's dad) became a writer and doubled up as stadium announcer for FC Volendam, a club now in the Second Division but which, until recently, flourished in the top flight with a team of homegrown players. Jan became a town councillor, a director of two factories and a much-loved healer. 'He had a box with everything in it, a kind of medicine cabinet,' Arnold remembers. 'People came to him with bad legs, arms and anything and he would fix them. If he couldn't fix them, he'd say they had to go to the doctor, but you had to be nearly dying for that to happen.'

In the tourist season, beside Volendam's pretty harbour, locals in traditional costumes sell cheesy souvenirs and freshly caught fish. Freshly caught in the North Sea, that is, and brought by truck from Amsterdam because few villagers now follow their forefathers' trade. Tourists can also take scenic boat trips to nearby Marken (an even smaller ex-fishing village with wooden houses but no notable footballers). In the gathering gloom of a chilly October evening, after interviewing Arnold at the stadium and before catching the once-an-hour bus back to Amsterdam, I cannot resist the lure of this ferry. Volendam used to be beside the salty Zuiderzee. Then a dike connecting north Holland to Friesland was built in the 1930s and the Zuiderzee became a giant freshwater lake called IJsselmeer. In freezing weather this water can turn into a sea of ice. This evening it's merely chilly. The boat chugs its slow arc across the great flat water under a huge, grey sky. Pavarotti sings arias from Puccini on the captain's tape machine, a serenade for his few passengers, the wheeling gulls, the sunset and the gentle lapping waves. On the horizon are windmills and trees and far-away Amsterdam. The captain turns out to be a distant cousin of the Muhrens, too. 'They are special boys,' he tells me. 'People here like them so much.'

Gerrie was the left-midfielder in the golden-era Ajax team. When Rinus Michels asked him to play for Holland in the 1974 World Cup, Gerrie declined because his baby son was unwell. 'My wife and father said: "Go! Go! It's the World Cup!" I am crazy for football, but my family is more important. I would do it again.' In 1976 he joined Seville, where his artistry made him a cult figure and he was voted Spain's Player of the Year. Five years younger than Gerrie and even more left-sided, Arnold played with his brother in the Ajax team of the early 1970s, later moving to FC Twente and later still, in 1978, to England, where his calm mind, perfect technique and visionary passing made him a star for first Ipswich and then Manchester United. At the age of thirty-four he returned to Ajax under the supervision of new coach Johan Cruyff, who had long admired Arnold's game. In Euro '88 Arnold, then thirty-seven, played a tournament of silky perfection and provided the cross from which Marco van Basten scored his miracle goal in the final, the screaming dipping volley from an impossible angle. 'Everyone said it was the best cross I ever made but that's nonsense,' says Arnold modestly. 'Marco made a not very good pass look very good. Before the ball reached my feet, I saw him running free near the penalty

area. If I'd controlled the ball, there would have been another
situation, so I decided to play it first time. I was trying to play the
ball about two yards in front of him. I thought he would control the
ball and bring it back into the penalty area. But he finished it! I've
never seen anything like it.'

The Muhrens – like all the Dutch greats of their era – learned
their football on the streets. Arnold: 'My brother played with his
friends, and when I was five or six I started joining in. I started off in
goal but I could never stay there; I was always running all over the
place and eventually they said I could play with them. We weren't
exceptional. Everybody could play football at a very high level. At
the time there was little else to do but play football. If you couldn't
play football, bad luck: you had to go in goal. We played every day.
If it was raining, we played in the bedroom. At school we played
football between lessons. When school finished, we played on the
street again; there was no traffic. We played with anything as long as
it was round – rolled-up papers tied with string, anything. Some
people's parents had money and could get hold of a proper ball, but
mostly it was tennis balls. You develop great technique like that.
The ground was hard, so you didn't want to fall because it hurt; so
you have good balance. And the game was very quick because the
hard ground makes the game quicker. No one ever told us how to
play. It was all natural. When we joined Volendam when we were
twelve, we already knew how to play. Now you can join a club
when you're six years old and you can train once or maybe twice a
week, but there's a lot of difference between [that and] playing
every day, seven days a week.' There's a difference, too, between the
attitude of Arnold's generation and that of today's young players.
He met his wife when he was nineteen, and never lost his focus on
the game. 'I was only interested in football – I lived like a monk! No
smoking, no drinking, go to bed early. People said I didn't have a
youth but I've had the best life. I've seen the whole world. It was a
great experience to be in England for seven years and to live on the
other side of Holland when I played for Twente. I've seen so many
things, met so many interesting people. A lot of people in Vo-

lendam stay in this village. They think it's the best place in the
world. Maybe it is, but there are other places as well.'

   Arnold's hair is no longer dark and long as it was in the 1970s; it's
short, greying and swept back from his open, intelligent face. For a
footballing legend he works in surprisingly unglamorous surroundings, as an assistant coach at FC Volendam, where we talk in a
humble press room underneath the main stand. 'I don't want to be in
the limelight. I did that for thirty years, so now I want to do
something in the background,' he explains. His travels have given
him a broader perspective on his singular home town. 'Everyone asks
me how is it possible that such a small place produces so much.
Volendam people are very skilful at everything. What their eyes can
see, their hands can make: building houses, making music, doing
sport. You mention a sport and we've got it: football, running,
underwater hockey – everything! And everyone works hard. People
here want to reach the top no matter what they do. Everyone wants
to own their own house, so they have to take a mortgage for thirty
years, but that doesn't matter to them. Everyone works from seven
a.m. until four and then at five they start again until nine, working for
their friends or family. They pay black money so they don't have to
tell the tax people about it. Of the 18,000 who live in our village, I
think 1500 have their own business. At four o'clock if you stand at
the roundabout at the entrance to Volendam and see what's coming
into this village it's unbelievable – all the coaches and trucks. Traffic
jams! And we are so competitive: "If he can do that I must do it
better." That's why our football club always had Volendam players
and we were known for our good football. Everyone thinks, "I want
to be better than you, so I have to train harder than you." People
here want the best for themselves and for their family.'

   There can be a price to pay for all this striving, though. 'Sometimes
people work too hard. You can work from seven until nine every day
but if you do that for twenty years . . . well, you're knackered, as they
say in England. People don't see their own children growing up.
That's not the right way to live.' He maintains that playing football
simply because he enjoyed it was the key to his success. 'It started off as

a hobby, to take part with a group of players. When I ended my career it was still a hobby – a well-paid hobby. You have to see it as a hobby. You win something together, you lose something together, you live as a group, you laugh with each other, you create things together.'

At Ipswich Arnold is still remembered with awe. He recalls that when Bobby Robson signed him in 1978, the difference between English and Dutch football struck him immediately. 'My first game was against Liverpool, who had Terry McDermott against me. He was a very good runner and we ran up and down the wing all day. Neither of us touched the ball because it kept going over our heads. After the game I went to see Bobby Robson and said: 'It's better to put the linesman in instead of me. He can run up and down all day, too. If you want to get the best out of me, you have to give me the ball. That's what I need. That's why you bought me.'' Ipswich soon learned to give the ball to Arnold, and later to his fellow countryman Frans Thijssen (who arrived in 1979) – and they were richly rewarded. The Dutchmen gave Ipswich what Dennis Bergkamp gave Arsenal nearly twenty years on: poise, intelligence, a different dimension of vision and skill. Yet Muhren genuinely admires English players. 'They have things I didn't have. So strong in the air, strong tacklers. You can run all day. If you could combine the best from the English and the Dutch, you would have the best footballers in the world. If you could put Dennis Bergkamp's skills with Tony Adams's strength and spirit, you'd have the complete player.' Another job for the geneticists . . .

I meet Gerrie a week later in a motel in the endless flat landscape outside Volendam. When I get off the bus at an isolated stop, it feels a bit like that scene in *North by Northwest* where Cary Grant gets attacked by a crop-dusting plane. Except instead of being parched and menacing, this landscape is the richest green imaginable and laced with ditches and farm animals. Hendrika the cow must have fallen into her canal not far from here.

Gerrie was a superstar in Spain and now works as a scout for Ajax, spending much of his time in Africa. But he always comes home, and lives a stone's throw from his brother in the village. When I ask him his theory about Volendam's creativity, his answer surprises me. 'We're all Spanish, really. A few hundred years ago, there was always war between Holland and Spain, and they say the Basques from Spain created Volendam. We are the only place in this part of Holland that is one hundred per cent Catholic. Marken is one hundred per cent Reformed. Among our neighbours there are no Catholics; it's only Volendam. When I lived in Spain for three years, I saw many similarities. Everyone here can go into each other's houses to eat together, just like Spain.' I tell him it would be hard to imagine anyone who looked less Spanish and more Dutch than himself. 'Yes! But the fact that we are all Catholic – that's unbelievable, no? And the talent that we have. Yes, I think we are Latins. You see it in the music and our painters and everything for such a small place.'

As a boy, Gerrie supported Real Madrid. 'When I was young, we saw Real on TV. They played nice, attacking football. To see them on TV all in white, it was unbelievable. It was my dream to play good soccer against Real Madrid in the same way that every opponent dreams of playing well against Ajax – because we let them play and then we play. And later on, when I grew up, I played seven times against Real Madrid. And I won seven times.'

He may be 'Spanish' but his ideas about celebrity and status are decidedly egalitarian and deeply Dutch. 'A doctor came to me to ask me for my autograph and I asked him for his autograph instead. It is only luck that we could play soccer. If there was no crowd, we could not earn money from soccer; we could not see how good we were. We needed the crowd; the crowd needed us – we are part of each other. I always think it's unbelievable when a player these days refuses to give his autograph to a child. But the times changed. Players don't have time any more. You have to call the agents before you can speak to the players – I don't like that. Even now when I come to Seville, they treat me like a king. I don't like it. It's better to be modest. In Holland they are a little bit cool and I prefer that. No one here has ever asked me for my autograph. I am one of them. In Volendam it is normal; everyone lives normal lives.'

3: the beauty of thought

'Football is not art — but there is an art to playing good football'

Ruud Krol

Every player in Holland has a dream of beauty or glory. The tiny and strangely gifted Abdellah Belabbas, surely the quirkiest footballer in the country, has two. First, he wants to win the World Cup, preferably for the USA. This might be a little tricky: he will be thirty-four years old by the time of the next tournament; he doesn't play for a professional club (or any club at all, in fact); and he is Algerian. Abdellah's second goal is a little more attainable but far more dangerous. He yearns to juggle a ball with his feet as he holds himself hundreds of metres above the ground, clinging with only his bare hands to the underside of a helicopter. 'I know it's a little bit crazy, but I want to do it because it is difficult. You must have muscles for this and I train hard and work for this every day. To hang under the helicopter needs trust. I have a friend with a helicopter in Kansas. He sent me an e-mail yesterday. He wants to take me to do this in Chicago. For me, it's not dangerous. The wind might make it hard to control the ball, but between hanging and controlling the ball I will be thinking of my family.'

You've probably seen Abdellah if you've been to the Leidseplein, the little square surrounded by cafés, restaurants, clubs and cinemas in the centre of Amsterdam. Skinny, bedraggled-looking, track-suited and about five feet tall, Abdellah is a football juggler and one of the most noticeable characters in a place that is full of them. There's the nearly naked acrobat who climbs a rope and performs under a tree opposite the Stadschouwburg, the national theatre. There's cowboy-hatted 'Alex de Fotograaf' who'll sell you a red, red rose sheathed in plastic or an instant portrait from his ancient Polaroid camera. There's Jerrol, a fabulously dreadlocked Surinamese cyclist with a green parrot living on his head. They are all artists in a way, and so is Abdellah. He is of less flamboyant appearance than some, but he has a strange smile and light in his eyes. He usually sits or stands on (or dangles above) a little patch of cobbled stone on the east side of the square between the tram tracks and the Heineken Hoek Café. He makes his living as a football busker, earning guilders from tourists who gather in little circles to watch his astounding feats of ball control. Sitting on his little rubber mat, Abdellah can keep a football in the air almost indefinitely. He makes the ball bounce hypnotically, metronomically, unceasing . . . pap, pap pap . . . from instep to forehead to thigh to toe . . . pap pap pap . . . instep, forehead, knee, instep . . . pap pap pap pap . . . When he gets bored, he crosses his legs, apparently defying the laws of gravity, and lets the ball almost reach the ground before flicking it up again with his wrong foot. 'I do this sometimes for twenty-four or thirty hours without stopping. I don't know why, but I never get tired. It is an art, like meditation, like philosophy,' he says. He can even juggle from a position half underneath a table, lobbing the ball precisely from one side to the other with his head or foot. His favourite trick is to climb up a wrought-iron lamppost and carry on juggling with his feet as he holds himself ten feet above the ground.

Abdellah grew up in Algeria in the village of Mendes near Oran. He says he knew at the age of four that he had a gift for football. He played in the street and later for the village team, where he always felt an outsider. 'The others in the team only wanted to score goals, but football is not a question of scoring goals. That doesn't matter. Football is like a communication. It's a question of how you look in a team and between friends.' After technical secondary school he went to Spain looking for work. Life was hard and often lonely. He took jobs in bars, shops, supermarkets and played football on the streets or beaches. One day, while working in a lemon-processing factory in Alicante, he was struck by the thought that his route to fame lay in devoting himself to his art, his football, before he got too old. 'I'm going away and you'll see me on TV one day,' he announced to the factory's owner. 'Why?' she asked. 'Have you killed someone?'

He headed north – 'Holland was a little bit of a free country; different and free' – and found himself a little niche in the market. His fame has since begun to spread. His idol, Maradona, has apparently seen a video of him in action and been impressed. Abdellah has been filmed for an Adidas commercial for Euro 2000. He meets players, too. 'Celestine Babayaro and Tijani Babangida; they are OK. Stefan Schwarz is nice. Edgar Davids is OK too. But we are different. They are in business because everything in football is money, money. I am not like that. For me football is like meditation, a thing of the brain. If you have not a good brain, you can never be special in something.'

So what's the philosophy to partner his skills? 'Football is dancing,' he says. 'What is dance? Dance is rhythm. Everything is rhythm. If you can dance, you can do everything. Just the way you move your body. The public like the way I move. They don't know how I do it, but they don't need to know. Every day people ask me strange questions. Is the ball magnetic? Is it a trick? Is it something with the shoes I wear? What I do is clean football. I help people to play clean football. Not dirty, not muscles. What I do is something really new, something created by me. It is not easy. It is education for football. It makes you. I learn a lot when I watch people watching me – all the different mentalities. There is some-thing funny, too. My football is for comedy, for joking. People like it. One man gave me 2000 guilders. I don't mind if they give me one guilder or a hundred. People give what they give.'

Abdellah's greatest frustration – and source of bewilderment – is that in a land he knows is supposedly dedicated to beautiful football, no one wants him in their team. Absolutely no one. 'Nobody in the world can do what I do, except Maradona. I thought I could learn and study football in Holland. I want to play in a team but football here is about quick running and big muscles. They think I don't have enough muscles. I can do anything with a ball but they think I'm strange and difficult. They don't understand me. When they see me, they say no.' He has performed in the Amsterdam Arena, where Ajax play, but only to entertain a group of businessmen. 'I spoke to this man. I said: "Maybe I can train with Ajax?" He said he would call. He didn't call.'

It's not surprising the Ajax official didn't call. Abdellah Belabbas may be entertaining; he may even be an artist. But what he does has nothing to do with the Dutch understanding of football. The Dutch see his kind of technique as the football equivalent of the card memory tricks Dustin Hoffman's character performs in *Rain Man*. '*L'art pour l'art* is nothing here. It's not appreciated,' explains the elegant Auke Kok, who is currently writing a book about Dutch football's loss of innocence. 'Art must have a goal. We say: What is the function? That's a very deep Dutch principle. What's the use? What's the purpose? What's it for?' Barry Hulshoff makes the point emphatically: 'Lots of people think being able to keep the ball in the air by kicking it up 3000 times is football. But that is not football. The good player is the player who touches the ball only once. And knows where to run.'

Here's another popular vision of football beauty that doesn't do much for the Dutch. The talented former Haarlem player Dennis Purperhart recalls with deep pleasure a goal he saw as a teenager in his native Surinam. 'An attacker is through, he beats the defender and is through on goal. He dribbles around the goal-keeper and there's an empty goal. So what does he do? He takes the ball back, does it all again and only then he scores. In Europe to score a goal is all that matters. It doesn't matter if you do it with your shoulder or your knee: a goal is a goal. In South America it has to be a very beautiful goal or it's not worth much. It's not a real goal.' Similar stories are told in Georgia, where individual artistry is prized above all. And the Dutch are the Brazilians of Europe, aren't they? Well, up to a point. Consider the case of Georgi

Kinkladze, the Georgian one-time darling of Manchester City fans, a footballer of such rare gifts and evident genius that he was once nominated by Maradona as his natural successor. Kinkladze was loved in Tbilisi and at Maine Road for his incredible ability to run with the ball and dribble at opponents, sometimes charging straight through a massed defence on amazing jinking runs. In 1998 Morten Olsen, Louis van Gaal's successor at Ajax, paid £5 million to take Kinkladze to Amsterdam to play for the club he had supported and adored from afar as a boy. It looked to be a match made in heaven: the natural football artist together at last with the club that loves artistic football. It was a disaster. In two years 'Kinky' played only a handful of games. He didn't understand the Ajax system. He was baffled and alienated by the Dutch and their ugly, incomprehensible guttural language. Within a year he was utterly depressed, his only comfort watching videos from home with his cannier countryman Shota Arveladze. In retrospect, it was obvious Kinkladze was never going to fit. As one Ajax scout scathingly observed: 'Oh yes, he's a great player. Lots of technique. But if you ask him in the shower after the game: "Hey, Georgi, what was the score?" he wouldn't be able to tell you.'

Almost every Dutch fan agrees with Johan Cruyff that 'Football should always be played beautifully, you should play in an attacking way, it must be a spectacle.' And everything you've ever heard about the Dutch love of spectacle and attack is true. The *Oranje legioenen*, the hordes of mainly non-Amsterdam fans in lavish orange costumes and perpetual carnival mood who follow the national team, spend most games yelling '*Aanvalluh!*' ('Attack!'). In 1973 Ajax fans famously came home subdued and disgruntled from seeing their team's third successive European Cup win, this time over Juventus in Belgrade. Ajax scored with a Johnny Rep header after five minutes, and instead of trying for an equaliser, the nervy Italians carried on defending. Ajax simply played keep-ball until the ninety minutes were up. Yes, Ajax had made history: they had become the first team since Real Madrid to win three European Cups in a row. Nonetheless, their fans' pleasure was muted: the game had been dull and the manner of the victory was considered miserable.

Frankly, the Dutch can be a little picky about what constitutes a truly good footballer.

Goalscoring, for example, is never quite enough. Unlike the other outstanding German talents of their era, Franz Beckenbauer and Gunter Netzer (who were both esteemed), Holland's 1974 nemesis, the terrifyingly effective Gerd Muller, was only grudgingly considered great because he was virtually a passenger outside the penalty area. Johan Cruyff when he took over at Barcelona wasn't too thrilled by Gary Lineker, either, because Lineker was hopelessly limited: all he did was score goals. Cruyff admired his speed, though, so he put him on the wing. Lineker still hasn't forgiven him. Jan Mulder says of his former colleague Ruud Geels, the goalscoring sensation who between 1974 and 1978 scored a staggering 153 goals in 166 games for Ajax: 'Oh, a top scorer! At every club he played he scored thirty goals a season. In front of goal he was incredible! He was a fine technician, too. He was a great goalscorer, but nothing more. He had no passing, no dribbling. In the game, he didn't do much.'

There may be an art to ferocious defending, but if there is, the Dutch are largely blind to it. Cold ruthlessness in the style of Juventus and Italy's notoriously ungentle Claudio Gentile or the 1978 Argentina captain Daniel Passarella is deplored. Dogged marking à la Berti Vogts when he played Cruyff out of the 1974 final is detested. Tony Adams is admired for his fighting spirit, but English centre-halves remain on the whole the objects of ridicule. Jan Mulder loves England. 'Football is atmosphere. The crowd, the whole environment and England is much *bigger* than here, *much* better. Yes! But you have right- and left-backs who can't control the ball! That's so unbelievable! I once saw Barcelona versus Manchester United: 4–0 to Barcelona! Who were those big guys in the Manchester United defence? Pallister and Bruce. Oh yes! Steve Bruce! [Makes a face like he has eaten a sack of lemons.] And every English team has its Bruces and Pallisters! They never learn. To see

Romario against Bruce and Pallister. Oh, it was gorgeous! That is
the only weak thing in the English game: the centre-backs! But
don't change it, I like it!' He enjoys Adams, too. 'It's great that they
have too much spirit and not enough technique. Who was that
other Arsenal player? Steve Bould? [Chortles, grimaces, laughs
uncontrollably.] He's a fine gentleman . . . but one would like
to play against him, yes?'

The number of tough natural defenders produced in the Netherlands is small. The Ajax sweepers in the golden age were the
Yugoslavian Vasovic and the German Horst Blankenburg. When
Barry Hulshoff was injured for the 1974 World Cup, Rinus Michels
made an untested central defence out of Arie Haan, a midfielder
who had never played in defence before, and the uncapped Wim
Rijsbergen. PSV's European Cup win in 1988 owed a lot to their
inspirational right-back Eric Gerets, a Belgian. 'Iron' Rinus Israel,
the rock of the Feyenoord defence in the 1970 European Cup-
winning team, is remembered with affection. So too are the father
and son Ajax 'stoppers' from before and after World War II
respectively, both called Wim Anderiessen. Adri van Tiggelen
and Berry van Aerle from 1988, and the 1995 Ajax pair Winston
Bogarde and Michael Reziger, now at Barcelona, are also excep-
tions. Jaap Stam – one of the finest natural defenders and an Old
Trafford cult hero – on the other hand, is considered dull, his
'provincial' virtues prompting condescension rather than admiration in the capital. 'He's just a good defender; very big and very
strong. There's nothing interesting about him,' says Henk Spaan,
football commentator of *Het Parool* and editor of the literary football
magazine *Hard gras*.

What the Dutch really prize is their *techniek en taktiek* – technique
and tactics. 'The one who can achieve something by thinking is the
hero,' says Auke Kok. 'The crowds of course adored Johan
Neeskens and Wim Suurbier, who were hard and mean. But they
loved them partly because they helped and protected the creative
players.' Dennis Bergkamp, the coolest, most austere aesthete of
current Dutch players, has said that 'Behind every action must be a

thought.' As Johan Cruyff puts it: 'Every trainer talks about movement, about running a lot. I say don't run so much. Football is a
game you play with your brains. You have to be in the right place at
the right moment, not too early, not too late.' *Observer* columnist
Simon Kuper observes: 'When the Dutch say that someone can play
football, they are referring exclusively to his technique and his
reading of the game. Courage, desire to win, pace and height mean
nothing to them. In Holland, they say that someone like Oliver
Bierhoff can't play football. They never thought Ruud Gullit was
up to much, either. And they didn't really appreciate Gerald
Vanenburg, who was always the one who could do the most with
the ball.'

Of course, physical grace and virtuoso play – individual 'artistry'
– are respected in Holland as they are everywhere else, especially in
the big cities. The Italian-suited Faas Wilkes is still revered as a
'dribble king' who could drift effortlessly past four or five defenders
to score. The folk memory of Ajax's first beautiful team, the World
War II-era *Gouden Ploeg* of Jan de Natris and Jack Reynolds,
lingered for decades. In the 1920s Ajax's American-born Jewish
right-winger Eddy Hamel had his own fan club. The Hamel
connoisseurs would assemble on the strip between the halfway
line and the corner-flag to watch their man in the first half, and then
switch to the opposite corner of the stadium at half-time. Hamel
was eventually murdered in Auschwitz, but his tradition persisted.
Between 1957 and 1973 Sjaak Swart, a half-Jewish right-winger,
inherited a following of fans who changed ends at half-time. It was
the same at De Kuip with Feyenoord's great left-winger Coen
Moulijn. In the late 1970s, former Swart fans found a new hero in
Tscheu la Ling and followed him round the ground until anti-
hooligan fences ended the practice in the early 1980s.

When, in the late 1970s intellectuals, artists, writers and students
flooded to De Meer for the first time to watch the nascent Total
Footballers in action, the idea began to take hold that what Cruyff
and the others were doing was something more than football. It was

no longer men kicking a ball around a muddy field. It was something refined and intriguing. It was Art.

One key debate of the time was whether Piet Keizer or Cruyff
was the greater artist. Cruyff was electrifying and the most dramatic
presence on the field; Keizer better fitted the bill as the moody,
elusive and almost dilettante creative genius on the field. The oddly
upright, long-striding Keizer had a precise, accurate, near-visionary
style. He had a unique scissoring run, could dribble past several
defenders at once and delighted in deceptive curled crosses and
passes. He was also a humorist. One favourite trick was to look one
way and flick a perfect pass in the opposite direction. He could do
Charlie Chaplin-style football comedy at vital moments. In a match
against PSV he leaned forward as if to hammer the ball in with his
head, only to stop stock still and exaggerate the gesture. The ball slid
from his forehead and floated gently into the far corner of the net.
Jan Mulder recalls a goal Keizer scored as Ajax beat Feyenoord 5–1
in Rotterdam: 'In front of goal, he stuck his leg out and the ball
went very slowly in . . . but enough! The crowd went mad and he
stood as if to say, What have I done? But there was no accident
about it. It was absolutely on purpose.' Nico Scheepmaker, author
of the quirky 1972 biography *Cruyff, Hendrik Johannes: Phenomenon*
and the first Dutch writer of note to take a literary approach to
football, wrote an article entitled 'Rembrandt Never Played Football' (poor Rembrandt, he reckoned). He also teasingly failed to
answer the Cruyff – Keizer conundrum. His enigmatic verdict was:
'Cruyff is the best, but Keizer is the better one.'

Keizer, four years older than Cruyff and an established star before
the latter's debut, had a reputation for being mysterious and prima
donna-ish at the peak of his career. Instinctively uneasy with
journalists, he hated the media spotlight and never gave interviews.
When someone mooted the idea of collecting a book of poetry
written in his honour, Keizer consented on the proviso that the
book had a tiny print-run and was given no publicity at all. He
never got on with Rinus Michels, either. On the field, he disliked
being told to run back for defensive duties and was uncomfortable

with Michels's 'system', harsh management methods and discipline. When Michels went to Barcelona in 1971, Keizer celebrated by dancing on a table. At the 1974 World Cup Keizer played only once and was dropped after an ineffective game against Sweden. Michels preferred Rob Rensenbrink on the left-wing, and in the final he replaced the injured Rensenbrink with the quicker but much less creative PSV winger Rene van de Kerkhof. Keizer never forgave Michels this treatment, though in the opinion of other players he was by then past his peak.

Ajax football was clearly art. But which art? The most obvious candidate is ballet. The idea that footballers in general and Johan Cruyff in particular were balletic first took root in 1972 as a result of Maarten de Vos's film about Cruyff, *Number 14*. (Fourteen was Cruyff's lucky shirt number.) De Vos's film was made at Ajax's peak, in 1972–3. What is most striking now – as it was then – is neither its *Thomas Crown Affair*-style split-screen tricksiness nor the footage of Cruyff as dad with baby son Jordi; its interviews with Cruyff driving his sports car or watching himself on one of the first-ever Philips video recording machines. The most indelible images are of Cruyff's extraordinary grace captured in slow motion.

Choreographer Toer van Schayk was fascinated by the Ajax footballers. 'Cruyff was an artist, though I don't think he ever realised it himself. He just played football as best he could. He had such incredible speed and he was so much in control of his body and movements that it was beautiful to watch what he did. You can see how graceful he was. Unconscious grace is much more beautiful than conscious grace.' Van Schayk was inspired by newspaper photographs of the players. 'When I started choreography I used to cut out extraordinary action photographs of players creating compositions and groups you could not possibly have imagined: several bodies jumping in the air at the same time and colliding. Sometimes I was able to use these compositions, recreate them in dance.' The ballets, though, were more deeply inspired by the Club of Rome and explored Van Schayk's fears of environmental apocalypse. 'My early ballets were to do with all the futile activities of man which had seemed for centuries to build up to a brighter future but turned out to be also self-destructive. The violence of some of the accidental bodily compositions in football was useful for me in those ballets.'

For dancer Rudi van Dantzig the beauty was in the football itself – and especially in Cruyff. Cruyff and he became friends after Van Dantzig made a TV film about the training of ballet dancers and young footballers.

'Normally, footballers are boring, but with Cruyff and the others it was like fireworks. Or like Maria Callas singing. Cruyff was a Callas on the field. Callas was the first to bring fire to a role in opera, and you felt the same passion in Cruyff and the others. There was something very dramatic in him, like a Greek drama – life or death, almost, even when they played ordinary Dutch League games. You see it in him even now, just in his face when he's just sitting watching – that alertness! It's fantastic to see.

'But the whole group of players were inspired. Their agility and virtuosity made for incredible explosions of bodies together. Somehow they all dared a lot. There was something special about that whole generation. Piet Keizer was more of a big block, the way he moved. Cruyff was very delicate and graceful, like a fish in his movements. He had this swiftness and – phwhoosh! – he would do something totally unexpected! He would go in one direction and suddenly change direction completely. I think those kinds of surprise also made the fantastic pictures. Players now are rougher, more to do with strength and speed. Much less interesting.

'In dance every movement is studied so it can sometimes become very boring and bad. Football is the spur of the moment; you can never tell what's going to happen. But Cruyff always seemed to be in control. He made things happen.' Van Dantzig was a close friend and colleague of Rudolf Nureyev and created numerous ballets for the charismatic Russian star. Nureyev, he recalls, was fascinated by Cruyff. 'Rudolf said Cruyff should have been a dancer. He was intrigued by his movements, his virtuosity, the way he could suddenly switch direction and leave everyone behind, and do it all with perfect control and balance and grace. He was amazed that Cruyff's mind was so swift. You could see he was thinking so fast ahead. Like a chess player.' Nureyev never went to Ajax games, but he watched on television. 'The performance of Cruyff is something that he would have loved to be able to do. That magnetism! And in a way, I think Cruyff was a better dancer than Nureyev. He was a better mover.'

For the TV-watching world, the greatest Johan Cruyff moment was the 'turn' he performed in Holland's 1974 World Cup match against Sweden. As he probed for an opening on the left side near the Swedish penalty area, Cruyff found his way blocked by Sweden's sturdy and experienced right-back, Jan Olsson. Cruyff checked back and shaped to cross. What he did next was voted one of fifty 'greatest moments ever' by readers of *Total Football* magazine in England. It has been taught to generations of schoolchildren as the 'Cruyff turn'. Even Olsson, a friendly-sounding man, who now designs computer systems for Electrolux and raises sponsorship for his old club, Atvidabergs, cherishes the memory. Olsson recalls moving instinctively to block Cruyff's cross. 'At that moment I thought, "I have him," but . . .' Instead of crossing, Cruyff, seeming almost to twist himself inside out, flicked the ball behind himself, changed direction completely, and in a split second was three yards clear and dancing towards the goal-line. Bewildered, Olsson stumbled and fell and could only watch helplessly as Cruyff raced clear and delivered a perfect curved cross with the outside of his right foot. The chance was headed over the bar. Only later when Olsson studied Cruyff's move on TV did he understand what had happened to him. 'People often ask me about it. I say that I played eighteen years in top football and seven times for Sweden, but that moment against Cruyff is the proudest memory of my career. I thought I'd win the ball for sure, but he tricked me. I was not humiliated. I had no chance. Cruyff was a genius.'

The mild-mannered Gerrie Muhren, one of the greatest technician's of all the Dutchmen of his era, says opponents often tried to make Ajax play on a bad pitch. 'At De Meer it was like a billiard table, the pitch was perfect. And we always liked to play with the Derby Star ball. With this ball, you can give a centre with love. You can chip a high ball over ten metres. If a ball is too hard. You can never give a short ball over the opponent from the ground. We could do everything with that ball. We never had words with it.' Sometimes, bad weather and rotten pitches would be turned to advantage. For example, Piet Keizer often calculated the strength of the wind, precisely over-hitting the ball in the knowledge that it would be blown back to the correct position. In a famous 1968 European Cup match on a swamp of a pitch in Istanbul (the 'Hell of Fenerbahce', as it became known), Keizer created one of the greatest Ajax goals ever by lobbing a high ball into the thickest mud on the field. The Turkish defenders, expecting a bounce, were wrong-footed as the ball stuck where it landed. Cruyff also read the conditions perfectly and glided on to the ball without breaking stride, flowing on to score gracefully. (After the game a watching Kuwaiti emir was so moved by Keizer's performance that he gave him the gold watch from his wrist.) In another match, this time against Panathinaikos, on a pitch damaged by rain, the Ajax players continually played passes into pools of water in the middle of the field. It took a while before the crowd or their opponents understood what was happening: the Ajax players knew the ball would stop in the water but the Greek defenders continued running to where the ball would have been if it had been dry.

Sculptor Jeroen Henneman believes, 'With the Dutch, the beauty is in the pitch. In the grass, but also in the air above it, where balls can curl and curve and drop and move like the planets in heaven. It is not only the field. The folding of the air above it also counts. That is why the Arena stadium is so horrible. It is ugly and it seals off the heavens.' Cruyff has been known to pass footballing judgement on the basis of sound alone. Ajax historian Evert Vermeer remembers him criticising a player's technique while looking away from the pitch. 'He said: "His technique is no good." "How can you tell?" Cruyff said: "It's obvious. When he kicks the ball, the sound is wrong."' Henneman reckons that without knowing it, what the average Dutch footballer most wants 'is silence, a kind of quiet on the pitch, to feel the beautiful green grass and fresh air and the passes he receives. When you kick well, you have to touch the ground, to dig a little under the ball as in a golf shot. And you hear it. And it is nice to hear.' Gerrie Muhren agrees: 'Wind is the biggest enemy because you cannot hear the ball. You have to hear the ball during the game. You can hear from the sound it makes on the boot where the ball is going, how hard, how fast. You can tell everything. If there is a big wind, you are angry with the ball. You kick the ball but it doesn't listen to you.' Muhren used to find crowd noise unhelpful, too. 'I didn't like the crowd making a noise. You have to be able to listen. Atmosphere is good, but if there was a noise near me, I wanted to go to the other side of the stadium. I want to hear the game, the players, the ball . . .'

Arnold Muhren was famed for both his technique and his singularly Dutch ability to approach the game as if it were a kind of physical chess. 'It's a thinking game. It's not running around everywhere and just working hard, though of course you have to work hard too. Every Dutch player wants to control the game. We play the ball from man to man; we wait for openings. That's how to play football: with your brains, not with your feet. You don't have to be a chess player, but you must think ahead. Before I had the ball I knew exactly what I would do with it. I always knew two or three moves ahead. Before I get the ball I can already see someone moving in front of me, so when the ball arrives I don't have to think about it. And I don't have to watch the ball because I have the right technique.' If ball control comes naturally to a player, he needs only one touch to get it where it needs to be. This is not the case if a player in possession has to stop to think. A pass which is a fraction of a second too late will have repercussions in the pass after that, and so on. 'English players don't think until they have the ball at their feet. You have to give the ball at the right moment. In Holland we don't think about the first man. We think of the third man, the one who has to run. If I get the ball, the third man can run immediately because he knows that immediately I will pass to the second man, and he will give it to him. If I delay, the third man has to delay his run and the moment is over. It is that special moment, that special pass.'

Ruud Krol was one of Ajax's best attacking defenders and later developed into a truly wonderful *libero*. He knows a thing or two about fine football and great art. When he retired in 1983, he took three years off to visit the art galleries and museums of the world he had never had time to visit as a player. He says carefully: 'Football is not art. But there is an art to playing good football. Michels taught us always that simple football is the best. It is also very difficult to play simple football. It's the same with artists. The best work is not difficult, it is very simple. We could play every kind of football. We could play tough. We could play technical. We were not afraid. In the beginning the Italians were dominating and physical. But we were not afraid of them. Not even of the Argentinians. If they played physically, we could do that. We trained on it. If you want to become stronger on the ball [slams fist into palm] you do it. We trained a lot on this. One against one. Three against three. Always very strong games. We had a way of playing that was very Amsterdam. It is a different mentality. Arrogant, but not really arrogant. The whole way of showing off and putting down the other team, showing we were better than them.'

The Argentinian coach, football writer and former World Cup striker Jorge Valdano has speculated on the nature of football genius based on his analysis of his friend Diego Maradona's goal against England in 1986. (Not the 'Hand of God'; the other one. The one generally reckoned to be the greatest goal of all time, involving as it did dribbling past six English defenders in a run from inside his own half.) Valdano was in a good position to observe the goal as he was just a few feet from Maradona the whole way down the pitch. In the shower after the game Maradona told him that the initial objective of his run was to set up Valdano for a shot on goal. Only when he'd beaten the last English defender and was bearing down on Peter Shilton did it occur to him that he could score himself. On a visit to London in 1998, Valdano recalled: 'He told me that at that moment, he remembered a game seven years earlier at Wembley when he'd been in a similar position and had played the ball to Shilton's left and missed the goal. He assessed the current situation and decided that he didn't need me; he could solve the problem of scoring himself. In a quarter-final of the World Cup, after a seventy-metre run, he was able to recall a situation from years earlier, analyse it, process the information and reach a new conclusion. And he did it in a fraction of a microsecond. That is genius.'

There are many perspectives on the 'art' of Dutch football; what links them all is that they value intelligence as the key ingredient.

'We think football is a passing game,' says Gerard van der Lem, who is now in charge at AZ Alkmaar. Van der Lem's teams, like those of his friend and mentor Louis van Gaal, are based to an extreme degree on possession of the ball and switching it around the field at extraordinarily high speed, probing for weakness and space in the opponents' defence. Creating fast, compact passing-triangles has become one of the central dogmas of Dutch coaching in the last decade. This requires intelligent, quick-thinking players who, when faced with several options (run with the ball? or pass? if passing, who to?), are able to choose immediately and correctly the right option for the team and the system. 'The most difficult thing in life is choices,' says Van der Lem. 'Every player usually has three options on the field. I try to explain it very simply to my players. I say: 'If a man outside the stadium offers you a free BMW Cabriolet, what would you do?' And of course they say: "Take the car." Right answer. But then I say: "What if the man asks you to choose between a BMW Cabriolet and a Mercedes Cabriolet and they seem the same. Same performance, same price, same everything. What do you do then?" "I don't know." And I say: "But you must choose and in soccer you have to choose very fast. It happens in an instant. And I will evaluate you on the choices you make on the field." They have to know when to leave the man they are marking to press the ball. It's difficult. We lost a game against Ajax because our defender left his man to press and found he couldn't. He made a mistake. He didn't succeed in pressing the first man, so the ball was able to travel to the next man, who was free and who scored the goal. Players have to make their choices all over the field. Every player has to understand the whole geometry of the whole pitch.'

Ever since the 1970s, awed South Americans have referred to the Dutch national team as '*Naranja Mécanica*' – 'The Orange Machine' – or, more colourfully, 'The Clockwork Orange'. The phrase does not signify young Malcolm McDowell performing ultraviolence in Kubrick's movie. It means the Orange system, individuals functioning as a perfectly integrated whole machine. 'We are the Brazilians of Europe,' claimed Kees Rijvers. But the description would better fit the moody footballing virtuosos of Yugoslavia or Croatia or Georgia than the Dutch. There is something slightly mechanical about Dutch football's system-building. Teams are planned and manufactured. The point of the vaunted youth-schemes is to churn out numbered products for the machine. A number 8 from the second youth team can step neatly into the shoes of an injured number 8 in the first team and will know precisely where to fit in, how to mesh with the team's other moving parts.

The significance of numbers dates back to Rinus Michels and his notion that on the field players were numbers and not people. Within Michels's system, each number denoted particular respon-sibilities and obligations. By contrast, Cruyff as coach always saw his players as people. Louis van Gaal, on the other hand, took Michels's number system and refined it. Van Gaal is the most extreme version yet of a Dutch coach who sees football almost entirely as a highly ordered collective endeavour: 'Football is a team sport, and mem-bers of the team are therefore dependent on each other,' he says. 'If certain players do not carry out their tasks properly on the pitch, then their colleagues will suffer. This means that each player has to carry out his basic tasks to the best of his ability, and this requires a disciplined approach on the pitch.' Yet there is a beauty in his sleek, powerful machines, both the one he built at Ajax to win the Champions' League in 1995 and the one he has assembled at Barcelona using some of the same components and which is designed for the same purpose.

Van Gaal's Ajax of 1994–5 won the Champions' League, took the Dutch title without losing a single game and is perhaps the ultimate example of what discipline, a sophisticated design and intelligent system-building team can achieve. An analysis of the team's basic structure and operating principles was written for coaches by Henny Kormelink and Tjeu Seeverens: 'Each position is linked to a fixed shirt number for the sake of clarity. In turn, each shirt number is associated with several basic tasks, which the player wearing the shirt has to carry out. There are tasks to be carried out when Ajax is in possession, and others to be carried out when the opposition has the ball. Ajax's youth teams play in the same manner with the same tasks. This ensures the desired continuity. Ajax usually builds up its moves from the back. The goalkeeper only rarely kicks the ball long. Usually he plays it to one of the more creative defenders. It is noticeable that the whole team moves in set patterns. If one player comes back to make himself available to receive the ball, another makes a run towards the opposition's goal-line. The wide midfielders make a lot of forward runs, creating space for the long pass from the back to the advance striker by pulling wide. The same midfielders always remain behind the winger when he receives the ball so that they do not curtail his action radius. The role of the midfielders is therefore always to support the strikers, and they must not overlap their wingers . . . If an attack cannot be pursued down one flank, the task of the midfielders in Van Gaal's system is to ensure that the ball is switched to the other flank as quickly as possible. Ajax almost always plays in a small area of the field in the opposition half. In this restricted space, a good positional play and the ability to create space for others are of great importance for the team. This also applies to wing play. The two wingers stay wide to create space for the advanced central striker. The favourite ploy is for the centre-forward to run into space when he receives a long forward ball, which usually comes from the heart of the defence.'

The blueprint may read like a factory manual, but in practice Van Gaal's Ajax could be spectacular. The players and passes flowed with such blurring speed and precision that it sometimes appeared as though they were shuffling the surface of the pitch the way an experienced dealer handles a pack of cards. Ajax could deal out their tricks, trumps and goals almost at will. Van Gaal's team won praise and the highest prizes all over the world before it was broken up by economic pressures. Most of his players figured in the Dutch World Cup team of 1998.

At least one influential Dutch writer and commentator loathes 'set patterns' and everything else in this mechanistic approach to foot-ball. The Byronic Jan Mulder, a brilliant centre-forward in the 1970s ('the best I ever faced,' says Arsenal's 1971 Double-winning captain Frank McLintock), prefers passion to possession. 'In Holland we are system mad and the world doesn't know it. The world thinks we always play attacking football. But we play with the handbrake on. All this passing at the back . . . tick-tock, backwards, sideways, tick-tock . . . it's boring! Too much fear, too much caution. Van Gaal . . . Beenhakker . . . handbrakes!'

With his lined face and rumpled hair, there's something compel-ling about Mulder which is hard to convey in print. He's a romantic, a nostalgic, an idealist who punctuates his conversations with dramatic pauses and impulsive surges of his voice. Mulder adores Cruyff, with whom he played for a short time, and the other great artists of Dutch football, and insists the game would be better – more *beautiful* – without the coaches. Warm, darkly dressed and smoky-voiced, Mulder is on TV every night, the most volatile and magnetic personality in Frits Barend and Henk van Dorp's chat-show on the commercial RTL4 station. He's a TV star, but he really ought to be in movies. If anyone ever makes a Dutch film of *Dracula*, he'd be a great Count. Come to think of it, why not cast him in the next English version – actors Rutger Hauer and Jeroen

Krabbe have made a decent living from their Dutch-accented charisma. But maybe Mulder would miss his football too much to spend long in Hollywood.

Over morning coffee amid the art deco splendour of the large Café Wildschut near the Concertgebouw, Mulder invokes the spirit of Sir Stanley Matthews: 'An English journalist once said to him, "Please, Stanley, would you show me your famous body swerve?" And Matthews said, "I'm sorry, sir, but I can't do it in cold blood." I can't do it in cold blood! Well, there is too much cold blood in Dutch football. Much too much! Ajax won the European Cup in 1995 but it was boring, boring! Yes! They won everything they could win, but the football of Van Gaal in those years was dull football. Dull! I like Van Gaal personally but not as a coach. I admire him. He got results at Ajax but they didn't play as well as one thinks. They outplayed opponents, but it had no soul. All this passing, passing . . . tick tock tick tock. Frank de Boer? Boring! Yes, OK. Frank de Boer can play the good long ball, in a game maybe once. Ronald Koeman did it a little more often. But Gunter Netzer did it far more, you know. Far more! Or Ruud Krol. He was a big player! But the game changed.'

Mulder loathes the coaches' idea that football is a science. 'Of course, one has to have a leader, someone has to organise it, but in a loose way. With a team like Ajax, it was easy for a coach. Cruyff was the best player in the world. With Cruyff up front, you could play any way and win. An unbelievable player with this devastating acceleration. Cruyff was so much more important than Michels. It wasn't because of Michels that Barcelona were champions in Cruyff's first year. It was Cruyff. Michels was coach already but Barcelona were bottom of the table when Cruyff arrived. Michels is my hero, too, but not because of his coaching – as a character. I love his humour. But the position switching, the fluid game? It didn't come from Michels. It came from Cruyff and Neeskens. They had so much. And Suurbier was very quick. The backs were so dangerous. It was their character, Suurbier and Krol, beautiful players, charging forwards. They liked to score goals, and they did.'

In September 1999, Holland and Belgium played one of the most old-fashioned games seen in Rotterdam in years, a rip-roaring, chaotic 5–5 draw which could not have been less like the two sides' dreary 0–0 World Cup encounter fifteen months earlier when the Belgians' fearful blanket defence smothered Holland's listless attack. Now attackers surged forward with abandon, defenders made schoolboy errors and Edgar Davids, in his new black goggles looking like Zorro, scored an astounding goal in the style of Maradona, slaloming at speed through four Belgian tackles before stroking the ball in with the outside of his foot. The crowd enjoyed it, but the press and coaches slated bondscoach Frank Rijkaard and his new Belgian counterpart Robert Waseige. 'Shaming – beach football' was 'Don Leo' Beenhakker's verdict. Mulder was delighted. 'Ninety-nine times out of a hundred when a coach has influence, it is negative influence. They make defences strong. This was beautiful because the coaches didn't care very much. 5–5! They laughed. But it was a beautiful game played without complexes.'

Mulder complains that even when Ajax won the UEFA Cup in 1992, the hand of the coach was too visible. 'They did not play with passion. Van Gaal is a teacher but doesn't give his players much freedom. OK, it works. In the modern game, results are the most important thing. But I love football and I see too many restrictions and obligations on players: too much handbrakes.' What about Cruyff as a coach? 'It has to be a myth a little bit. But he was a coach at Barcelona and I didn't follow it very well. He does like attacking football with wingers and so on up but it doesn't always help, you know. Modern coaches are too tactically involved. Too much systems. Yes! Even Cruyff! They think too much about this simple game. The talent of the players is decisive: one should always play naturally. No thinking, please! No thinking!'

11: the eleventh commandment

'There is no medal better than being acclaimed for your style'

Johan Cruyff

'Winning is not the most important thing. The most important thing is to play a good game.' It is almost impossible to imagine an English Premiership manager ever saying such a thing. (Or, needless to say, the equivalent in Germany, Italy or Spain.) Nonetheless, these are the words of one of the Netherlands' most admired, intelligent and best-loved coaches, Foppe de Haan. De Haan, who has spent fifteen years guiding the tiny Frisian club Heerenveen to a place among the élite of Dutch football, and then keeping them there, is no oddity. The vast majority of Dutch coaches, players, journalists and fans feel exactly the same way. Johan Cruyff struck a chord when he said during the 1998 World Cup that although his beautiful *totaalvoetbal* team had lost the 1974 final to the Germans, they had achieved a victory of a kind by playing football the world still talks about. The Dutch look down upon the cynical defensive tactics of Italy, Spain, Argentina or Belgium. The English are considered stupid. And the 'ugly' (i.e. defensive, physically powerful and hard-running) German style is beneath contempt. To win at all costs and by any means necessary is considered shameful and indecent.

'Decency is a very deep and very Dutch characteristic,' says writer Auke Kok. 'So it is also very deep in Dutch football culture. If you do something, you do it "decently". You keep the pavements clean. You keep the windows clean. You keep the play clean.

Holland has been decent through this ideal of purity since the seventeenth century, so we demand pure play. Even when they had English coaches, Ajax never played kick-and-rush; nobody in Holland did. Dutch crowds don't like it when southern European players come here and introduce diving. Machlas [a Greek striker] or Dani [who is Portugese] say: "At home, we are heroes if we win a penalty." But in Holland the crowd doesn't like it at all. If an English defender kicks the ball into the stands, he gets a big cheer. Do that here and you get booed by your own fans. It's seen as destructive. In every Dutch team the defenders, even the goal keeper, must be able to play football.'

To play in a beautiful, attacking way has become the Eleventh Commandment for the Dutch. Defensive tactics have been despised for a generation. In 1977 the respected Yugoslav coach Tomaslav Ivic won the championship with Ajax and was promptly sacked. His crime? Making Ajax play defensive football. The name of Arie Haan – probably the most underrated hero of the Golden Age of the 1970s – still arouses splutters of righteous indignation in Rotterdam where Feyenoord fans blame him for 'negative' tactics when he was in charge in the early 1990s. Dennis Bergkamp has said: 'I suppose I'm not that interested in scoring ugly goals.'

The importance of Johan Cruyff's influence in shaping this Dutch football idealism cannot be overstated. While the Michels/Kovacs era at Ajax established the idea that football could be art, and the concept was reinforced by the 1974 World Cup, these artistic standards were allowed to wither somewhat in the late 1970s and early 1980s. Coaches started playing 4–4–2 and defensive attitudes were dominant. Then Cruyff returned for three seasons as a player, first at Ajax and then for one season at Feyenoord, where he won the Double. In his remarkable Indian summer, Cruyff stimulated the careers of all the players who were to make Holland European Champions in 1988. Marco van Basten, Ruud Gullit, Frank Rijkaard, Ronald Koeman and Gerald Vanenburg all played with him and learned from him. So too did key Danish players, such as Soren Lerby, Jesper Olsen and Jan

Molby, who later helped to make their national team one of the most interesting of the decade. Even more crucially, as coach at Ajax between 1985 and 1988, Cruyff developed his system, using many of the key elements of the Kovacs/Michels teams to create what became standard Dutch attacking orthodoxy – the 'Dutch style'. The key elements in this – three defenders, two wingers, possession football, the footballing goalkeeper playing far out of his goal as an extra defender – were put in place during this period. In 1987 Ajax, with Van Basten and Rijkaard as key figures (and the seventeen-year-old schoolboy Dennis Bergkamp on the right wing) won the Cup Winners' Cup, raising Dutch football's profile to its highest level in nine years. Cruyff also revamped the club's youth-training and talent-spotting systems.

In 1996 Cruyff returned to Holland after seven years coaching Barcelona, having turned the Catalan giants into Europe's leading club and, arguably, the Continent's standard-bearer for beautiful, attacking football. Since then, Cruyff has developed a unique role as the soul, conscience and guiding spirit of Dutch football. He invariably uses his weekly TV appearances doing big match analysis for NOS on Champions' League games (and his regular columns for the influential *Voetbal International* magazine) to preach the same message: a sort of sermon on the right amount of football virtue. To him this means possession of the ball, to take risks, to play with right- and left-wingers, to be the boss on the field, and to have more players in midfield than the other side. Cruyff is an idealist. But he also believes in winning. As he has explained: 'Professional football means money. It means achievement. Idealism, of course, means loving beautiful football. And it means never in your life making concessions about one or the other. They are equally important.' Asked if they weren't really opposites he says: 'I don't think so. They turn out not to be.'

De Haan recalls the bafflement of the former East German coach Hans Meyer, who was sacked by FC Twente in the summer of 1999 because of his defensive approach. 'Hans is a very good technical trainer but couldn't understand that Dutch mentality in soccer.

From a trainer's point of view, he is excellent, he's very good on how to build up training. But he was not good in the eyes of the people because his way of thinking about football was totally different. He wanted to play 4–4–2 with certain variations, and he tried to teach that to the players. The Dutch journalists didn't like it because he was boring and the way the team played football was boring. One day he came with me to see NAC Breda play NEC Nijmegen. The game was played at high speed with a lot of mistakes and it finished 5–3. Everyone was very enthusiastic and liked it very much. Everyone except Mr Meyer. He hated it, but he said: "Now I understand what the Dutch journalists like. They like a lot of adventure in football. They like a lot of goals. It has to go from end to end." But he couldn't make a team that played that way, so he was sacked.'

When the thoughtful De Haan outlines his vision ('to be a nice club playing nice football. In future we want to be not really at the top but about fourth or fifth place') he is not displaying a lack of ambition. Quite the opposite. Once a senior figure in the KNVB, he is an imaginative and resourceful pragmatist. Even with a population of 50,000, Heerenveen is a village rather than a town, so even to survive in the top division is something of a miracle, and to prosper there is astounding. With his chairman, Riemer van der Velde, De Haan has guided Heerenveen away from forty years of provincial obscurity to become one of the country's leading and best-loved clubs. 'If you look at our public, they always want to see very good players who are almost more artists than they are footballers. The Dutch papers and journalists are the same.' All over the Netherlands people have adopted the 'sympathetic' Heerenveen, who play in the colours of the Frisian flag, as their second team.

De Haan has also nurtured some terrifically talented players but knows he will lose them to the Netherlands' big three clubs – Ajax, PSV and Feyenoord – who, in turn, lose their good players to the big spenders of Italy, Spain and England. If De Haan had been able to hang on to the likes of Russian midfield artist Igor Korneev, Danish striker John Dahl Tomasson and Jan de Visser (all

Feyenoord), midfielder Ole Tobiasen and defender Tom Sier (Ajax), or brilliant striker Ruud van Nistelrooy (PSV), Heerenveen would be playing in the Champions' League. But De Haan remains clear about his priorities. 'Our first aim is to be attractive, to amuse the public a little bit by being artists. Tactically, we play the Dutch style. Cruyff style. The two wingers; a centre-forward. Sometimes we have one midfield player behind the centre-forward and also in front of defence. It's always either 4–3–3 or 3–4–3. The way Cruyff likes it. We do it with our youth team all the way to the first team.' De Haan tries to teach his players to be fighters, but insists: 'We have to play in a positive way. We don't have a lot of yellow or red cards. We don't fight with the referee because we think that is not what we stand for. We have an image and the PR with the public that everything we do we have to be positive. Last year we won the Fair Play Cup. Now we are again at the top of the Fair Play Cup. We also have to qualify for European football. Perhaps we can win the Dutch Cup and maybe, you never know, the Dutch League.'

His football ideal is the 1974 Dutch World Cup team. 'That is the ground where I start. I'm trying to do that, though of course you have to look at the players and see what they can do.' In 1974 he was thirty-one years old. He had worked for sixteen years for the KNVB's trainer-development programme and decided to take a bus to Dortmund to see Holland play Bulgaria. 'I went only to look at the football from a technical point of view, not as a supporter. I was definitely not wearing an orange shirt. I would never do that! But when Holland started to play, I became a fan. I couldn't help it. I was singing just like everyone else. They played so nice! And when they lost in the final to West Germany, I was watching television on my own. I had sent my wife and two kids out. When we lost, I was crying. It hurt very much. Holland played football and they lost.'

Throughout the 1990s the Dutch commitment to the ideal of beautiful, attacking football, which was enormously stimulated by the success of the less popular Louis van Gaal's Ajax, has barely wavered.

*   *   *

The Dutch are devoted to their good football (a phrase with distinct Calvinistic moral overtones) and also have an equally Calvinist urge to proselytise their beauty and goodness to the world. As Feyenoord boss Leo Beenhakker observes: 'At a World Cup or a European Championship, ninety per cent of the teams are there to win. But there's always one country who only wants to show how good they are. And that's Holland. It's our drama. With all our talent, our technical and tactical skills, our offensive football, we have only once won a major tournament [in 1988], and that was by accident. We love the game, but we lack something. We are like a boxer who boxes very well but doesn't have a knockout. We don't have the mentality to take him by the throat, but sometimes you have to . . . [squishes throat]' Strangle? 'Yeah. We have no killer touch. That's been our problem during the whole history of our football. We've played in tournaments when Germany or Brazil or somebody was champion. And look at what happened in France; look at the French team and look at the Dutch team. There is a lot of difference. But the French are the World Champions. And we win nothing at all.'

The Dutch were (again) the classiest football team of the last World Cup – 'Masters of the Ball', Jorge Valdano called them. They played exquisite, elegant, attacking football, but they did not have the mentality or killer instincts of street fighters. Before their semi-final against Brazil in Marseilles, national coach Guus Hiddink explained the Dutch moral obligation to play beautifully whatever their opponents (notionally the team defending Pelé's concept of the 'beautiful game') planned to do. 'Brazil, sadly, is no longer swinging and flaming. I see defenders boot the ball away shame-lessly. Holland must never play like that. If we did, people would murder me, and they would be right to do so.'

In the same week Johan Cruyff explained why style is more important than winning: 'I don't go through life cursing the fact that I didn't win a World Cup. I played in a fantastic team that gave millions of people watching a great time. That's what football is all about. The Dutch team of the seventies was fantastic to watch. People say that to me every day here in France. They talk about us in awe. That is the biggest reward I can have as an ex-player: I played my football in a thrilling team. And I coached Ajax and won the European Cup playing that way, too. Then I went to Barcelona as coach and we won many trophies. But the best reward for me was that people said we were producing the best football in the world.

'There is no medal better than being acclaimed for your style. As a coach, my teams might have won more games if we'd played in a less adventurous way. Maybe I'd have earned a little more and the bonuses would have been bigger, but if people say that Barcelona were playing the nicest football in the world with me as coach, what more can I ask for? If you're appearing in the World Cup final it may be the biggest occasion of your life, so why be sad and fearful? Be happy, express yourself and play. Make it special for you and for everyone watching. For the good of football, we need a team of invention, attacking ideas and style to emerge. Even if it doesn't win, it will inspire footballers of all ages everywhere. That is the greatest reward.'

Against Brazil, the Dutch spent the whole night attacking in wave after wave of surging, intricate orange. Brazil played *catenaccio*, stacking ten men behind the ball and leaving only Ronaldo upfield to poach a goal, which he did at the start of the second half. Holland pressed continuously, scored an equaliser with four minutes to go and should have had a penalty when Van Hooijdonk was pulled down in the last minute. The Dutch played with style and passion but, at the end of extra time, when it was time for the penalty shoot-out, the result was a foregone conclusion. The Dutch touchingly – or arrogantly – always believe they can win matches in normal time. Despite having lost their Euro '92 semi-final (against Denmark) and Euro '96 quarter-final (against France) on penalties, they still instinctively regard shoot-outs as somehow beneath their dignity. Accordingly, they hadn't bothered to practise. Assistant coach Johan Neeskens tried desperately to get on to the pitch to explain how to do it under pressure ('If you're not sure, just hit the ball as hard as possible. If you don't know where it's going, nor will the goalkeeper'), but was stopped by FIFA officials. Winning on penalties may not feel to the Dutch like proper winning; but losing on penalties is authentic defeat. In Marseilles the Brazilians, who had practised, scored all their spot-kicks. For the Dutch, Bergkamp and Overmars scored, but it was apparent from the uncertain body language of Philip Cocu and Ronald de Boer, whose attempt to dummy the goalkeeper went horribly wrong, that they were going to miss. And they did.

Simon Kuper was struck by the lack of obvious Dutch grief at losing. 'Brazil won on penalties because they wanted to win more. They could not go home after a lost semi-final. Holland could because they had played Good Football. De Boer and Cocu put in weak shots that were saved. Both could go home with the requisite moral victories anyway: Ronald de Boer had scarcely lost the ball all tournament, and Cocu had excelled at centre-forward, in midfield and at left-back. Of course it hurt. Frank de Boer walked off the pitch berating his twin. But it plainly had not hurt that much because for a good fifteen minutes after the penalties, players from both teams stayed on the Marseilles turf to hug one another. Ronaldo embraced his former PSV Eindhoven team-mate Zenden, Seedorf and Roberto Carlos of Real Madrid intertwined, and so did almost everyone else. At last the Brazilians and the Dutch had met opponents they respected. The Brazilians know Good Football when they see it – "*o jogo bonito*", they call it – and differ from the Dutch only in their belief that winning is more than just a bonus. Zenden later ran into his friend Ronaldo in the corridor between the two changing-rooms under the Stade Vélodrome. The two twenty-two-year-olds talked for a long time, about football and other things. At the end Ronaldo clasped his friend's shoulder and said, in his broken Dutch: "Third place for Holland – good, I think!" He was right. To go down with honour is all the Dutch want.'

Third place would have been nice. All the Dutch wanted was to go home after the Brazil match, but they were obliged to stay a few humiliating extra days to face Croatia in what they saw as the meaningless third-place play-off. The Dutch wanted to treat the game as an open, flowing exhibition match and were baffled and irritated to find the technically inferior but hard-tackling, deep-defending, counter-attacking Croats fighting for the result. So Croatia won 2–1, which meant the Dutch, the best team in France, had finished fourth in the tournament. Hiddink claimed a moral victory anyway. 'After the disappointment, you have to say that our style, our philosophy, has impressed the world and that's what I'm proud of.' The Dutch played attacking, attractive and creative football. 'It was very important to keep to the philosophy. I don't know if I'd have been happy with a World Cup won in a bad way. We couldn't have done that.'

One of the most notable opponents of this way of thinking is Feyenoord coach Leo Beenhakker, a passionate man who has managed Real Madrid, Ajax and the Dutch national team. The Dutch ideal of playing beautiful football – good football – is now so deeply entrenched that many coaches, journalists and fans insist that winning is less important than playing well. 'Don Leo', however, tears his yellow-white hair out at this approach. Been-hakker (who is one of Cruyff's principal targets in his weekly TV sermons) secured the Dutch Championship in 1999 for Feyenoord with a style he freely admits was 'practical', winning lots of games 1–0 and relying on his brilliant Argentinian striker Cruz to grab most of the goals. Beenhakker has been around a bit. A former Ajax and Dutch national coach – he was in charge during the 1990 fiasco – he has also coached around the world in Mexico, in Turkey and, most notably, at Real Madrid in the late 1980s. There he assembled a brilliant attacking team considered at the time the best Real Madrid team since Puskas and Di Stefano. But his tactics at Feyenoord have won him few plaudits in the Dutch media.

'I am one of a small group of coaches who says: first you have to play to win. After that, if it's spectacular, fine. But you must win. A lot of my colleagues don't agree; a lot of people criticise me for it. People say I have to play more open, more offensive. I say, just a moment, just a moment. When I came here one and a half years ago this club was a disaster. What was my first main goal? To bring enthusiasm back to the club. How do you do that? To play fantastic football and lose 5–0? Or to put us again on the map and say: "Feyenoord is still here and we are the champions." Last year, we played very practical football. I know. Practical: you play to win. OK. In the beginning, of course, people accepted it, but then they were wanting more: "Why don't you play more open, more attacking?" I say, "OK, OK, I will try to be a little bit more. But the first thing is to win, to win, to win." Because this is big business. We are not talking about only a game any more. If I can survive in the Champions' League into the second round, it's another ten million guilders for the club. What should I do? Entertain people and say, well, bad luck, we're not in the next round? No, no, no! But a lot of coaches here say – and I never understand this – no, we have to let the people enjoy it. But when do the people enjoy it? When their club wins. I never see happy people after a defeat, huh?'

He has a point. Defeat rarely produces gorgeous football. Consider the fate of the heavily Dutch-influenced Danish 'Dynamite Team' at the 1986 World Cup. Three key members of the side – Soren Lerby, Jesper Olsen and Jan Molby – were direct Cruyff protégés, who had played with him at Ajax. Others, including captain Morten Olsen (the future Ajax coach) and coach Sepp Piontek, were devout admirers of the Dutch system in the 1970s. In the first round in Mexico, Denmark played a compelling brand of delicious-looking Dutch-style Total Football – the most artistic football of the tournament – and swept aside West Germany 2–0 and demolished the tough Uruguayans 6–1. The Danes were beautiful and seemed to be heading for glory. In their second-round match they took an early lead against Spain. Then a penalty miss and a careless back-pass by Jesper Olsen let Spain equalise and inaugurated one of the strangest massacres in World Cup history. The technically superior, more creative Danes continued to attack while their defence was ripped to shreds by smart, lethal Spanish

counter-attacks led by Emilo 'The Vulture' Butragueno. Long
before the end, the Danes were dejected and befuddled rather
than beautiful. Spain won 5–1. The only other Danish team of note,
the side that surprisingly won Euro '92 (putting out the brilliant but
over-confident Dutch in the semi-finals), was based on very
different principles: a packed midfield, tenacious defence and clever
counter-attacking with two quick strikers, Flemming Povlsen and
Brian Laudrup.

Benhakker continues: 'In Spain or in Italy they only talk about
one thing and that's winning. Just win the game; don't be so
difficult. If you play well – OK, fantastic. If you don't play well,
well, it's bad luck. But win. If you have a few Dutch players in
such an Italian or Spanish team or an English team, they pick it up
and go with it, the neurosis disappears. Yet for some reason, when
the Dutch are together, the main thing is "Let us show the world
how good we are". In 1990 I went to Italy with a fantastic group
of players [Van Basten, Gullit, Rijkaard, Koeman, Wouters, etc.].
But it was never a *team* because everybody wanted to show "I am
the man". It was terrible. We had a fantastic preparation. Then the
three from Milan arrived. They came and something happened,
something entered into the team. They didn't want to be the big
leaders, they just wanted to play. But from that moment on, I felt
the same atmosphere that I know so well from Holland: "Well,
let's just go to Italy, let's participate, let's play well . . ." Not:
"Let's go to Italy to win, to be World Champions!" No, no no:
"Let's play and we will see how it goes." It was terrible, unbelievable!'

He compares the Dutch mentality with the ruthless stars from his
great late-1980s' Real Madrid team. 'Every Dutchman has an
opinion about everything. When you go to a hotel with the Dutch,
one player says "Hey, it's too big", and the other says it's too small.
"It's too hot", "It's too cold", "It's too . . ." We are busy with
everything, ev-er-y-thing! But when I went to a hotel with a
Spanish team – and they're all big stars, Hugo Sanchez, Butragueno,
Gordillo, Michel, Camacho, Santillana, Juanito, great players – they

come in and it's: "OK, this is fine. Where's my room? OK. Bye."
They sit quietly and they don't talk about the bus, and about the
driver and the driver's wife . . . No! Come on! They think: "We are
here to play a football match. We play and we kill them. And then
we go home." That's the difference.

'I can only say that we don't have the mentality because as soon as
we have to play really important matches, in the World Championship or whatever, for some reason, we are no longer a team because
we have no servants on the pitch. We have only stars and it kills us.
Every tournament for the last fifteen years, player for player we had
the best, but we always had a very bad team. In some way we are
not able to forget ourselves, not to talk about "I" and "me", but to
talk about "we" and "us" for two or three weeks. In a tactical way
it's the same translation. Most of the time we like to demonstrate
how good we are, how "Total" we are. We hate to close a match,
to say: "Hey, listen, we are playing in the World Cup now, we are
winning 2–0, there's half an hour to go, let's close all the doors, have
a nice match, bye-bye, but it's over." You understand what I mean?
The Germans or Italians can do that. Fantastic! And that's how you
have to play a tournament, or a big international match. But we
can't do it.'

De Haan is also aware of the problem. 'Louis van Gaal told me
before Ajax played Juventus in the European Cup final in Rome
[in 1996] that he was not afraid of Juventus's idea of football. He
said: "Our idea is much better, but they have players like Vialli and
Ravanelli. And those two have a mentality we don't have. They
never stop; they go always, always to the border of what is
tolerated. And maybe our players cannot handle it. They are
not hard enough, not used to it. We will be the best team, we will
play the better football, but the chance that we'll lose is big. We
don't have those kinds of killer." It is always a problem for us.
Dennis Bergkamp is a very good player but he is not a fighter. And
if it isn't there, you can't teach it. Bergkamp didn't learn it in Italy
or England.' De Haan blames the safe Dutch way of living. 'We
have arranged everything very well. When something goes wrong,

you can go to *that* school. And if something goes wrong, you can
go to the other school. Or another. There is always a safety-net. A
place you can go. Football is the same. Look at our youth [teams].
We have to work very hard to teach them to give everything they
have. They are not real fighters; but their talent and the things they
bring from home are enormous. The boys here are tall, strong and
quick and have good skills. They are real footballers. Everything is
good. We can train twice every day, but we cannot teach them to
be killers.'

With the single exception of Edgar 'Pitbull' Davids, the current
generation of Dutch footballers are polite, intelligent, modest,
ironic, 'ideal sons-in-law'. They aspire to being great artists. Yet
the genuinely greatest Dutch football artists – the stars of the Total
Football era in the 1970s – had a very different agenda. They were
only trying to win. They could play rough and hard. And they
attacked relentlessly because it was the best way to dominate and
overwhelm, not simply because it was beautiful. They saw themselves not as artists but as winners.

'Anyone who says the only important thing is to play beautiful
football, well, they are crazy,' says Johnny Rep, still Holland's top
World Cup-goalscorer. 'But I don't think they really mean it. Yes,
we liked to play too, but our character to win was 200 per cent.
With so many great players in one team you make art; you don't
mean to, but you do. It's different now – good players like
Bergkamp and Kluivert lack the hardness to win. Bergkamp is a
very big player but he doesn't have the character in his body.' When
Holland played World Champions Brazil in the 1974 World Cup
semi-final, the two teams produced a game of almost frightening
physical intensity. There's a piece of film showing Rep tussling with
Rivelino, the Brazilian captain. Rivelino jostles Rep. Rep waits a
few seconds, checks to make sure no one is watching, and then
delivers his retaliation – a well-aimed elbow in the face. When I
remind him of this, Rep beams. 'Yes! He had done it to me before
and that was my reaction. Of course, you look to make sure the

referee doesn't see it. But he started it! Rivelino is now a good friend of mine. Of course! Always! That's football.'

Sjaak Swart, 'Mr Ajax', demonstrates Ajax's essential approach to their games in the late 1960s and early 1970s by pounding the table with his fist: 'Boom! Boom! Rinus Michels always said from the start of the game this is how we play: Boom!' He hits the table again. 'Like this to the other side. That's not a system, it is an attitude – every player knows what he must do. Very aggressive. We went for the goal. First we make three goals and then, yes, we can make some nice combinations, something you wouldn't normally do. You can make a show for the public. We were all winners; we weren't trying to be artists. We just wanted to win.' So people have remembered that team wrongly? 'Right.' When people say, 'Ajax is art', that wasn't the idea at all? 'No. Not at all.'

Dutch penalties were different then, too. In the 1970s the Dutch had lethal penalty-takers. The fearsome Velibor Vasovic and later Gerrie Muhren banged them in for Ajax. For the national team they could depend on Johan Neeskens, who scored three in the 1974 World Cup, and the phenomenally cool Rob Rensenbrink, who missed only two in his whole career and scored four in the 1978 World Cup. Rensenbrink actually enjoyed penalties, and when he was at Anderlecht practised taking them for ten to fifteen minutes at the end of every training session. His method was to tell the goalkeeper in advance which of the four corners of the goal he was going to put the ball, and then beat him there anyway.

Hugh McIlvanney savours the memory of the Dutch teams of the 1970s for their 'tremendous surging aggression which brought you to your feet all the time'. Some of the Dutch players could mix it like South American streetfighters. Suurbier, Neeskens and Van Hanegem were intimidating tacklers. Even now, in his late forties, Neeskens (who came from a broken home and grew up sleeping in a corridor) tackles with such ferocity that he has been known to injure national-team players in training. Neeskens and Van Hanegem were close friends but on the field they could knock lumps out of each other. In the 1971 Dutch Championship decider, which

Feyenoord won 3–1, their thudding midfield collisions were audible in the stands. Before the 1974 World Cup match against Bulgaria the Dutch prepared a special treatment for the one Bulgarian player they saw as a threat, their playmaker Bonev. Arie Haan recalls: 'Before the game, we drew up a list of our players who would hit him with hard tackles early on. Neeskens first, Van Hanegem second, then Suurbier, I think, Wim Jansen, maybe . . . I forget the order and exactly who it was. I think I was number five. But we never needed number five. After four tackles, Bonev didn't want the ball any more. He didn't give us any problems.'

In a team with such a winning mentality, there can even be a place for a spot of juggling. Abdellah Belabbas-style. Not because it's art, but because it is the ultimate put-down, the ultimate, aggressive assertion of dominance.

The most fondly cherished moment of Ajax's 'golden age' in the early 1970s was neither a great goal nor the lifting of a trophy, but a swaggering act of showmanship from the most unlikely source. In April 1973 in the European Cup Ajax, reigning champions who had thrashed Bayern Munich in the previous round, met the Spanish champions, Real Madrid, in the semi-final. Ajax won the first leg 2–1 in Amsterdam and faced a hostile 110,000 crowd for the return in the Bernabeu Stadium two weeks later. Gerrie Muhren scored in the first half to give Ajax a 1–0 lead. Early in the second half, as he was standing near the centre-circle, Wim Suurbier swept a high-arced crossfield pass to him. Gerrie Muhren caught the ball on his left foot and, incredibly, started to juggle with it. Pap . . . pap . . . pap . . . pap . . . All with his left foot. The huge Madrid crowd, briefly stunned, rose and roared. To dare to do such a thing! In the Bernabeu! In such a match! Applause rolled like thunder around the giant terraces. After what seemed like an age, Muhren allowed the ball to drop and played a simple pass to Krol, who had come charging up from left-back. Inspired by his team-mate's effrontery, Krol himself swept past two Madrid defenders and shot, narrowly missing the bar.

After the game, the Muhren brothers walked away from the stadium together and were surrounded by Madrid fans. 'The Spanish people didn't recognise us, but they came up to us and wanted to talk,' Gerrie says. We didn't speak Spanish, so they started juggling. They were excited. They thought we were Ajax fans. Arnold pointed to me and said: "This is the guy who did the juggling." The fans laughed at him. They didn't believe it. They couldn't imagine that a soccer player would walk on the streets with normal people. They were smiling and laughing. Arnold was saying: "Really, it was him." And they didn't believe it.' Not everyone was happy, though. On the pitch Barry Hulshoff had been appalled and immediately ran across to remonstrate. 'Gerrie was my best friend, but I shouted at him and we fought about it. I said it was a mistake because it made the Spanish players angry. Afterwards they started to kick some of our players. I'd do the same because it was an insult. If someone did that to me, I'd kill them. When a team becomes aggressive, you never know what they can do. If someone is sleeping, don't wake them up! We still fight about it. He said: "Well, the occasion was there." I like it now, too, but I still say it was wrong.'

For Gerrie Muhren the meaning was different. As a child he had idolised the Real team of Puskas and Di Stefano, fuzzy, black-and-white superstars of the first European football to be televised in Holland. 'It was always my dream to play good soccer against Real Madrid. When the ball came to me from Suurbier, I saw Ruud Krol in the corner of my eye, coming up. I wanted to control the ball and wait. I knew I was going to give the ball to Krol but I needed some time until he reached me. So I juggled until he arrived. You can't plan to do something like that. You don't think about that. You just do it. Yes, it was an expression of superiority. But it was the moment when Ajax and Real Madrid changed positions. Before then it was always the big Real Madrid and the little Ajax. When they saw me doing that, the balance changed. The Real Madrid players were looking. They nearly applauded. The stadium was standing up. It was the moment Ajax took over.'

12: the snake man

'He was as good as Cruyff'

Raymond Goethals

'It was *this* close,' says Ruud Krol, and shows me by holding his thumb and forefinger about a millimetre apart. 'No, more like this.' The gap is down to a couple of microns. 'If it goes in, it is finished.'

Buenos Aires. The River Plate Stadium. 25 June 1978. Just after 5 p.m. It's the last minute of a frantic, tainted World Cup final and the score between Holland and Argentina is 1–1. The home team (whose fascist government, it will later emerge, almost certainly bribed their last opponents, Peru, to smooth Argentina's safe passage to the final) took the lead in the first half through Mario Kempes. Throughout the afternoon the Dutch have had to put up with punches in the face, blatant gamesmanship, scandalous refereeing and perhaps the most hostile and frenzied crowd in the history of football. They have spent the entire second half attacking. Seven minutes ago they finally equalised through their lanky substitute centre-forward Dick Nanninga. Now, standing in the centre circle, Ruud Krol, Holland's captain and sweeper, famed for the precision and range of his passing, unleashes a raking sixty-metre ball which pierces the Argentina defence. The pass reaches Holland's player of the tournament, the goalscoring left-winger Rob Rensenbrink, in a position just wide of the Argentina goal, close to the goal-line on the left. Fillol, the Argentinian goalkeeper, rushes from his near post. Rensenbrink snakes out his long left leg and guides the ball past Fillol and towards the empty net. The ball bounces slowly on its way to the goal, seeming to deviate fractionally to the left . . . and hits the post.

The ball rebounds to safety and Holland's chance evaporates. The game goes to extra time and Argentina eventually win 3–1, Kempes driving through the centre to score the second; Bertoni hitting the third after apparently controlling the ball with his hand.

'*This close.*' The difference between justice and despair. Between joining the immortals and being forgotten by history. There are many in Holland who believe that if Rensenbrink's shot had gone in, the Dutch would still have been denied victory somehow. The Italian referee, Sergio Gonella, a man whose appointment the Argentinians had allegedly demanded in place of the respected Israeli Abraham Klein (a demand to which FIFA had preposterously acceded), would have played enough extra time to award Argentina a penalty. Or Rensenbrink's goal would simply have been disallowed. Or there would have been a pitch invasion. Or something worse. There remains a suspicion in Holland that there was no way Holland could have won that game and left the stadium alive. But Ruud Krol says: 'I didn't have that feeling on the field. Of course we felt the referee was not with us; that's for sure. Everybody knew that on the field. We spoke at half-time about it: "That fucking referee – is he playing for Argentina too?" That's a normal reaction from players. Whether it is right or wrong at the moment, you can judge later.' Krol insists the Argentinians were blatantly cheating 'in everything'. 'We were in a hotel outside Buenos Aires and they took us a very long way round to the stadium. The bus stopped in a village and people were banging on the windows, really banging and shouting: "Argentina! Argentina! Argentina!" We couldn't go backwards or forwards. We were trapped. For twenty minutes we stood in the village like this and some players were really frightened because the crowd was really banging and pushing on the windows of the bus.' In the stadium the teams did not enter the field together. Holland came on first and Argentina delayed their entrance by five minutes, keeping the Dutch waiting, surrounded by military police and a wall of hostile noise. When they did finally appear, the Argentina captain, Daniel Passarella, demanded Dutch winger Rene van de Kerkhof be banned from the game because of a small protective plastic cast he had worn in five matches since injuring himself in Holland's first game of the tournament. 'I am sure they prepared everything beforehand,' says Krol. 'They made us wait and the referee did nothing. And there was already a discussion before the game about the referee because FIFA wanted Klein, the Israeli, for the final. But Argentina had lost against Italy when Klein was the referee, so they wanted Gonella. How is that possible? Then we discussed Van de Kerkhof's cast. After fifteen minutes I said: "OK. Enough is enough. If he cannot play, we are going off." I was angry. And then within two minutes we were playing. Only he had to put on another bandage. He already had three bandages, so they put on a fourth. They were trying to unnerve us. They did everything to win. You can understand that, but it was not done in a sporting way. And they were already cheating in the semi-final. I don't know if they bought Peru, and of course the Argentine players have always denied it. But they needed to win 4–0 and they had never beaten Peru before by more than 2–0. And now it was something extreme: 6–0, I think. That was a lesson to FIFA to start games at the same time in future.'

Although Cruyff and Van Hanegem missed the 1978 tournament, that year's Dutch team, led by the Austrian former Feyenoord boss Ernst Happel rather than Rinus Michels, is fondly remembered around the world as being of the same bottle as the 1974 vintage. In Holland, surprisingly, they don't make that connection and 1978 arouses much less feeling. There the golden age of Dutch football seemed to be already over by then. Feyenoord and Ajax were shadows of their early-1970s selves. And although the team in Argentina included Neeskens, Haan, Rep, Jansen and Jongbloed who, like Krol, Rensenbrink and van de Kerkhof, had played in 1974, the Dutch started poorly in the mountains in Mendoza on a bumpy pitch. They beat Iran 3–0 with a Rensenbrink hat trick, then drew 0–0 with Peru, and could have gone out to Scotland when they lost 2–3, despite Rensenbrink's early penalty. Peru had won the group and the Scots had to beat Holland by three goals in order to reach the second round in their place. When Archie Gemmill scored a famous solo goal, the Dutch were briefly 1–3 down before Johnny Rep scored to make them safe.

Things improved in the cooler, damper conditions of Cordoba in the second round. Revitalised by the injection of two younger players, PSV's defender Ernie Brandts and the FC Twente midfielder Piet Wildschut, the Dutch ignited, exploding to beat Austria 5–1 (with goals from Brandts, Rep with two, Willy van de Kerkhof and another Rensenbrink penalty), fighting back to draw 2–2 with West Germany (thanks to Arie Haan's phenomenal long-range strike and Rene van de Kerkhof's late jinking run). And then, in what was effectively the semi-final against Italy, Brandts scored, bizarrely, for both sides, before Haan settled it with arguably the greatest long-range goal of all time, beating Dino Zoff with a straight drive that was still rising as it went in off the post despite being struck from near the centre-circle. (Nearly twenty years later, when I spoke to Haan by phone on a bad line to Greece, where he was coaching Thessaloniki, I mentioned that I got goosebumps whenever I saw that goal shown on television. He said: 'So do I,' as if some higher power than his right leg was responsible, and I immediately got goosebumps again.)

Despite arriving with a below-strength squad and being so long and so far from home that some players were homesick, the Dutch had reached their second successive World Cup final. Krol: 'For us it was very good to get that far. We were unlucky to play two times against the home team in the final. And that never happened, ever. Never before and never after.' He still thinks Rensenbrink could have scored at the end. 'Maybe if he took a little more time, he could make it because Robbie, like Van Basten later or George Best, was a person who could score unbelievable goals from technically impossible angles. I haven't watched it again too many times, but maybe if he had come inside . . . I don't know. I would have to see it again. Look at it closely; see how he was standing, how he could have made a step . . .'

This close. If Rensenbrink had scored, Holland would not only have been World Champions. It would have been the brilliant, self-effacing Rensenbrink – and not Mario Kempes – who entered history as the star of the tournament. Rensenbrink had scored five times in Argentina. With a winning goal in the final, his total of six would have eclipsed Kempes's five and handed the Golden Boot to the Dutchman. Rensenbrink would probably have had Dutch streets named after him by now. Instead he is remembered, if at all, as the 'anti-hero' who hit the post. That he was one of the game's all-time greats has been forgotten. Even during his career, Rensenbrink was seen as a loner and an outsider, and was under-estimated in Holland. This was mainly because, although he learnt his football on the street among the tenement blocks of west Amsterdam and started his career with DWS, his best years were spent in Belgium, first with Bruges and later as the central figure of the great Anderlecht team that reached three and won two European Cup Winners' Cup finals between 1976 and 1978. Belgian TV was not watched in most of Holland at the time, so few Dutch fans ever knew how good he was.

Nor did he ever play as well for his country as he did for his club. In 1974 he didn't enjoy having to learn and adapt to the demands of Total Football. 'Tactics didn't interest me,' he explains. 'I had to learn a lot quickly. Physically, it was difficult to come back to defend, but mentally it was not difficult. At Anderlecht and Brugge we played 4–4–2. Most of the time I was thinking only about getting past my man.' At Anderlecht Rensenbrink was given the freedom to operate as more of an old-fashioned inside-left than a winger. In the national team this spot was Cruyff's domain and Rensenbrink was pushed to the wing. 'I never argued with Cruyff about this. For me it was no problem. We had success in every game. But I didn't play really at the level I did in Belgium. I played much better in '78 because Cruyff wasn't on top of me, but also because I was four years older.'

Rensenbrink never had what the Dutch call the 'gift of the voice'. When he spoke with his feet, however, it was with an eloquence that could move men to tears. Jan Mulder played alongside him for a season at Anderlecht in 1970–71, and says: 'Robbie Rensenbrink was as good as Cruyff – only in his mind was he not. He was a little like George Best, a great technician, a wonderful dribbler. He was better than Piet Keizer. Rensenbrink! Oh, he was a player for those times. He could dribble! Take six or seven men in a slalom! And he was a winger. But he would score twenty goals a season. As a left-winger! Rensenbrink was one of the all-time great players, but he had complexes with Cruyff in the national team; he was always in Cruyff's shadow because of his character. He was a very silent guy. I enjoyed watching him at training sessions . . . whoah! These movements! Some players have that. *La beauté de geste*, they call it. The splendour of the gesture. It's nothing, but the way he puts his foot against the ball. So different! When Robbie Rensenbrink did it . . . ahh! [Sharp intake of breath] He only was kicking a ball, but I was moved to tears. [Laughs]

'I say this twenty years later, but I think there is a bit of truth in it. *La beauté de geste*! He had such an elegant way of passing the ball. Just with his body . . . his foot . . . yes, *elegantly*. When I do it, OK, bang. It's OK. It's a human being who kicks a ball. When Robbie Rensenbrink does it, it's art. No, not art but something other. It's more beautiful, more precise. It's like handwriting. He had beautiful handwriting. All with the left foot. And he was quick. He had an acceleration. A very lean man. '*De Slangemens*,' they called him: "The Snake Man"! "The Serpent"!

'I saw him once against Bayern Munich in the Super Cup. Incredible! Against Beckenbauer and Breitner and Schwarzenbeck. He dribbled all the time. And once when he was at Bruges I went to see him play against Ujpest Dozsa, which was a good team in those days. 6–0! And Robbie scored five goals. Incredible goals from forty metres! He could shoot, too. Robbie has been forgotten a little bit, but he was a much better player than Van Hanegem. Different from Van Basten but at the same kind of level.'

'He was as good as Cruyff,' says the legendary Belgian Raymond Goethals, Anderlecht's coach in the 1970s who later led Marseilles to their 1993 European Cup-final win over AC Milan. 'But completely different. Cruyff was a coach on the field; Rensenbrink was an introvert.' In Rensenbrink's greatest year, 1976, he was probably the best player in the world.

Since quitting as a player, Rensenbrink, whose introvert modesty makes Dennis Bergkamp look like Dennis Rodman, has kept an extraordinarily low profile. He still lives in Oostzaan, a village just north of Amsterdam, in a hard-to-find house he bought for himself in 1970. He lives on the money he made – and invested astutely – when he was a player. He is rarely interviewed, never appears as a TV pundit and has little connection with football. On the pitch he used to look like Cruyff's bigger, bonier elder brother. Now his hair is greying and swept back, there are bags under his eyes, he is wearing a cardigan and his midriff is generously padded. He still has no desire to become a coach – 'coaches age faster' – and has spent much of the last twenty years fishing. 'I like fishing, but not every day. I have a garden. I have a house. I have family. I live. I have fun. I prefer to be quiet.' He watches football, but is amused by the 'nonsense' talked by most pundits: 'They talk about it like it's an academy subject, but in the end it's a simple game. After all the theories, all you need is eleven good players and a trainer who tells them to stand in the right place.'

He insists he is not haunted by those few microns from more than twenty years ago: 'If it had gone in, we would have won. We would have been World Champions in Argentina. It's a pity. Though they were pretty crazy, those Argentinians. If we'd won, going back to the hotel would have been a dangerous trip. Even though we lost, there were still thousands of people chanting at us outside the hotel. Inside the stadium, the noise . . . it was a blue sea and we felt it. You couldn't block it out. Anyone who says the noise was stimulating to us is bluffing. We had shots and chances in the first half; it could have been 2–0 to us before half time . . . I think "if only" thoughts, of course.' And the last-minue chance that hit the post? 'But it was not a chance. I did well to hit the post. The ball was almost on the goal-line. I had no space to do anything. I had no chance to control the ball and come inside. There was a defender in front of me. I had to shoot first time. The goalkeeper left a very narrow opening. Sometimes I think it would have been better for me to miss completely. Then people wouldn't ask about it. If it was a big chance, I would still suffer from it, but really it was impossible to score.'

16: here's johnny

'The book isn't really a history of all of Dutch football. Just the highlights. And for me, you are in most of them.'
  'That's true. You can't say it isn't true.'

It's hard to believe Sloterdijk Station exists in the same universe as Amsterdam's over-photographed, tourist-friendly town houses and canals, let alone in the same city. But here it is, wedged among the endless neat apartment blocks and poplar trees and graffiti and canals in the city's north-western suburbs: a railway station quite unlike any other.

In the half mist of a late-autumn afternoon, the building seems a study of cool white and blue steel, curving glass canopies, and concrete. Sleek silver super-trams and blue and yellow double-decker trains whisk in and out on three levels simultaneously. Elevators and escalators hum. Business commuters, teenagers in anoraks and neat Dutch mums with kids scurry between the many platforms and across the flat, grey marble concourse.

Café Het Station is chilly and fantastical, a stark blue and white space with huge windows, which seems to float between the curves of the station and the huge, bleak spaces of the adjacent pale bus station. A tubular white sculpture curls snakelike outside the window. In the middle distance, huge concrete housing blocks rise out of the mist.

I'm here today with Ingrid, a Latvian psychoanalyst on a flying visit to Amsterdam. Intrigued by my eager, boyish talk of a football legend, she has invited herself along to my interview with Johnny

Rep, imperishable Total Hero of Total Football, the most elegant and deadly of Dutch strikers of the 1970s.

Once seen as Holland's answer to George Best, the clever, tousle-haired blond pin-up, whose image was later copied by Benny (or was it Bjorn?) from Abba, remains Holland's top scorer in World Cups. He was a key man in the tragic Lost Finals of both 1974 and 1978.

In Britain, Rep is perhaps best remembered for the sumptuous thirty-yard strike that put Scotland out in Mendoza in '78. In the Netherlands there's a wealth of other Rep memories to call upon. In one of Rep's first senior matches, the momentous World Club Cup final against Independiente in 1972, the nine-teen-year-old boy-wonder scored two graceful goals, the second of which was a run from the halfway line, ending with a shimmy past the goalkeeper. Then there was the looping header that won Ajax their third European Cup against Juventus in 1973. The four goals he scored on the way to the World Cup Final in 1974 and the three tragic chances he missed in the final. Three goals in the first three minutes when he played alongside the young Michel Platini for St Etienne in the 6–0 slaughter of PSV in 1979 . . . The grace with which, almost single-handedly, he steered Mafia-run Bastia of Corsica to the UEFA Cup final in 1977.

Café Het Station is a convenient location for Rep, being as it is halfway between his home in Zaandam and the training ground of Almere, the Second Division team he now coaches. Somehow, the scene and the concrete remind Ingrid of Soviet Russia. The station feels sinister, like a film set. *Brief Encounter* meets *Scanners*. Johnny is late, and as I grow a little anxious – 'Is this the right place?' – Ingrid, who has never seen a Total Footballer before, not even on television, weaves absurd movie fantasies: 'These big windows . . . sitting here we're so exposed . . . a good place for a hit, yes? I think we sit further away from the window . . . That man with the briefcase . . . is that him?'

'Too short.'

'And him, the one in the raincoat?'
'Too old. And black.'
'Maybe he looks different now. Maybe he changed.'
'I think I'd recognise him.'
'He could come in disguise. That's possible . . .'

Ahh, here's Johnny. With a friendly smile and a modest air, the great man arrives, his hair now not long, tousled and blond but short, dark and greying at the temples and long creases in his face. Unassuming in jeans and an Italian check jacket, he is warm and twinkly. As he begins to chat, his still–luminous piercing blue eyes dart frequently – nervously – to the window. He leans across and peers into the distance. 'I am looking out for the police . . .'

DW: Theun [de Winter, Johnny's best friend] told me your long blond hair was a little bit from the bottle.

JR: Yeah, just a little bit. Hydrogen peroxide, you know, just to help nature . . .

DW: The book isn't really a history of all of Dutch football. Just the highlights. And for me, you are in most of them.

JR: That's true. You can't say it isn't true.

DW: Did you make your debut in the World Championship game against Independiente?

JR: It was my first big game. I had played some games in the European Cup and in the League but this was my first big game.

DW: And you scored those two goals?

JR: Yes, the second goal was a nice goal.

DW: Someone told me that when you were first in the team, you were considered arrogant. And that Johan Cruyff taught you a lesson by always passing the ball a little in front of you, so it made you look bad when you couldn't reach it. It was to make it look like your mistake, but actually the pass made it impossible . . .

JR: Yes. But I was not arrogant. No. I had problems with Johan. I was a little bit young and Johan was always telling me what to do. Do this, do that. And I was a boy but I spoke back to him . . . He was stubborn and so was I – that was our problem. And Johan doesn't like that. You must always say OK. But I did it instinctively because I didn't like him telling me what to do. He thought you had to do what he said.

DW: What was it like growing up in that team?

JR: I was about sixteen years old. I came from Zaandam, the Second Division club, to Ajax. I was one year in the youth team. Two years in the second team. And when I was nineteen, I got to the first team. I was never with Michels.

DW: One has the impression that the players ran that team in the time of Kovacs.

JR: Kovacs was a good coach. He was the boss. But the players ran the team. Kovacs was a very good coach for us after Michels. He gave us more freedom. That was very important. The players were fed up with the hardness and discipline of Michels. It is good for the team that Kovacs came at that moment. After two years, it was enough.

DW: Why did it fall apart, break up?

JR: The biggest problem was that everything was so easy. It was such a good team. The players had won everything. The players needed another challenge, another team, another club. Every team has the same problem when they win everything. They had won the European Cup three times. For me it was the first time. It was nice.

DW: But Liverpool managed to stay together.

JR: Yes, but how long did they play well? Three, four, five years? That is the problem. Then you must change your team. Because it gets stale, a little boring.

DW: Gerrie Muhren says you could have won the European Cup throughout the seventies if you had stayed together.

JR: Yes, but the ambition was gone. We had won everything. I was very happy in 1973. That was my first time [winning the European Cup]. The other players were happy, but the third one was not like the first one for them. So the team did break up and Johan Cruyff went to Barcelona, and then Johan Neeskens. And then we had a problem. Cruyff was very important to us.

DW: You are a little famous for your mouth. Apparently you used to say things to referees and other players.

JR: When I played against Independiente. Three days later I had to play with the second team. And that was very difficult . . . I didn't play very well. Well, then I would say things to the referee. I was not happy. If you played one day against Independiente and then three days later in the second team . . . Yes, I got some yellow cards. Did Theun say that? Not too much, but that was the problem: I should have been in the first team. Swart was thirty-four years old. He wasn't playing badly but I was so strong at that moment. I was twenty years old. I had been at Ajax since I was seventeen or eighteen. It was very difficult but the next season I was OK. A month later I was in the team.

[I tell Rep a story Jan Mulder told me: 'Johnny Rep was a fantastic player and such a great mouth. In one game I remember the referee, Frans Derks, our first gay referee, gave a wrong offside decision. We were all arguing with him and then Johnny came over and said to him, very seriously, very aggressively: "Frans, you do that one more time and I won't give you a blow-job tonight." There was shocked silence for a second and then Frans burst out laughing. It was fantastic!']

JR: [Laughs] Oh, maybe. I don't remember. Jan Mulder said it? I think that I didn't say this. No . . . Jan Mulder thinks that. But I never said that.

DW: But Derks tells the same story, according to Theun.

JR: Yes? It's a rumour. Rumour and humour.

DW: Why don't you say that you said it? It sounds good. It's a great line!

JR: I'm not saying nothing! I know how it is, that's for sure. Yeah, it's a good story, but I never said this. I was too young!

DW: There's another story about you from the famous game at Wembley in 1977, when you were beating England 2–0: that you went across to Kevin Keegan and said – very sympathetically – 'You've got some problems here, haven't you?' Is that true?

JR: Oh, maybe . . . I don't know. I don't remember it. I had a lot of sympathy for Keegan. He's still a good player. But the English team was not good. Maybe that's what I said to him. You have problems with this team.

DW: So you weren't doing it to put him down? It was a nice thing?

JR: Yes, sure. I would never do that.

DW: That Ajax team had an incredible personality. Everyone has stories about this great energy to win but also to play with style.

JR: It was always Ajax, football with style. Not every year, but Ajax is a club where the boys played football with style.

DW: Is that more important than winning?

JR: Winning is always important.

DW: Because now people like Co Adriaanse and Foppe de Haan say that the only important thing is to play beautiful football.

JR: Well, they are crazy. But I don't think they really mean it. Heerenveen often play defensively. They don't always play on the attack. Willem II like to win, too.

DW: In the Champions' League, for example, they played suicide football.

JR: But that is different from our championship. The Dutch League is a lot less difficult than the Champions' League. It's different.

DW: But people always refer back to the Ajax team of the early seventies and the national team of 1974. They say: that is art and that's how we want to play.

JR: Sure. But there were so many good players together.

DW: Where did you learn to play?

JR: On the streets, on the field. We played all the time. With my friends. We always played football. We love to do it. I like to do it.

DW: What is the difference between that 1974 World Cup team and the earlier Ajax?

JR: Just the players: Van Hanegem, Jansen, Rensenbrink, Rijsbergen . . . and the goalkeeper. Good players. Van Hanegem played for Muhren, Jansen played for Arie Haan and Haan played *libero* because our *libero* was Blankenburg, from Germany. Rensenbrink for Keizer, who was over the top a little. Van Hanegem was one of the best players in Holland, better than Muhren – harder, more of a winner. He ran less but he was more of a winner. Not so quick, but harder: more important for the team.

DW: What about the tactics? Was it difficult for Michels to come in and say to the other players . . .

JR: No, it was the same.

DW: Did he say: 'We are going to play in the Ajax style'?

JR: It was just our normal manner of playing. So that's not a risk. The trainer was there. Michels was very important for us, his discipline was very good. We had our tactics from before, that was normal. We were speaking about the team we were to play against, but our manner of play was always the same.

DW: What was the best game for you?

JR: For the people, the best game was against Brazil. For me, it was Uruguay. The first game, I made two goals. But Netherlands and Brazil was one of the big games of the tournament.

DW: Beating Bulgaria 4–1?

JR: OK, but it was easy. Against Sweden [0–0] was a good game. A very good game for the public, a very *spannend* [exciting] game. Very quick, many occasions in front of goal.

DW: In England it's remembered for the Cruyff turn.

JR: Oh, yes, he did that many times.

[Ingrid stands up to get him a coffee; again Rep looks nervously to the window. 'I'm looking out for the police . . . for my car – you cannot park there.'
There's laughter. I explain: 'I thought you were on the run . . .']

DW: I have to ask you about the final against Germany.

JR: It was terrible. For us it was not good to score in the first minute. We went on to make fun with the Germans. We didn't think about it, but we did it. Passing the ball around and around. And we forgot to make the second goal. If you see the film of this game, you can see that the Germans get more and more angry. You can see it. It was our fault. And we came to half-time losing 2–1. In the second half we played well but it was too late.

DW: No one said, 'Let's keep the ball'?

JR: No, it just happened. It would have been better if Germany had scored in the first minute.

DW: You got frightened?

JR: Yes.

DW: Because you thought, 'My God, we're winning in the World Cup final'?

JR: No, at that moment, no. Because you know the ga[...] minutes. But later, when we lost . . . we were so stu[...] such a strong team. And against the Germans is mor[...]

DW: You missed two or three very good chances.

JR: Yes.

DW: One just before the German penalty.

JR: Yes, the good chance. I went a little bit to the left. I was not very good in the game at that moment. Not many balls, nothing important and then you have a very good chance. In the second half I had some very good chances but [they went to] the goalkeeper, or on the post. We were not lucky in the second half. We did everything, but [German goalkeeper Sepp] Meyer played very well. It was a big shame.

DW: Do you blame Haan, for example, for not stopping the Bonhof run for the second goal, or was Cruyff at fault for playing too deep?

JR: There were some mistakes. Hoeness was too quick for Van Hanegem. And Jongbloed. And the German penalty was not a penalty. You can see it. For the referee, it is difficult. But Holzenbein made a show. A *Schwalbe*, in German, as we say.

DW: Was that the worst thing that ever happened in your career?

JR: Yes, yes. Sure . . .

DW: Did beating Germany in 1988 make any difference?

JR: No. No, of course not. OK, it's nice to win against the Germans. But *we* played in 1974. It was different.

DW: What did you mean when you said it was more terrible to lose against the Germans?

JR: When you can win the World Championship, it's even nicer if you can beat the Germans.

DW: Why?

JR: It is always particular against the Germans.

DW: Van Hanegem lost most of his family in the war. For him, it was the war. But for other players . . .?

JR: No. It wasn't the war. Our parents were always speaking about the Germans. We have to do something against the Germans. Go to war. That's normal. But we weren't thinking about that on the day. No.

DW: What about later? Many years later. How would you look back on it now?

JR: It's because we lost the Championship.

DW: People say it was much more painful than losing to Argentina.

JR: That's true. But not because of the Germans. Because we had such a good team in '74. We should have won. In 1978 we had a good team but we were happy just to play the final. And we could have won the final. If Rensenbrink could have made it in the last minute.

DW: Though a lot of people think that if he had scored, the game would have gone on longer. The referee would have given a penalty to Argentina.

JR: Maybe, maybe. But we don't know that. Maybe we wouldn't have got out alive from the stadium. People say that, too.

DW: Did you feel that?

JR: Yes, it was not a good atmosphere. It was too hot. All the *militaire*, not a good atmosphere. It was too heavy.

DW: It was terrifying just to watch on television, thousands of miles away.

JR: It was *kokend*, boiling. When we went to the stadium there were so many people on the street. And all the people banging on the windows of the coach. We had twenty kilometres driving through very small streets. And a lot of people always against the coach, shouting: 'Argentina! Argentina!' Almost the whole way. It took an hour.

DW: And then the business about Van de Kerkhof's bandage . . .

JR: For us, that was not so important. When we played, we played well.

DW: You're remembered for that goal against Scotland. If you hadn't scored that goal you would have gone home.

JR: With 4–1, we go home. It was 3–1 and Scotland had played very well. And then I scored a little bit of a lucky goal. When you shoot from twenty metres you have to have the luck.

DW: But you went all the way back into your own half to get the ball. It looked as if you thought, 'I've got to try to do something now'.

JR: No, it was just instinct. I went back to the ball, looking to dribble, to give the ball to somebody. No one tackled me, so I have a shot.

DW: Did you used to do a lot of position switching?

JR: When a defender is marking me tightly, I go looking for space. So I can have the ball, make a dribble or something. If the players don't give me the ball there and the defender is always close to me . . . So give me the ball and I can dribble him. Defending is nice to do but when you play in attack, you have always to run behind your opponent. But as the defender, you always have a lot of ball. It's easier, you can see the whole game.

DW: Total Football – was that real? Or just an image, an idea for the media?

JR: The players were so good. Suurbier, Ruud Krol. It was not the trainer who did that. It was natural for those players. When Suurbier went on an overlap, I took his job. It was natural to do that. You understand when you begin to play with them. If I go there, you take my place.

DW: Later it became a system with Van Gaal. What do you think of that?

JR: It's not so nice. We don't like that. I think it's a little bit boring. Van Gaal doesn't like dribbling in case you lose the ball. Not nice for the players and not nice for the public.

DW: It was strange to see players like Finidi George and Marc Overmars have to turn back if there were two defenders and pass back.

JR: Michels used to say to me: you play this way. But don't dribble too often. It's not that he was so flexible, but he accepted that it was my personality. When you are in good form, you can dribble two or three [defenders]. But when I didn't play well, I played easy. So you don't lose the ball every time. Because then you have a problem with all the team. *Yes!* Come on! With Ajax? With the Dutch team? With Johan? Oooh. If you lost the ball too much, oooh! You'll get it from everybody, and not only Johan. If I gave the ball and then you have the ball – like a team – it's easy to play passing. But when you lose the ball, you have to run all the time.

DW: So if you lost the ball, you would get into trouble?

JR: Big trouble! At half-time they would say . . . phhhooo! Yes, *big* trouble with all the players. But that is normal. Not necessarily with other clubs, but with Ajax and the Dutch team. That was special. You're not allowed to lose the ball very much. It is precious. You don't give away. You are allowed to lose it, but not much. Do it too often, and the trainer will take you off the pitch.

DW: Would these conversations carry on after the game?

JR: When you are winning, it's OK. But when I didn't play well, Johan said something. Sometimes that I had to play with more intensity. Sometimes it was too easy for Ajax when we played in the Championship. He said things to make me sharper. He was important for me; I learned a lot from him.

DW: Was he your hero?

JR: Yes, he was my hero when I was young. I always went to see Ajax. Johan and Keizer were my heroes, both.

DW: And when things went wrong, as they sometimes did, like in Yugoslavia in '76?

JR: That was a disaster, yes. Knobel was the trainer. He was a really nice person but he was not so respected by the players. He was the trainer at Ajax when the team fell apart. After Kovacs. He didn't do that very well, either. I think he had too much respect for us.

DW: Was he a little bit frightened of the players? Nervous of them? He was just this guy from the south?

JR: Yes, a little bit.

DW: He said in a big newspaper, a scandal newspaper, that Ajax was kaput because of drinking and women. Did he mean you?

JR: No. I have two children – I was married very young.

DW: You have a reputation for your women, as a bit of a playboy.

JR: I don't understand that. People see me like that. That was my image. But I never understood it. It was always my problem that people thought of a man [who was] a different person than I am . . .

DW: You were seen as naughty, a bad boy.

JR: No, not a bad boy. An *enfant terrible*, like George Best. Not quite the same way. I had two children, but people always thought I was with women, or girls. I was married when I was twenty. Two children, and always I lived for football.

DW: Do you want to coach a bigger team?

JR: That's my problem. They think I'm not serious.

DW: You should try in England. You have a big reputation there.

JR: I am ten times better than Gullit and many other trainers there. But I'm working now in the Second Division.

DW: Would you like to come to England?

JR: I always liked to play there. There are some traditions. I liked the crowds.

DW: I had forgotten there was a connection between you and Michel Platini. I saw a connection between the 1982 French team and the Dutch teams of the seventies. The French also played an attacking, pressing game – and then they lost to the Germans.

JR: Platini and I played for two years together. And we lost against them in France, which meant we did not qualify for Spain in 1982. We lost in Paris because of a very big mistake by Van Breukelen. He allowed Platini to make the first goal. There was a free kick. Krol was on the near post. Breukelen was supposed to be guarding the far post. But he also came to the near post. Platini curled it into the far corner. He curled a fantastic free kick – he made a lot of goals like that.

DW: How much did he learn from you?

JR: He was twenty-four and I was twenty-seven when we played together. Maybe he learned from me a little more character. That was his problem a little bit in the beginning when he played at St Etienne. He was a big player but he was too easy, too nice. Wrong character: you have to be a little hard. In the third year he did that. He changed when he had problems with his wife. She was having an affair with Larios [a fellow midfielder at St Etienne]. After this affair he got harder. They stayed together – it's OK now.

DW: So this is what we have to do with Dennis Bergkamp?

JR: Yes. But he's thirty years old now, or twenty-nine. Maybe it's too late!

DW: You played together with Mario Kempes at Valencia. And before the 1978 final you gave him a kiss?

JR: Sure, he was a good friend of mine.

DW: And after the final?

JR: Sure.

DW: What did you think of his goals?

JR: Our goalkeeper didn't do very well. If [Piet] Schrijvers had played, Kempes would not have scored two goals. Schrijvers was strong but he was injured in the semi-final against Italy, so Jongbloed came instead. I think he was forty-two – or was it thirty-eight? He wasn't that good a goalkeeper. In 1974 he was OK for us. Only, in the final, maybe he could have got the Muller goal. But he was not a 'wrong' goalkeeper. In 1978 he was our second goalkeeper. I think it was his fault a little bit, the two goals. It was too easy.

DW: When you were at Valencia, did people compare you to Faas Wilkes?

JR: Yes, he was a real hero to the people in Valencia. When I was very young, I saw him come on the television. He was thirty years older than me. He was a very good dribbler, a very good player. I know how good he was from the people in Valencia. Whenever we went to a restaurant, a football restaurant, there was always a picture of him.

DW: Did they see you as a new Wilkes?

JR: Maybe. I was not the same style exactly, but a little bit like him. He was more a midfield or No. 10. I was not always on the right. I played in the centre in 1978 with Rensenbrink on the left and Van de Kerkhof on the right.

DW: Rensenbrink was better in 1978?

JR: He scored more goals – on penalties, mainly – so people thought he was better.

DW: He said he had a happier time.

JR: Because Johan was not there. Johan was always going to the left and Robbie was not happy with that, he didn't like the way he had to play but he was important, too.

DW: Tell me about St Etienne–PSV.

JR: It was 3–0 in the first three minutes.

DW: Was that one of your better games?

JR: No, but it was very nice. I didn't play so well, actually. Later I saw the video and we were very impressive and scored three goals in the first three minutes. I was not so good but the scoring sequence was fantastic. That game cost me a lot of internationals because Kees Rijvers was the PSV trainer and he had played for St Etienne in the fifties or sixties. I made a real atmosphere in the newspapers in St Etienne against him. To whip up the public a little. We had lost 2–0 in Eindhoven, so we had to win 3–0. It was not easy. And PSV were a good team. I don't remember what I said. It wasn't so nice, but it wasn't terrible either. I said he was a terrible or old guy, something like that. It wasn't dirty or anything. But he was not happy. After the game he said, 'It will never be good between us.' And he did not forget. When he was the trainer of the national team, for his first game he said: 'No more Rep.' Only when it was not going so good for qualification for Spain, he called me back. I played four games but then we lost against France and I was thirty years old and I didn't play any more.

DW: That was crazy. Is that the same problem that Arnold Muhren had with Rijvers?

JR: No. Only me.

DW: Didn't he have a policy of not taking people who were playing abroad?

JR: That was not the problem. There was a young generation coming. Vanenburg . . . But at that moment he was not good enough. But I think it cost me fifteen or twenty caps. He dropped Ruud Krol also. He said if we win qualification to Spain, we all go together to Spain. But if not, it's finished for the old guys. He is going to build a new team. But I was playing so well and I was only thirty years old. All because of that 6–0 against PSV! That was my present from him. But that's trainers for you.

DW: Holland should have played in 1982.

JR: But France had a good team also. Rijvers also made big mistakes before the France game. He was playing the young players in the beginning. They lost against Ireland. Then he called us back but it was too late. They lost against Belgium also. We won every game at home. We beat Ireland, France, Belgium – but we needed to take a point from France. Then we would have to play a game against Ireland for Spain. And if we took a point from France, they wouldn't go to Spain. But the French won in Paris and it was finished for us.

DW: In '82, '84, '86 . . . Holland just vanished from international football . . .

JR: Yes, but we still had good players. If we had gone to Spain, we would maybe have reached another final. Because we still had a good team: Krol, me, Neeskens, who was back for some games. He had too many problems at that moment. He was very young when he started at Ajax. He was very good very young. Van Basten came later . . . but we should have played in Spain.

18: death wish

'I hate it, I hate it! But I love it, I love it!'

Leo Beenhakker

'The logic of suicide is different,' wrote A. Alvarez in *The Savage God*. 'It is like the unanswerable logic of a nightmare, or like the science-fiction fantasy of being projected suddenly into another dimension: everything makes sense and follows its own strict rules; yet, at the same time, everything is also different, perverted, upside-down . . . As in love, things which seem trivial to the outsider, tiresome or amusing, assume enormous importance to those in the grip of the monster, while the sanest arguments against it seem to him simply absurd.'

So it is with Dutch football. Why does a person kill himself? Why have the Dutch never won the World Cup, despite having so many wonderful, intelligent players and such a deliciously original and beautiful conception of the game? To an outsider, the manner in which Dutch national teams regularly fail in major tournaments is hard to comprehend. What weird, remorseless, fatal inner logic causes Dutch players, coaches and the federation to exhaust themselves in pointless petty feuds about tactics, power and money? Why, when it so obviously defeats the purpose of achieving success, do the Dutch so often pick the wrong coach or spend all their time and energy complaining about the coach they do pick? Why do their gifted teams so often fall asleep against inferior opposition? Why do their stars walk out on the eve of major tournaments? Why don't they ever seem to ask themselves why?

Whatever the reasons, it's a pattern unique in world football: a quintessentially Dutch combination of ill-discipline, complacency and lack of will or nerve. The Dutch seem to have an allergy to authority, leadership and collective discipline. Their teams behave like armies of generals. When I ask Dutch people why it happens, they tend to shrug their shoulders and tell me that it's 'typically Dutch'. Even Wim van Hanegem, who famously hated to lose, chuckles when I ask why the Dutch make life so difficult for themselves in major tournaments: 'For Holland, problems are normal and healthy. If things around the national team are quiet, everyone thinks everyone is sick. If we don't have a problem, we have to create a problem. Personally, I think it's better when things are quiet. But for every World Cup or European Championship we have to have problems. I don't know why.'

On paper – and usually in performance, too – the Dutch have had more than enough talent to win four World Cups (1974, 1978, 1990 and 1998). And they can blame only themselves for not winning at least two more European Championships (1976, 1992 and 2000) than their solitary 1988 success. The pattern in this, as in so many other aspects of the Dutch game, was laid down in the 1970s. With hindsight, it seems odd that Georg Kessler's team, containing as it did talents such as the young Johan Cruyff, Wim Jansen, Rinus Israel, Piet Keizer, Van Hanegem, Jan van Beveren and Coen Moulijn, should lose to Bulgaria and fail to reach the 1970 World Cup in Mexico. Where the Bulgarians wilted in the heat, the Dutch, buoyed by Feyenoord's European Cup win a month before the tournament, would surely have flourished , or at least learned some valuable lessons. But the Netherlands then had no tradition even of competing at top level. Four years later, the agonising near miss in Germany could perhaps also be attributed to beginners' bad luck. By 1976, however, it was clear that darker forces were at play. The crazy Dutch antics at that year's European finals in Yugoslavia became a kind of template for all future patterns of self-destruction. Old hands shudder at the mere mention of the tournament, which turned into a theme park of all the bad things the Dutch do to themselves. Personal feuds aplenty, scheming and divided leadership, ill-discipline, bad luck, arrogance. 'Tja . . .' (as the Dutch strangely say with a shrug when they consider a subject closed), Euro '76 had it all.

These days, the European championships are structured like mini-World Cups, but in 1976 the tournament consisted of just four matches: two semi-finals, the final, and the third-place play-off. Holland were to meet unfancied Czechoslovakia in their semi-final in Zagreb. Hosts Yugoslavia faced West Germany in the other match. Since Cruyff and his colleagues were at the peak of their considerable powers and had demolished Belgium 5–0 and 2–1 in the quarter-final, the Dutch arrived as red-hot favourites. Everyone assumed they would meet – and beat – West Germany in the final and revenge the traumatic defeat of 1974. As usual, not all was well in the Dutch camp. There had been infighting during the qualifying rounds. In 1975, between losing 1–4 in Katowice and beating the Poles 3–0 in Amsterdam, the question of who had the real power in the Dutch team was settled when the country's best goalkeeper, Jan van Beveren, and his PSV colleague Willy van der Kuylen, walked out in protest over the all-encompassing influence of Johan Cruyff. The technically able and amiable coach George Knobel was no leader in the style of Rinus Michels. Three years earlier, when he had taken over from Stefan Kovacs at Ajax, Knobel had alienated and lost control of key players following the interview he gave complaining about his stars' drinking and womanising. It was said that Arie Haan engineered Knobel's dismissal from the club; with Knobel in charge of the national team, Haan didn't get a game for nearly two years.

More critical was the long-running and damaging conflict between Knobel and Jacques Hogewoning, the old-fashioned, Bugs Bunny-toothed 'regent' who ran the KNVB. Hogewoning loathed his chief coach and deeply disapproved of the power Knobel allowed his key players. Several times Knobel had asked to sever his contract. The two men had also clashed over the granting of club coaching licences and over Knobel's demand for a top-flight assistant. The final dispute concerned the appointment of a *chef d'équipe* for the team, whose job was to make arrangements for hotels and suchlike. Cruyff and Knobel wanted Jack van Zanten, a friend and business associate of Cruyff's, who had done the job in Germany in 1974. Hogewoning refused. Knobel claims now that, unknown to him, Hogewoning and Van Zanten had fallen out over a business deal. The matter came to a head in the week before the Dutch team flew to Yugoslavia. Knobel met Hogewoning and his fellow KNVB official Dé Stoop, and again asked for permission to end his contract; again they turned him down. During a phone call a few days later, after the team had flown to Yugoslavia, Hogewoning accepted his request because of the argument over Van Zanten, and confirmed his decision in a letter that Knobel would receive when he returned home.

Knobel's resignation was supposed to remain a secret until after the tournament, but there were some at the KNVB who were determined the story should break on the day of Holland's first match. Two journalists, Lex Muller of *Algemeen Dagblad* and Jan de Deugd of *De Telegraaf*, were aware of the story but were reluctant to publish it for fear of wrecking morale in the Dutch camp. Muller recalls: 'Jan de Deugd and me knew about eighty per cent of the story but had no confirmation. People had asked me to keep it secret so as not to destroy the team's chances of success. The day before the game against Czechoslovakia, some KNVB officials – I can't say who – warned me that it would be better to publish because the other paper was about to publish. They played with both of us. They told Jan that *Algemeen Dagblad* was about to print the story, and they told me I had to publish because *De Telegraaf* knew everything. It was unbelievable. I remember that afternoon very well. They asked me to come alone to their hotel and they told me everything. It was not one KNVB official; it was several, and they were all very keen to tell me all the details and make sure I published the story.' As soon as news of what was in the first editions spread from Holland, reporters drove in the middle of the night to the training camp at Samobor, outside Zagreb, to quiz Knobel and his staff. 'We had to know the whole story,' says Muller. 'As you can imagine, the game the next day seemed not so important. What mattered was to find out the truth about all these conflicts.' De Deugd and Knobel now confirm Muller's account, though Knobel had always assumed the story leaked accidentally from one of the twelve members of the KNVB's 'amateurish' professional football board, whom Knobel considered incapable of keeping a secret for more than three days. Mr Hogewoning declined to comment. First he asked me to fax him a list of detailed questions so he could refresh his memory and consult with former colleagues. Then he said he was bound by the KNVB's 'code of honour' not to comment on events of the past: 'Since I retired as a member of the board, I have never given any interview about the inner circles of the Royal Association. That's my principle.'

Things weren't exactly harmonious in the dressing-room, either. Wim van Hanegem remembers: 'There was a bad atmosphere between Knobel and the players, and before the game there were the big problems between him and people from the KNVB. They spent the whole evening before the game talking. The players thought: maybe he's out. I didn't like him. Knobel was not honest with the players; he was not straight about many things. I told him: "You're not a straight guy", and that made him angry. He said I couldn't play, so I was substitute. But after ten minutes, Rijsbergen came off and I had to go on.' Knobel says: 'There are a lot of stories about what happened in those championships, but the real story is that the players went to Yugoslavia thinking: "We'll beat the Czechs and be in the final against the Germans." I had a bad feeling deep inside two weeks before we went to Yugoslavia. The players were only thinking about the Germans, not about the first opponents. They thought only of revenge for 1974. I tried to warn them, but most of them were in their late twenties, almost thirty. They weren't children any more. They had had a lot of successes, made a lot of money. They had their own opinion about things. You can't do anything about it because arrogance is part of the Dutch character. Personally, I respect all opponents because no game is ever decided in advance.' Of Van Hanegem, he says: 'He was a good player but with a bad temperament, like Paul Gascoigne.'

If all had gone well against Czechoslovakia, perhaps none of the behind-the-scenes intrigue and chaos would have mattered. Instead, the game, which was played in constant driving rain and wind, was calamitous. Far from being a pushover, the determined Czechs hustled the Dutch out of their rhythm and took the lead early in the first half. Referee Clive Thomas, chosen by UEFA because of his disciplinarian reputation, booked seven players, including Cruyff, and sent off Johan Neeskens and the Czech defender Pollak before Holland scraped into extra time via a Czech own-goal.

The decisive moments came near the end. Moments after Thomas had failed to punish a heavy foul on Cruyff, Nehoda scored the second Czech goal and, during the heated Dutch protests, Van Hanegem got himself sent off. The two men still disagree about the incident. Van Hanegem: 'I protested about the bad foul on Cruyff, but that wasn't the problem. The problem was that Clive Thomas told me to take the kick-off. I said: "Why? I'm a midfield player. Ruud Geels is the striker – he should take the kick-off." Thomas said: "Come over here." Normally the referee comes to the player, so I stayed where I was. He said again: "Come here." I stayed where I was. [Actually, Van Hanegem did a little more than that: he crooked his finger at Thomas, beckoning the referee to come to him.] Then he sent me off. If I had made a bad foul and Thomas had sent me off, that would have been OK. But this was about nothing. At the time, I wanted to kill him. Even now it makes me angry. Clive Thomas was already not my friend because he had disallowed a good goal for Feyenoord against Benfica in the European Cup three years before. In this game he made problems out of nothing.'

Thomas remembers: 'I'll never forget that game. It was one of the hardest of my career. My job was to ensure the game was played in the right manner, but some Dutch players wanted to play it their way. Some of them were ill-disciplined that night. They would not accept my decisions. When the Czechs scored their second, I gave the goal and walked back to the halfway-line. As I'm walking back, Van Hanegem says to me: "No goal – very bad decision." So I said to him: "Do not say that again." Anyone can say something in the heat of the moment. I gave him the opportunity to calm down. But he said it again. I showed him the yellow card. He continued to disagree with my decision. I said: "I'm going to the halfway-line. If you step one foot over that line, I will show you the red card." He did that, so I showed him the red card: off. He said he wasn't going to go. I suddenly had a right production in the middle of the field with all the TV cameras and everyone in Europe watching. The player refuses to go, so I pick the ball up and start to walk off the field. I was going to abandon the match, until my linesman, who could see what was happening behind me, told me Van Hanegem was coming off the field, so I went back on. I doubt anything like that has ever happened in the history of top-level professional football. Usually I found the Dutch a pleasure to referee or to watch because they were all top-class players. But if things started going wrong, they'd lose control with the referee and with each other. They were all prima donnas. Their attitude was: "Don't you know who I am?" and "This shouldn't be happening to us." I've never lost control of any match. Whether players disagree with my decisions or not, they have to respect me. I'm fair-minded. I've looked at that tape and I know I was right. I've made mistakes in my career, and I've learned by those mistakes. But that wasn't one of them. I slept that night.' Two minutes from the end, Vesely made it 3–1 to the Czechs. Three days later, in the meaningless third place game, the deflated but much calmer Dutch played Yugoslavia without Neeskens, Van Hanegem, Rep or Cruyff – who had flown home to Barcelona for a knee operation – and comfortably won 3–2.

Although Holland were desperately unlucky in the 1978 World Cup final, they were weakened by the absence of key players such as Cruyff, Geels, Van Beveren. Van Hanegem pulled out on the night before the Dutch squad flew to Argentina. Ruud Gullit did something very similar on the eve of the 1994 World Cup. He and bondscoach Dick Advocaat had been at daggers drawn for over a year. Gullit refused to play for the national team after Advocaat substituted him in a qualifying match against England at Wembley in 1993 but the two men seemed to have settled their differences in time for the World Cup. Gullit, past his best by then but still a potent and charismatic presence, rejoined the squad as captain a month before the tournament. Then, on the eve of departure for the USA, he walked out of the training camp. Fans burned their Gullit wigs and many have still not forgiven him. Gullit promised to explain his actions when the tournament was over but never fully did so, though he did give an interview in Italy during which he criticised Advocaat's attacking tactical approach, which he thought would be exhausting in the Florida sunshine. Advocaat's version is that Gullit never talked to him about that or any other problem.

The Dutch began Euro '96 in England as tournament favourites. But the team – and the image of the Netherlands as a harmonious multi-cultural society – was wrecked by a bitter conflict between black and white players in Guus Hiddink's Dutch squad. The black players complained, with some justification, that Hiddink did not listen to them, that they were not served Surinamese food in camp, and that Ajax paid them less than white players. In a radio interview Edgar Davids suggested that Hiddink take his head out of the white players' backsides. In what was intended as a piece of firm leadership, Hiddink kicked Davids out of the squad, a move that didn't address the black players' grievances and left the team even more divided than before. In one match, the black Clarence Seedorf could be seen trying to decide whether or not to pass to his white midfield colleague Ronald de Boer. The Dutch were still busy fighting each other when they faced England at Wembley. With a display of intelligence and ferocity, which came as a total surprise to the Dutch, England won 4–1, exacting some revenge for nearly twenty years of humiliations. In their next match, Holland went out of the competition on penalties against France, Seedorf missing the vital kick. Later Patrick Kluivert, Winston Bogarde and Michael Reiziger were reported as saying they would prefer to play in an all-black national team, though they now insist they were misquoted. The tensions continued in a World Cup qualifier in Turkey, when Holland were awarded a penalty and Seedorf, spokesman for the black players, grabbed the ball. As he prepared to take the kick, the De Boer twins demonstratively turned their backs and Seedorf struck the ball several metres over the bar.

In 1988 the Dutch won the European Championship with generous helpings of luck, having played uncharacteristically below their capacities. 'It was by accident, I tell you,' says Beenhakker. 'We lost the first match [against the Soviet Union]; and we were very lucky against England. And we won the third match against Ireland with a header by Wim Kieft that was never a header: the ball hit his ear and went in the goal eight minutes from time.'

For once, though, the Dutch were disciplined *and* ambitious. TV anchor Kees Jansma spent June 1988 with the Dutch national broadcaster NOS: 'The players were very determined and obsessed by the thought that they could win in Germany because they knew they were very good.' Before the tournament, coach Rinus Michels, then sixty years old, briefly addressed his players: 'If there is anyone in this team who wants to leave because he doesn't want to obey orders and abide by my decisions, please say it now so he can leave.' (He had used a similar speech to end pre-tournament feuding and sharpen minds in 1974.) The players laughed and set to work. The day before the final against the Soviet Union, and three days after their titanic victory over West Germany in Hamburg, the players expressed their appreciation for Michels by giving him a gold watch. Team captain Ruud Gullit told him: 'You are the best coach we've ever had.' Michels replied: 'I appreciate the watch, but if we lose tomorrow against Russia, I will give it back to you.'

Two years later, for the World Cup in Italy in 1990, with most of the same players present, a totally different spirit prevailed. Even with Gullit nursing a knee injury, the European Champions had by some distance the most impressive collection of talents in the competition and were more experienced than ever before. Gullit, Van Basten and Rijkaard were world football's biggest trio, the heart of AC Milan, the world's best club team, with whom they had just won a second successive European Cup. Ronald Koeman, Jan Wouters, Adri van Tiggelen, Berry van Aerle, goalkeeper Hans van Breukelen and the Ajax winger Johnny van't Schip were all at or close to their peaks. But instead of continuing the spirit of 1988, the team was a shambles. The tone had been set eight months earlier when the players had held a meeting at Schiphol to vote for the man they wanted to lead them in Italy. It was an extraordinary declaration of player power and an echo of the 1973 election at Ajax. This time Cruyff won, and by a huge majority – though he was not present, had not been consulted and was not helped by the result. If the stars wanted Cruyff to lead them in Italy, the officials at the KNVB had other ideas. The key man at the KNVB's headquarters in Zeist was Rinus Michels, by now the head of the committee that appointed the national coach. Instead of Cruyff, Michels picked Leo Beenhakker, allotting himself an advisory and supervisory role. Beenhakker accepted the poisoned chalice. 'I had no chance,' he says now. 'I knew it before the tournament. But there was a special circumstance why I accepted the job. I will never tell the reason; but there was a special reason to accept. The only thing you can hope for then is that it will work out because there is a very talented group. I hoped the group would take the responsibility because of the ambience of the tournament. We did that in the first serious match in the eyes of the players, the game against Germany. And we lost a very unlucky game. So we lost. But that was my hope. With such great players, the coach is not so important and I hope that they take the responsibility, especially the big stars to say hey come on, we are all in the same boat, just let's go for it.'

Jansma recalls the poisoned atmosphere: 'In 1990 the same players from 1988 were a completely different team. They were not a team at all. Every player had his own ideas, everyone was the hero by himself. Too many opinions. Too many islands. No atmosphere of togetherness, only superstardom. There was an A group in the team, a B group and a C group. I think the A group was the players from Milan. The B group might have been Ronald Koeman, Wouters and so on. The players have always denied this but I watched them. They played a horrible game against Egypt. 1–1. Horrible! Against England, 0–0. Also horrible. With Ireland, the same, a 1–1 draw. They played quite a good match against Germany but it was too late by then. The atmosphere of 1988 was absolutely gone. The boss was Beenhakker, but with Michels also there it was unworkable. In 1988 it was a family. In Italy it was nothing.' After the victorious final in 1988, Gullit had carried Michels on his shoulder in joy and triumph. By 1990 in Italy relations had soured to a barely believable degree. Journalist Dick van der Polder remembers conducting an interview with Michels after the Egypt match. Instead of using the official area reserved for press, the two men were speaking on a training pitch that no one was using. During the interview, the KNVB's senior press officer, Ger Stolk, ran up bearing a message from Ruud Gullit for Michels: 'I'm afraid that in this area it is forbidden to conduct interviews. I must ask you to terminate the interview now.'

With three fortuitous draws, Holland scraped into the second round and faced Germany in Milan. Beenhakker: 'Before the game, Franz Beckenbauer comes to me and he says: "Leo, I'm going to tell you something." I said: "Tell me." He says: "The one who wins this game will be the champion." ' At this point Beenhakker mimes his poker-player face he adopted for the brief encounter with the German coach. ' "OK," I said. "Have a nice match. Let's go for it." ' The Germans won 2–1 through second-half goals by Klinsmann and Brehme; but the lowest moment came early in the first half when Frank Rijkaard was seen to spit in the face of Germany's Rudi Voeller after they had both been sent off. Beenhakker simply shrugs at the memory: 'It was just typical of the atmosphere in the whole team at that time.' At the press conference after the game, Beckenbauer spoke privately to Beenhakker again. 'He said: "Now watch me. Now we will be the champions. And if you had won this match, you would have been World Champions." And after the final, again he said it to me again: "If it wasn't us, it would have been you because you still have the best players there are." But having the best players is no guarantee to have the best team. And that's always the problem in Holland.'

The Israeli-born paranormalist Uri Geller reckons there could be a curse on the Dutch football team because of 'some devastating occurrence that happened many years ago'. 'It may sound very bizarre to you, but these things happen. I don't know what it could be, but I will check the history.' He senses 'a very powerful wave of lack of confidence' among the Dutch players, which is passed down from generation to generation. He also thinks there's a problem with the Dutch fans. 'Orange is a very powerful, assertive colour and Dutch supporters make a lot of noise, but there is something dead in them. There's no life, no spirit. If they had the spirit, then they'd start winning. Maybe it's in the psyche of the Dutch people. Someone has to teach them the power of prayer, belief and faith. If you could teach the players also and combine that with the fans, then you would definitely start winning cups.' Geller suggests a televised ritual involving chanting of 'key words' before a match might get the whole country behind its team.

There are surely more rational explanations for this Dutch affliction – and less exotic cures.

The most obvious diagnosis for the Dutch tendency to fail at the vital moment surely lies in the nature of Dutch individualism and antipathy to autocracy. Holland's democracy, individualism and profound distrust of authority all have deep historical roots. Since the Middle Ages, the bourgeois Dutch traders and merchants developed both a healthy sense of independence and a tradition of deal-making and finding solutions to make accommodations with their neighbours and trading partners. Herman Pleij, a historian and professor of medieval Dutch literature, argues that this history is a function of geography: 'From the Middle Ages on, we had to develop democratic institutions to keep the country dry. We had to co-operate and develop democratic institutions. More importantly, we had to become traders because you couldn't live off this land in any other way. It made us very independent. There was never any possibility that a king or the church or a person of high rank would rule here. The way we ruled ourselves always involved talking, talking and more talking.' One of the reasons Dutch power declined in the seventeenth century, says Pleij, was that it was usually difficult, if not impossible, to make quick decisions. 'It's not surprising that the Dutch team is always arguing about how to play and how to work together. No wonder being coach of the national football team is a thankless task.' He adds: 'We are very keen on being equal and because we all feel equal, Dutch teams always find it very difficult to acknowledge the authority of a coach.' He sees a 'clear parallel' between vacillating Dutch football coaches and William the Silent, that 'archetypal Dutch leader, always hesitating and talking and wondering what to do next'.

Total Football was profoundly imbued with democratic impulses. It prided itself on being the most cosmopolitan, creative conception of the game; a perfect balance between collective responsibility, equality and individualism, a system that allowed every player to excel and express himself. The flip-side of the system was that discipline and inner cohesion were always fragile. Democratic principle is the reason Van Hanegem cites for leaving the Dutch squad on the eve of the Argentina World Cup in 1978, a decision he came to regret. 'People think the problem was that I was second choice for Argentina, but that's not true. Happel told me he planned to leave me out of the first game with Iran because that wasn't so important, but he wanted me to play against Scotland and in all the other games. The real problem was money.' He says he was happy with the arrangements in 1974, when he, Cruyff and Neeskens were Holland's top stars but all the players' commercial earnings went into a pot shared equally by the whole squad and the backroom staff. In 1978 some senior players, notably Ruud Krol and Arie Haan, planned to keep the earnings from advertisements and so on for themselves. Van Hanegem says he was outraged. 'Everyone from one to twenty-two is important. Everyone should get the same, including the man who cleans the boots because if he's not there, I must clean my own. I went to Happel and said I was not happy with some players, and if we were away for three or four weeks, maybe we would have a lot of problems. Happel and I talked for one and a half hours with him trying to persuade me. But my feelings said no, and when I say no, I mean no. He knew it; I'd worked with him for four years at Feyenoord. He was the best coach in my life.' So the great midfield player sat out the tournament on a beach in Spain. 'I only watched one game, which was the final. I saw people playing so hard; I saw Neeskens and I thought: yeah, I should have been there.'

Hans Vonk, one of Holland's leading conductors and musical director of the St Louis Symphony Orchestra, says football requires the same approach as making music. 'In music there is a rule: the bigger the group, the less democracy you can have. With three or four musicians performing chamber music, yes, you can work according to democratic principles. With anything larger, there is only one possibility: one person who tells all the others how to perform. It has to be the same way in football.' In Russia after the Bolshevik Revolution, orchestras tried to run themselves as collectives without conductors. As a result, preparations for a single concert often took more than a month and the orchestras dissolved into chaos. 'Football is a kind of art, too,' Vonk continues 'Players should be free to express themselves and play their best game. But a coach, like a conductor, has to be a benign dictator who says: there's only one way, my way, and there's no room for discussion. You have to focus on one person and one idea, which is winning.

'In Holland, our national coaches – apart from Happel and Michels – have been weak. Men like Hiddink and Advocaat think and talk too much. They want to be liked, but that doesn't work at the highest level. As a conductor, the very worst thing I can do is to want to be liked. I used to want that, but I gave it up. Now I really don't care if they like me or not, as long as they do what I want.'

He thinks of Dutch footballers as being like Dutch musicians, only worse. 'Dutch musicians don't accept authority automatically, though it's possible to earn their respect through your knowledge and experience. But the prima donna behaviour of our footballers is far worse than anything I've ever seen in music.' Vonk adds: 'The young players are so materialistic, spoiled and surrounded by agents and other distractions it must be difficult for them to focus on football. It's extremely frustrating watching our national team: we see that Germany has mediocre players, but they always win; and we look at all the great Dutch players and know we're not going to. We have an incredible arrogance combined with a lack of self-discipline. It leads to fights, frustration and disappointment. Dutch people never play for their country – they play for their own wallets. We have incredible talent, but the patriotism you see from the Germans when they play for Germany is absolutely lacking with us. Look at our team before a game: they stand chewing gum and none of them has the first idea of the words of the national anthem. They may be thinking about the match; but they are definitely not thinking about playing for Holland.'

Critic and writer Anthony Mertens sees positive virtues in the national team's difficulties, since they usually reflect a society in transition (as with the insurrectionary spirit of the 1960s and 1970s, and the multi-cultural tensions in '96). 'Football is a safety valve,' he says. 'It plays the same role in Dutch society as literature. They are the only two fields which make it possible to discuss taboo issues which cannot be raised in other forums.'

Political scientist Paul Scheffer sees 'a clear, consistent pattern of self-destruction in our football' and diagnoses a particular Dutch neurosis about national identity as the problem: 'The Dutch take an almost nationalistic pride in denying that we have a national identity. We like to think of ourselves as an open, trading nation, a transparent crossing-point, a place mediating between our neighbours. We are world travellers, international traders who have overcome nationalism and made the nation state obsolete. We think the whole world should move in our direction – but of course we are not nationalists! The art of being Dutch is to transform our vulnerability into moral superiority. We are small and we lack power, but we think the whole world will adopt us as a model of enlightenment. We have such a strong sense of moral superiority that it's not so important to us if we win or lose. It's like the self-legitimation of a small country which says it's no scandal to lose against a superior military force when outnumbered. When we lose, it's always because of "brutal force". We never think we lose because of the elegance or creativity of another team. No, it's because they used brutal force, which is simply not relevant to us because we are playing a different, better, higher game, which the referee also happens not to understand. We won't lower ourselves to your level, but if it makes you happy to destroy our elegance, then go ahead!

'We think we are the best. Yet there is always a vulnerability, a sense that it's natural for us to come second. We think winning is a little bit ugly: it's only for other people, who need it to compensate for some other lack. When the national team is losing, their morale goes completely. They start insulting each other. They want to escape the collective responsibility of defeat. But the basic idea is that we are not going to compete with force because it's not our subject.' Another consequence of Holland's denial of nationalism is its underestimation of national energy of other countries. 'We lack the ability to describe who we are,' says Scheffer. 'We know who we are, but we deny ourselves the idea of describing it because we seek our identity in the denial of that identity. We make it difficult to mobilise our own national energy or use national symbols for ourselves. For a Dutchman to cry for the flag would be considered almost obscene. Yet there's a sense of uncertainty of our place in the world. We deny ourselves the possibility to reflect on who we are. Not every idea about nationalism is the same as hardcore nation-alism. Perhaps it's time to adopt a less schizophrenic attitude to this question. I never use the words "healthy nationalism" but that's what I mean. Not every patriotism or reflection about your own history or loyalty towards your history or community is *per se* blindness or closing yourself to the outside world.'

He thinks the Dutch conception of themselves as an open,

cosmopolitan nation paradoxically represents a narrow-minded view of the world: 'In this so-called modesty of ours there is the idea of not having any borders, of being everywhere and being an example to everyone. It would be a lesson of modesty to know our place in the world, to know where we differ from others, not in a sense of superiority but simply knowing that not every country is the same.'

Jan Mulder earlier suggested that when it comes to the World Cup, for all their apparent arrogance the Dutch have a deep-seated inferiority complex. 'It's the event which defeats us, not the opposition.' The Dutch mixture of arrogance and insecurity is decidedly odd, though. In Euro '92 they produced a performance of quite stunning power, grace and control to beat the Germans 3–1 in a group game. The Dutch prepared for what looked set to become an epic rematch with the Germans in the final, forgetting that they first had to win a semi-final against Denmark. As against the Czechs sixteen years earlier and the Croats six years later, the Dutch simply couldn't find it in themselves to take their opponents seriously. Even when Frank Rijkaard scrambled a desperately late equaliser to take the match into extra time, he reacted with an expression of disdain rather than joy. As his relieved colleagues mobbed him, the expression on Rijkaard's face quite clearly read: "Well, thanks, guys, but it's still only Denmark, you know." Denmark, inevitably, won on penalties. It's a deeply Dutch character trait. Patrick Kluivert displayed a similar attitude in a friendly game against Belgium in 1999. The Belgian goalkeeper parried a shot by Bergkamp which rolled gently to Kluivert moving unmarked and alone near the empty net. Instead of tapping in, Kluivert stopped the ball and stood, hands on hips, with the ball under his foot on the goal-line, insolently taunting the Belgians to come and tackle him. When they declined, he shrugged and stroked the ball home with a smile and a swagger. Enraged, the Belgians played twice as hard after the incident as before.

Psychoanalyst and novelist Anna Enquist has an intriguing theory about the unconscious motivation for the Dutch pattern of under-achievement: 'There is some kind of death wish in it connected to our Dutch, Calvinist shame of being good. Our Calvinist culture makes us deeply ashamed of being the best. It's a very common phenomenon in our cultural life. You see how anyone who is better than average is criticised and singled out in newspapers. Perhaps, in football, we have the unconscious feeling that it's shameful to proclaim ourselves the best in the world.' Despite secularisation, the influence of the Netherlands' historical Calvinist background pervades and underpins every facet of Dutch life at a deep, unconscious cultural level. 'Calvinism is a horrible religion,' Enquist says. 'It teaches that if anything good happens to you, it's a gift from God and you must be very humble. But when anything bad happens, it's your fault because you've committed some sin or you weren't good enough.'

There is a weird tension between the desire to succeed and the unconscious belief that success is morally wrong. So Clarence Seedorf's fatal miss against France in Euro '96 was no ordinary feeble penalty. It was a complex, masochistic psychodrama: 'Calvinism means that you have to be very humble, but in reaction, in transformation, you think you're the very best. You become arrogant, but that's not comfortable for you because arrogance is not deeply rooted in your character. That could have been the case with Seedorf. Consciously, he may have been attempting to break free from his conditioning by attempting to take a penalty. Unconsciously, he felt he had to punish himself for such feelings. That was really a masochistic action, not only by Seedorf but by the whole team. The rest of the team knew Seedorf was no good at taking penalties. They should have stopped him, but they didn't.'

English sporting failures produce tidal waves of national self-doubt. The English are, in fact, rather good at healthy – or, depending on your point of view, masochistic – self-criticism. Test cricket disasters used to generate a rich discourse on national decline and loss of moral fibre. When Holland knocked Graham Taylor's England out of the World Cup in 1993, the BBC cleared its TV schedules for a major debate on how to rescue English football from its mediocrity. (Oddly, none of the panellists mentioned what turned out to be the solution – selling the game to Rupert Murdoch and buying in lots of foreigners.) When Waddle, Pearce, Southgate and Batty missed their respective vital penalties in 1990, '96 and '98, columnists who didn't usually write about football queued up to offer theories about the deep underlying causes of these symbolic national bereavements.

The Dutch don't do this. They go numb and pretend it doesn't matter. They shrug and don't talk. Intriguingly, unlike Britain or America, psychoanalysis is exceedingly rare in Holland. Virtually the only people who undertake it are therapists, who are obliged to do so as an essential part of their training. (Watching *Analyze This*, the Billy Crystal/Robert de Niro film comedy about a gangster in therapy, in a Dutch cinema produces an odd realisation: the audience aren't laughing in the right places because they just don't get any of the therapy jokes. Talking cures just aren't part of Dutch culture the way they are in Britain and America.) Enquist thinks the attitude of the Dutch towards their football setbacks is disingenuous and destructive. 'Sometimes it is good to be relativistic and realistic, to take a step back and not take defeat too seriously. But it's a little sad if it leads to a lost World Cup.'

When I mention Enquist's theory to Leo Beenhakker, he raises his expressive eyebrows and chuckles. 'Yeah, well, there must be some scientific explanation for it somehow.' He's a practical man who wants results and despairs of Dutch self-destructive tendencies. He reflects on that Kluivert goal against the Belgians. 'Ahh!' he exclaims with a mixture of abhorrence and delight. 'That was so typical Dutch!' Not an Amsterdam trait? 'No. No. Dutch. You see it in all kinds of sports. We have a big success and after that – boom – disaster! Arrogance! That's it. In hockey, Holland is very strong now. A few days ago in the European Championships it was the same kind of match. They played fantastic: poom, poom, poom. One moment it is 1–0, the next 2–0. And then they start in a typical Dutch way, with an arrogance, and everyone is floating and boom! Boom! Within ten minutes it was 2–2. Hey, watch it! Watch it!

What's happening here? In 1974 it was arrogance too. But we are still sympathetic people, good people and we are not dangerous, you know. But we have that special feeling. That's the way we are. I hate it. I hate it! But I love it. I love it! Because we are *so* special!'

How many psychotherapists does it take to change a lightbulb? Only one. But the lightbulb has to really want to change.

8: a short interview
about killing

'I play a different kind of game'

Dennis Bergkamp

The terrific Dutch radio commentator Jack van Gelder probably captured the ultimate Dennis Bergkamp moment as eloquently as any human voice could. Almost twenty years to the day after Rensenbrink's hit post in the last minute of the 1978 final came its weird and perfect redemptive mirror image. Marseilles. The Stade Vélodrome. 5 July 1998. Just after 5 p.m. It's 1–1 in the last minute of an epic World Cup quarter-final between Holland and Argentina. Dutch defender Frank de Boer plays a sixty-metre pass, which finds a gap on the right side of the Argentina defence. At an unpromising angle, the ball drops from its high arc towards Holland's player of the age, Dennis Bergkamp, who leaps like a high hurdler and cushions the ball so it falls perfectly under control without breaking his stride. It's one of the most remarkable pieces of control ever seen on a football field. 'Very good by Dennis Bergkamp,' says Van Gelder, rather like an art critic describing the Sistine Chapel ceiling as 'nice'. But as Bergkamp uses his next two touches to cut inside the last Argentinian defender and then lash the ball across goalkeeper Roa and into the net, Van Gelder rises memorably to the occasion: 'Dennis Bergkamp takes the ball on . . . DENNIS BERGKAMP!' He begins to shout. 'D-E-N-N-I-S B-E-R-G-K-A-M-P!' He is now utterly ecstatic, hoarsely gulping lungfuls of air as he howls the name with joy ('D-E-N-N-I-S B-E-R-G-K-A-M-P!!!') before lapsing into a crazed joyful yodel: 'OHOHOHOHOOW!!!!!!'

The most commonly heard complaint about Bergkamp, in north London as well as in Holland, is that he doesn't do this sort of thing often enough. 'People always criticise Bergkamp,' complains Jan Mulder. 'But why? He did so much. The joy! His un-be-liev-able goals!' Absolutely right.

I'd gone through all the usual channels to try to get an interview with Dennis with a view to asking him all the usual questions about abstract space and beauty and the Dutch soul. But via his agent he had nixed my requests. Then he turned up almost on my doorstep in Amsterdam, at a press conference for the Dutch national team. After doing a pre-arranged interview with someone else, I found myself this close − *this close!* − to Bergkamp and I couldn't help butting into his conversation to challenge him on his alleged addiction to the exquisite. Everything I'd heard about Bergkamp's quiet shyness suddenly made sense: he's a strikingly gentle, quiet and calm presence. Not just a great footballer but a great soul, I decided on the basis of four seconds' acquaintance. Instead of ignoring me, he disarmed me completely by agreeing: 'I'm the biggest critic myself on that. I should be more of a killer. But it's just not a quality I have. Normally you find me just outside the area, outside the box, trying to score from there. When you try to score from there, usually those are beautiful goals. It's not that I prefer that, it's just that I don't have the killer instinct to be in the box at that time, at the right moment. I would like to score those goals but . . .' You'd like to be more of a Gerd Muller? 'Yeah, but I'm really not. I play a different kind of game. I think that you can add certain things. That could mean being a killer, going more into the box − that is something I would like to add. But it shouldn't be that I then forget to play my kind of game That's why I score those kinds of goal − I don't want to end up damaging my game.'

He's saying he'd much rather win than simply create beautiful moments. 'Definitely to win. because that's what your playing for. It's not good to lose. You're not happy.' So why didn't Holland win in 1998 when they were the best team in the tournament? 'It's difficult. Because we're not really a killer team. What I say about myself could be the same for the Dutch team as well. If we were a killer team, we might forget to play the football we're good at. You never know where that will end.'

15: the jewish club

'Hamas, Hamas – Jews to the gas'

Feyenoord fans

The Ajax fans sing: 'Jews! Jews! We are super-Jews!', which is strange because hardly any of them are. Welcome to the weirdest, least kosher Hebrew tribe in the world. Under Jewish religious law, anyone wanting to be a Jew must either have a Jewish mother or undergo a lengthy conversion process involving a lot of study and thought. A willingness to beat up fellow hooligans from Feyenoord isn't really relevant. Neither is wearing a T-shirt emblazoned with the Star of David, nor waving an Israeli flag at matches. A lot of Ajax fans do these things, and a lot of people wish they wouldn't. The Ajax president, Michael van Praag (the son of Ajax's golden-age Jewish president, the flamboyant Jaap), once said: 'Ajax is not a Jewish club and these fans are about as Jewish as I am Chinese.'

Apparently no one believes him. The modern 'Jewish Ajax' phenomenon initially developed in response to rival fans' anti-Semitic jibes, and was restricted to the club's noisiest fans, the 'F-Side' members, who have a notorious propensity to violence. In the 1980s F-Side skinheads were photographed with their shaven heads tattooed with what they considered to be the 'Ajax Star'. While such extreme manifestations are rare these days, the fact remains that each year increasing numbers of non-Jewish, mainstream Ajax supporters identify both themselves and the club as Jewish. On match days, kiosks around the Arena sell Israeli flags and T-shirts alongside traditional red and white favours. In 1999 the fans' chant to their much-loved Surinamese goalkeeper Stanley Menzo upon his retirement was their deepest compliment: 'Stanley's a Jew'. And when Israeli transsexual Dana International won the Eurovision Song Contest with the song 'Viva La Diva', the occasion was celebrated by Ajax fans with a song of their own: 'We are the champions! Jews win everything!'

It's hard to know whether to laugh or cry about all this. Either way, some historical explanation is required.

For centuries Amsterdam was as Jewish a city as New York is today. (Amsterdam's slang, the *bargoens*, as a result remains rich with Jewish words: the city's nickname, 'Mokum', is Yiddish for 'place'; people of all shapes and colours wish each other '*mazzel*', Hebrew for 'luck'; and so on.) When Spain and Portugal expelled their Jewish populations at the end of the fifteenth century, it was Amsterdam that provided them with a home. During the glittering age of the seventeenth-century Dutch Republic, much of Holland's intellectual energy came from Jewish nous and international contacts. Rembrandt painted his Jewish neighbours. Baruch Spinoza, the son of a Portuguese Jewish family, was considered the greatest philosopher the Netherlands ever produced (until Johan Cruyff's arrival, that is). In the nineteenth century a new wave of Jewish refugees fled the pogroms of Eastern Europe and came to Amsterdam. When the city became a centre of the diamond trade, it was Jewish workers who cut the stones and created Holland's trade union movement. By 1939 there had been Jews living in Amsterdam for hundreds of years. They were thoroughly integrated and their presence touched most aspects of life in the city.

Unsurprisingly, there was also a strong Jewish influence in Amsterdam's football. There were Jewish players, Jewish referees (such as the celebrated Leo Horn) and Jewish supporters. Also Jewish clubs, such as AED, Wilhelmina Vooruit, Hortus, and Eendracht Doet Winnen. (Only a fusion of the last three – WV–HEDW – now exists, and with few Jewish players.) Technically, Ajax was not a Jewish club, but its stadium on the Middenweg was close to the most Jewish parts of the city. The club was immersed in Jewish culture and had a huge Jewish following.

All this was destroyed and Amsterdam's heart ripped out during the Nazi occupation of World War II, when the vast majority of the city's Jews were rounded up, deported to Poland and gassed. Amsterdam was probably the least anti-Semitic city of all those lacerated by the Holocaust, and yet there the survival rate for Jews was pitifully low – worse than anywhere else in Western Europe. (Even in Berlin, proportionally far more Jews survived than they did in Amsterdam.) By the late 1940s there remained only some 5000 traumatised survivors of a pre-war Jewish population of around 80,000. These figures reflect those of the Netherlands as a whole. Seventy-nine per cent of Holland's 140,000 Jews were killed – almost twice the proportion of those killed in neighbouring Belgium, four times that of France, a larger percentage than in Germany. There have been many theories to explain this disaster: Holland's close contiguity to Germany; its lack of forests or other natural hiding places; the innocence of a nation that had not known war in 125 years and was therefore psychologically ill-equipped to deal with Nazi ruthlessness; or the compartmentalisation of Dutch society, which isolated Jews from other groups.

In Amsterdam to this day the popular perception of the city's catastrophe is that its non-Jewish inhabitants did everything they could to help and protect the Jews. This comforting theory stems largely from the February Strike of 1941, when the city briefly rose almost as one to protest against Nazi brutality against Jews. The event was led by Communist dockworkers and lasted only days before it was bloodily suppressed by the occupation, and is now commemorated each year on 25 February. Flowers are laid and speeches of thanks given at a statue of a hefty dockworker which stands in a square behind the ancient Spanish and Portuguese synagogue. In Amsterdam the February Strike is wrongly viewed as marking the beginning of Dutch Resistance.

Following the Strike, the Nazis in Amsterdam changed tactics.

They no longer employed crude violence, and instead devised a series of seemingly minor administrative measures as a means to harry and isolate the Jews. Identification forms specified who was 'Aryan' and who was not. Jews were banned from cafés, cinemas and parks. Dutch bureaucrats worked diligently on the Nazis' behalf to compile detailed and precise card-indexes listing the names and addresses of the city's Jews.

By 1942, the gas chambers in Poland were ready, and in the summer of that year the deportations of Jews began. There was no repeat of the February Strike. Amsterdam tram drivers drove their fellow citizens from the main collection point at the Hollandsche Schouburg theatre to the city's Central Station, from where workers and officials at every level of the Dutch railway system ferried the victims on to Westerbork transit camp – the first stage of their journey to Auschwitz, Treblinka and Sobibor.

There is a little-known Amsterdam memorial that recalls one of the period's most harrowing episodes. In the brick pavement in front of the Stopera (the combined opera house and town hall built on the old Waterlooplein) a white line marks the site of a Jewish orphanage from where children were deported to their deaths in March 1943. The monument is silent on the details of what happened there. When local residents came into the street to protest when trucks arrived to carry away the tiny victims, the Amsterdam fire brigade were summoned to regain order, and on arrival turned their hoses on the crowd.

Perhaps the most shocking betrayal of Amsterdam's Jews was by the city's police force. Of its 2400-strong membership, more than 1200 were ordered to round up the Nazis' victims – this they did under the supervision and with the encouragement of their chief commissioner, Sybren Tulp. Historian Guus Meershoek's book *Dienaren van het Gezag* (*Servants of Authority*) details the process. 'Because the police were known and trusted, because they came reluctantly, they persuaded their victims that resistance was pointless,' he says. 'In this way they were the most efficient executioners. The Germans could never have deported so many Jews on their own. Most of the police had serious qualms about arresting Jews, but their tradition of submissiveness won the day. Their occasional protests were too little and too late.' Patrolman Jan van der Oever was the only officer ordered to arrest Jews who refused to do so. He was sacked for insubordination. After the war, Van der Oever rejoined the force but colleagues were still angry about his 'disloyalty' and he was compelled to leave. There was just one active member of the Resistance in the entire police force: a detective called Cor Verbiest, who was never asked to take part in the arrests. In 1946 Verbiest demanded an investigation of police behaviour during the war and also found himself ostracised. An internal police report into his allegations of collaboration was produced and then suppressed for fifty years. Not one Amsterdam police officer was ever prosecuted.

When the war was over, the Dutch convinced themselves and the world that they had been a nation of brave anti-Nazis and Resistance members. This persisting image is slowly changing. In 1995 Queen Beatrix apologised to the Jewish people for Holland's wartime record. Writer Harry Mulisch once quipped that most Dutch joined the Resistance *after* the war. Despite this new awareness, however, many Dutch people remain uneasy and bewildered. German historian Gerhard Hirschfeld's 1988 book *Nazi Rule and Dutch Collaboration* was an important contribution to the reassessment of wartime activity in Holland. On the subject of Dutch discomfort with recent historic revelations he says, 'It's easier to live with what the Germans call "life lies". You aren't cheating but you stick to certain traditional interpretations: you had an uncle who was in the Resistance; a cousin or grandfather who was taken to Germany and worked as a slave labourer. It's nicer than having to explain away an uncle who was in the police.'

Amsterdam after the war was a city of ghosts, especially in the former Jewish districts. It still is. Although fragments of Jewish life in the city survived, albeit on a far diminished scale, the city's Jews seem always to have been missed. Yet there remains a current of pro-Jewish feeling in the city that chose to see itself as the home of the February Strike rather than the home of Sybren Tulp – a name that is virtually unknown – and his subordinates.

Like most Amsterdam institutions during the war, Ajax merely bobbed like a cork on the sea of horror. Ajax's English manager Jack Reynolds spent World War II in a POW camp; Eddy Hamel, a much-loved winger in the 1920s, was deported and murdered in Auschwitz. One of Hamel's former team-mates, centre-half Wim Anderiesen, was a member of the wartime Amsterdam police, though most of his service was spent guarding the national bank before he died of an illness in 1944.

After the war, Ajax's image as a Jewish club survived – in both Amsterdam and the rest of Holland.

Barry Hulshoff recalls fondly the club's Jewish climate in the 1960s and 1970s: 'That Ajax team never felt Jewish, but it was there nevertheless. It's an Amsterdam thing – many Jews always had a feeling for us. It was just part of the atmosphere, part of the personality of the team. A certain humour, a selling thing. It was partly to do with Jaap van Praag. And Bennie Muller. And Sjaak Swart was not really Jewish, though his father was Jewish and he really wanted to be, so it's not a problem!' Ruud Krol grew up in the Jewish district and his father hid and saved fourteen Jews during the war. 'The personality [of the team] was to do with laughing, always laughing,' Hulshoff says. 'We were serious also, but when we laughed it was often with a Jewish kind of humour. In Belgium and Holland, where do you hear the jokes first? In Amsterdam and in Antwerp – I feel my best in Belgium when I'm in Antwerp, which has a little of the same Jewish atmosphere. [At Ajax] we were in the middle of the Jewish community, so they brought it all to us. Quite a few of the players were Jewish in the youth teams and so on. It was not something you thought about consciously but it was always in this direction. Of course, no one carried Israeli flags at that time. Never. That came much later, in the eighties, and it's a mistake. It focuses too much attention. We never thought about those things. If someone had red hair, you called him "Red"; if he had a harelip, you'd call him "Arselip". No one cared about it, only the people concerned. But now they make too much fuss about it. That's never good.'

Salo Muller, the much-loved Jewish physiotherapist at Ajax between 1959 and 1973, recalls: 'The players liked to be Jewish even though they weren't. They liked to talk about it a bit. We had a Jewish butcher in Amsterdam – Hergo in Beethovenstraat. Before every European match they gave me an Amsterdam salami, a Jewish salami. And the boys said: "Oh, it's Jewish – we like it!" Dick van Dijk always joked about it. If there was another kind of salami, he'd say: "Hey, come on, throw it away – it's a Catholic salami. We like only the kosher one." Before every match Van Praag would come and tell a Jewish joke. We also had Co Prins, a typical Amsterdam player, a real Amsterdam boy. His family worked on the market with many Jewish men who had their Jewish words. So he was always using Jewish words. It was normal. He wasn't Jewish himself, but he was using these words because it was part of Amsterdam, part of the culture. They liked to tell Jewish jokes and use Jewish words.'

Muller was close to goalkeeper Heinz Stuy. 'One time people were teasing me, and Stuy said: "Salo, let them go, they are *goyim*." He didn't pronounce it right: he said *choyim*. And I said, "No, you have to say it right – if you use the word, use it properly, eh?" But now you couldn't do it, believe me! Nobody in the team understands Jewish words now.'

Rival fans – in particular those from Feyenoord – use the Jewish connection to taunt Ajax with a vile line in anti-Semitic insults. 'Hamas, Hamas – Jews to the gas' is a regular chant among the home fans at De Kuip at Feyenoord–Ajax matches. They also hiss in unison a 'joke' about gas chambers and shout, 'Trains for Auschwitz leave in five minutes'. The abuse is widely viewed as a symptom of childish football tribalism rather than anti-Semitism, and has become so commonplace that police hardly ever bother to prosecute. Hadassa Hirschfeld, deputy director of the Centre for Information and Documentation about Israel in The Hague, considers the trend 'dangerous' because it lessens the taboo against anti-Semitism.

The Ajax fans' attitude is confusing. When the Israeli media billed the 1999 UEFA Cup match between Ajax and Israeli team Hapoel Haifa as a 'Jewish derby', non-Jewish Ajax fans appeared on Israeli television saying how excited they were to be 'going home'. F-Side members, accustomed to being treated like dangerous animals, were in Israel given VIP treatment and received like long-lost cousins. 'Ronald' is one of the editors of *The Ajax Star*, the F-Side fans' magazine, which uses the Star of David as its logo. He insists: 'Calling ourselves Jews is normal now. Out-of-towners called us "Jews" as an insult. In the early eighties we decided to take over the insult word as our own. We started carrying Israeli flags [this was after seeing fans of the English 'Jewish' Club' Spurs doing the same], calling ourselves Jews. Every year more fans take the star for their own symbol. It is accepted. Of course the star is a dangerous symbol, we know that. But it doesn't mean anything to us . . . We are not Jewish, but I heard once that if you have just a single drop of Jewish blood, you can call yourself Jewish. We have no relation to real Jews or feeling about Israel or anything like that. We like to provoke a little bit with this symbol. Dutch fans are not very friendly to one another, and Ajax is one of the most hated clubs in Holland, and when you wear the star, everybody gets mad. We have lawyers, teachers, even a KLM airline pilot. There are people from every walk of life on the F-Side. We have Surinamese, Chinese, even a handful of North Africans. But none of us are Jews.' The F-Side has a bad reputation and 'Ronald' speaks on condition of anonymity. He fears he would lose his job as a computer systems developer with a large Amsterdam bank if his employers knew how he spent his leisure hours.

The postwar Jewish population in Amsterdam has recovered to some 20,000, and there are almost that number of Israelis now living there. The Jewish presence can be felt in the bricks and stones, the street-names and best-loved places, from the Sarphatipark to the Tuschinski Cinema (perhaps the most beautiful cinema in Europe – an art deco people's palace built in the 1920s by three Polish Jews, who were later murdered by Nazis.) It was no accident that the city had only Jewish mayors for thirty years from the mid-1960s to the 1990s. In the 1970s, more than thirty years after the February Strike, a loose coalition of post-Provo squatters, radicals, proto-Greens and local residents fought pitched battles with the police in the old Jewish district around the Nieuwmarkt to stop the city council destroying the area completely for a Metro line. (The result was a draw: the Metro was built but plans for a motorway, fancy hotels and office blocks were dropped, and the old street pattern was largely preserved.) There was among the leaders of this movement a profound awareness and sensitivity to the area's rich and tragic past. One of the most remarkable of them, Auke Bijlsma, is now a city councillor himself. Bijlsma has immersed himself in the city's Jewish past and proposed a stream of moving initiatives, such as a scheme (never implemented) for plaques to be put on houses recalling the names of their former Jewish inhabitants.

Perhaps the Ajax fans' strange adopted 'Jewishness' is an inchoate part of Amsterdam's deeply Jewish tradition. Could the waving of Israeli flags or the daubing of weird football graffiti (the Star of David with a letter F [for F-Side] is scrawled everywhere) be in fact some unconscious act of post-Holocaust solidarity with the city's murdered, missing Jews? I like to think so. I find it affectionate and warm, kind almost. But I might be entirely wrong. I'm a Jew but I'm also a foreigner, and foreigners often misread cultural signals – especially when they're as weirdly coded as these.

Many older members of Amsterdam's small surviving Jewish community are deeply upset by Ajax fans' antics. Bennie Muller, one of Ajax's handful of Jewish former players, now runs a cigar shop near the Central Station. He for one finds the behaviour disturbing: 'Sometimes when I'm sitting in the stadium and I hear those crazy people shouting "We are super-Jews" and "Jews are the champions" it's so bad that I just walk off and go home. And when Ajax play Feyenoord in Rotterdam . . . well, I won't go to those games any more.' About 200 members of Muller's extended family died in the Holocaust and he vividly remembers the day his mother was taken away. 'I had two brothers and two sisters – all of us were crying. The Germans said, "Oh, let's leave them", but the Dutch Nazis said no. My mother had eleven brothers and sisters.' His mother survived but, like 106,000 other Dutch Jews, her relatives were killed. 'Older people know what happened in the war. But these fans, they don't know. Maybe they learn a little in school, but they don't really know. They walk around saying "Jewish, Jewish". They wear Stars of David on their caps. It's nothing to do with being Jewish. I wish they would stop it but they won't. I talk a lot with Israelis here. They all seem to like it. They laugh about it. But for the Jewish people in Amsterdam here, it's so disgusting, it's unbelievable.'

Younger Jews tend to take a more relaxed view. Yves Gijrath, publisher of *Jewish Journal* magazine, says: 'The Ajax board should have said: "This is simply not possible" but they accepted it years ago. When other fans insult us, it's not because they hate Jews but because they hate Ajax.' 'I don't dislike the F-Side,' says Danny Jacobs, an Ajax fan and orthodox Jew who wears a *kipa* to the stadium. 'But if you ask the average Dutchman about the blue and white flag with a star on it, he thinks it's an Ajax flag, not an Israeli one.'

4: the boys from paramaribo

Forget Holland–Germany. For some Dutchmen, the local derby that stirs the deepest feelings is Holland–Brazil. Put those eyebrows down immediately. It's a simple matter of history and geography. One of Brazil's northern neighbours is Surinam, formerly known as Dutch Guyana, a Dutch colony or autonomous region until it gained independence in 1975. Surinam is a hot and often neglected politically troubled land full of rainforests and footballers. It's five times bigger than the Netherlands, has a total population of less than a million, and for the last two decades it has given Holland a startlingly large number of its best players. Dutch football would have been a good deal less interesting without players like Gullit, Rijkaard, Vanenburg, Davids, Seedorf and Kluivert.

Surinamese immigrants who arrived in Holland's big cities both before and soon after Surinam's independence had always loved football, but had traditionally looked south to Brazil for their sporting inspiration. Things later got confusing when the Dutch national team started to feature huge numbers of players born in Surinam (such as Edgar Davids, and Aron Winter) or Dutchmen whose fathers were from Surinam (Ruud Gullit and Frank Rijkaard, for example). 'In the World Cup, Surinam people are always for Brazil,' says Dennis Purperhart, a centre-forward for the Surinam national team, who plays for the top amateur club AFC in Amsterdam. 'Now there are a lot of Surinam kids in the Dutch team, people are for Holland *and* for

Brazil. In the last World Cup when Holland played Brazil, it was fifty-fifty, half for Brazil, half for Holland, but it didn't matter who won because they were both for us.'

The Surinam connection is now vital to the Dutch game. 'A Dutch team these days which had no Surinamese players would be a weak, soft, strange Dutch team,' says the sleek and engaging Humberto Tan, Holland's only significant black sports journalist, who has written a history of Surinamese players in the Dutch top division, the Eredivisie. 'It could never happen now. A Holland coach who dared to play without Davids and Kluivert and Seedorf and Reiziger would be committing suicide.'

Surinamese players marry the Brazilian South American style to cooler and more Dutch qualities. Tan: 'They enjoy the *panna* [nutmeg]. That is the flavour the Surinamese bring to the Dutch game. It's skill and a mentality of doing things relaxed and loose, without stress but with results. Dutch people like freedom, which is why they prefer to play in a technical way. So Surinam players blend into Dutch football easily. They share the philosophy. The only difference is that the Dutch players tend to think more in terms of concepts and solutions and are always businesslike. The Surinam player plays more because he likes it. He has more fun. Sometimes he plays not even to win, only to enjoy. The Dutch talk everything through, but the Surinam players play more intuitively. When you combine that with Dutch efficiency, it's lethal.'

Ruud Gullit is the perfect example: the son of a Dutch mother and Surinamese father, George Gullit (who played in the lower leagues in the 1960s and was famed for his powerful bare-footed shooting). 'In every aspect, Ruud Gullit is a blend. His game is joyful – "sexy" as he calls it – but he still wants that lethal Dutch efficiency.' People often look for the 'secret' of the Surinam players, but Tan says there is none. 'People talk about race theories, say that black players are stronger and all that stuff. I don't believe in that. There are lots of talented people in soccer, black and white. The talents who make it aren't the ones who are physically or genetically stronger: it's mental strength that counts.'

He compares the relatively minor impact of the much larger population from former British colonies in the Caribbean on British football. 'The first Surinamese player to play for Holland was in 1960. I think it was something to do with the joy the Surinamese had in their football and the open-mindedness of Holland. The first black English international was Viv Anderson, I think, in 1978. Why so late? You can easily imagine an English team without Andy Cole or Sol Cambell. But the Dutch without their Surinamese? It's unthinkable!' As was its predecessor, the Ajax team that won the European Cup in 1995, the Dutch national side is now heavily dependent on Surinamese players. When Holland beat Germany in a friendly in February 2000, six of the team, and the coach, Frank Rijkaard, were of Surinamese descent.

The Surinamese certainly didn't invent the playful, technical Dutch style, Tan says, but they played an important part in keeping it going. 'Without the Surinamese, Dutch football would have become a little more like German football.' Internationally, the Dutch may have overtaken Brazil as the leading standard-bearers for the concept of the beautiful game. 'Until the nineties, the Brazilian attitude was always: "You score three goals. We'll score six." But then it switched around. The Brazilians got fed up with losing. They started to think more about the result.'

Yet it has never been easy for Surinamese players to make their way in Dutch football.

The first of them arrived in the 1950s, but failed to make a permanent breakthrough because of a mismatch of attitudes and cultures. In Utrecht, Humphrey Mijnals's debut was a tragi-comic affair. Mijnals, a defender who combined a formidable physical presence with the skills of a John Barnes, was reckoned to be the best player in the colony. He had played for the Robin Hood club in the Surinam capital, Paramaribo, and was talent-spotted (though he was probably hard to miss) by a Dutch vicar called Graafland, who contacted the Utrecht club Elinkwijk. Following an exchange of letters, Mijnals arrived to try his luck in the Eredivisie, where professionalism had just been allowed for the first time. Elinkwijk's officials found the concept of a black defender hard to comprehend (a strange enough attitude in 1954, you may think, but one that persists: I was astounded to hear a Dutch reporter expressing similar sentiments in 1999). Accordingly, Mijnals was obliged to play his first game as a centre-forward. Out of position and wearing a hat and gloves against the unfamiliar bitter cold, he had an awful game. For his next game, Mijnals persuaded his employers to let him operate in his natural position – and was a revelation. Soon Elinkwijk had four black players from Surinam as Mijnals was joined by his brother Frank, a midfielder; Michel Kruin, a quick, goalscoring winger, and Charlie Marbach, perhaps the most skilful of the group. Elinkwijk played – as did many Dutch teams of the period – a form of English-style kick-and-rush to which the Surinamese players had to adapt. A famous match against a Dutch army team presaged things to come. In the first half the ball was mostly in the air (as usual), and by half-time Elinkwijk were losing 3–0. During the break, Mijnals led the Surinamese in a plea to be allowed to play their own short-passing, Brazilian-style game. They eventually got their way and Elinkwijk were transformed, the Surinam players leading the team to win 5–3. Newspapers raved about 'the black train'. But the virtuosity of the four (still remembered fondly in Utrecht) was a fleeting moment rather than the beginning of a revolution. In 1960 Mijnals became the first black player to represent Holland but, after only three caps, fell out with the national coach, Elek Schwartz, who had refused to put Mijnals in the starting line-up in a tour match against Surinam in Paramaribo (this to the crowd's annoyance, as well as Mijnals's). On his return to Holland, Mijnals criticised Schwartz in a newspaper interview and was never selected again. By the mid-1960s several dozen Surinamese players – including Herman Rijkaard (father of Frank) and George Gullit – were working in Holland and enjoying varying degrees of success.

*   *   *

The struggle for recognition endured by Mijnals and his colleagues, and their lack of financial gain, did not go unnoticed by the young Surinamese players. In the late 1960s, as Dutch clubs strove to catch up with professionalism, the prospect of travelling to Holland for meagre wages and harder work became increasingly unattractive, so the flow of talent from the Caribbean dried up. After the dictatorship of Desi Bouterse, which wrecked the once-thriving Surinamese economy, and especially after Surinam gained independence, many Surinamese went to Holland. Life in the Netherlands was not easy. 'In the 1970s Surinamese people in Holland had a bad name,' says Tan. 'A lot of people who came were disappointed in a society they weren't used to. They weren't successful, so some of them turned to drugs. There were dealers, pushers, pimps and addicts on the Zeedijk.' It was hard for Surinamese footballers to get through the door of Dutch clubs. The Welsh manager of Haarlem, Barry Hughes, had a tough time convincing his board to take a risk on a big young centre-half called Ruud Gullit. Gullit and his childhood friend Frank Rijkaard, made their debuts for Kees Rijvers's national team in 1981. They were both tall, black and had moustaches, and when Gullit came on as substitute for Rijkaard many fans couldn't tell them apart. Tan is reluctant to blame Dutch racism for slowing the advance of Surinamese players. 'I think clubs didn't want to invest in Surinamese players because of this bad image.'

In the early 1980s Thijs Libregts gave an interview while he was Feyenoord coach, making derogatory remarks about the mental reliability of black players. (He was sacked for it.) Controversy still surrounds the feud between black and white players which wrecked Holland's Euro '96 campaign in England. One still hears allegations of black 'cliques' and 'separatism', much of it based on misquoted or misrepresented interviews. It's strange that Clarence Seedorf should still be derided for his 'arrogance' in taking and badly missing a penalty in a World Cup qualifying match in Turkey – when Ronald de Boer and Marco van Basten were never pilloried for missing decisive penalties in both European Championship and World Cup semi-finals respectively.

Dennis Purperhart was rated the best young player in Surinam when he was a teenager, played for Haarlem at the beginning of his career and was good enough to score two goals against Van Gaal's Barcelona in a pre-season friendly for AFC. Despite all of this, he never quite made it as a professional. He says: 'It's twice as hard if you're black. There are plenty of very talented black guys who don't make it. Dutch people will drink with you, laugh with you, but behind your back they are saying stuff about you. That's normal for here. They are not going to say you're black so you can't play. It's nothing crude like that. But you feel it.' He relates an incident when he played for Heracles. 'I was walking in the street with a friend who was also black. It was dark. Four white guys were walking in front of us and we heard them talking and being very racist. But when they saw us, when they saw our faces, they said, "Oh, it's Dennis – he's our friend." I went to the local discotheque in a village. It's difficult for a black person in a place like that. Because they knew me as a football player, it was OK, but if I was someone else . . . There is a lot of hostility.' He believes successful and well-known black footballers are resented. Tan, though, sees it differently. 'Racism exists but it's more that in Holland you have a problem in general when you stand out. As the saying goes: "act normal; that's crazy enough". And if you're dark, you do stand out. Is that racist? Sometimes it is, but sometimes it's just Dutch.'

25: problems, problems

'You want Christmas all year round? We can fix that'

Jan Benthem

It would be hard to imagine two institutions with less in common than a football team and an airport. But those two era-defining Dutch icons of the 1990s, Ajax (whose De Meer stadium was built on a former lake) and Schiphol (the only airport in the world built on the site of a major naval battle), share much more than their obscurely watery pasts. They were both designed in line with some decidedly Dutch organising principles and they used similarly innovative approaches to solving problems.

Under Louis van Gaal, Ajax became, for the second time, the most admired and most eagerly studied team in the world as their clever, high-speed football swept aside all before them. To solve the problems of congested pitches and massed, mobile, modern defences, Van Gaal, working on the principles of Cruyff and Michels, developed a flexible, integrated system based on speed of thought, movement and passing. His players were schooled to think their way past their opponents, to understand the structure of both the whole team and the shape of the game, and to solve problems on the hoof. 'We teach players to read the game,' Van Gaal explained at the team's peak in early 1996. 'We teach them to be like coaches. When people ask what I have done for Ajax, I say the main aspect is the culture within the club. Coaches and players alike, we argue and discuss and above all communicate. Every match is analysed afterwards. We work to improve ourselves every day. If the opposition's coach comes up with a good tactic, the players look and find a solution.'

In the same era, Schiphol established itself as the world's most admired and eagerly studied airport. It grew rapidly and became a central hub of Holland's economy and transport system. In the late 1980s, to resolve the problems of ever-growing congestion, architects Jan Benthem and Mels Crouwel were given the job of enlarging and improving Schiphol. The partners have been dubbed the 'Houdinis of the Polder' by critic Art Oxenaar for their ability to solve complex architectural problems. They have designed such high-prestige buildings as the Anne Frank Museum and are now integrating a new subway line and bus station into Amsterdam's Central Station, a project likely to change the face of the city. For Schiphol, rather in the tradition of Wim Crouwel (Mels's father), who devised Total Design, and Cruyff and Michels, who invented Total Football, Benthem Crouwel conceived a Total Airport.

It's not a term they ever use themselves. However, instead of using separate buildings (or parts of buildings) for separate functions (arrivals, departures, shopping, etc.), the architects insisted on just one sleek grey-white steel and concrete building, in which everything was integrated. The airport's railway station – once a separate building – was relocated to basement level. From there passengers can be whisked all over Holland at minimum cost and maximum efficiency by Netherlands Railways (another Dutch system that, by British standards, seems miraculously efficient and intelligently organised).

'Normally, everything is split up and problems are solved separately,' says Jan Benthem, the airport's chief architect since 1985. 'That makes individual problems easy to solve, but the connections between the problems become very complicated and something simple ends up in a real mess. If you integrate it in the first place, that turns out to be the most simple solution.' Benthem is famed for his ability to negotiate the morass of the carefully balanced Dutch consultation system to achieve the solution he wants. 'You have to think ahead,' he says. 'And you must always expect the unexpected.'

Schiphol's integrated structure allows huge volumes of freight and passengers to circulate at high speed and with remarkable precision. The simplicity and flexibility of its basic grid design (the grid is even visible on the airport's floor-tiles) means different elements in the building can be switched around constantly to meet ever-changing needs. The complex and huge flows of people and cargo are shifting constantly. Even small changes in one area will ripple consequences through the entire system. For example, if fewer passengers use one 'finger' of the site, the customs desks, shops or bus station all have to be modified. The key to solving these problems is a mixture of quick thinking and careful preparation: 'You must have a plan, but you also have to be ready to change it at the last minute or to make a decisive, sudden completely unexpected movement to arrive at the place you want.' A rigid approach would be doomed. 'You must never say: "I've done my work in advance and nothing will keep me from my path." We don't plan the track; but we plan where we want to be. We have several tracks in mind and we are always ready to change track to re-group or have a new solution or be able to react at the last moment. We tried to make Schiphol so flexible that you can always change course. You need a simple system where, if something goes wrong, you always have a second, a third or a fourth solution at hand. For example, we always insist the buildings have strong floors. When you build an area you must always expect that it will be used for something else. It starts out as a waiting area, but maybe they will want to build shops there. Maybe they want a bank, too, which has a very heavy safe in it. When the traffic-flow changes, it becomes perhaps a baggage-handling area with heavy machines or a big hole on the floor.' Benthem insists that unlike, say, Paris's 'bombastic' Charles de Gaulle Airport – conceived in part as a statement of French technical brilliance – Schiphol was always seen purely as a traffic machine. And he does not see himself as an architectural artist but as the director or facilitator of an architectural 'process' whose task is simply to solve problems. 'What we like to do is very functional, rational, pragmatic. No grand visions, but clever solutions. I think that is why we get commissions: the Dutch have this tradition.'

Louis van Gaal is generally considered the creator of a football system or machine. It might be more accurate to describe him as the originator of a new *process* for playing the game. His underlying tactical principles were much as those of Michels and Cruyff: relentless attack; pressing and squeezing space to make the pitch small in order to win the ball; spreading play and expanding the field in possession. By the 1990s, though, footballers had become stronger, faster and better organised than ever before. Van Gaal saw the need for a new dimension. 'With space so congested, the most important thing is ball circulation,' he declared. 'The team that plays the quickest football is the best.' His team aimed for total control of the game, maintaining the ball 'in construction', as he calls it, and passing and running constantly with speed and precision. *Totaalvoetbal*-style position switching was out, but players still had to be flexible and adaptable. Opponents were not seen as foes to be fought and beaten in battle; rather as posing a problem that had to be solved. Ajax players were required to be flexible and smart – as they 'circulated' the ball, the space on the field was constantly reorganised until gaps opened in the opponents' defence.

Gerard van der Lem, Van Gaal's right-hand man at Ajax and Barcelona, explains: 'The main principle was possession of the ball. We trained on this endlessly. In some European Cup and Dutch League games we had seventy per cent ball possession. Seventy per cent! You need a lot of technical skills to do that. We almost always had the ball and we were always trying to find solutions. People think our system was rigid, but it was not. It could not be rigid. We could play with three strikers, or with three in midfield, with or without a shadow *spits* [striker]; whatever you like. The thing was to understand what consequences these formations have for the team. The players must be tactically very skilful and they have to be thinking spatially in advance. When we won the European Cup, everything fitted. Everything fell like a puzzle. Every player knew the qualities of his fellow players. Each player knew how to play a ball to his fellow players. In defence, they knew exactly how to press. They all knew the distances . . . Yeah, it was like solving a puzzle.'

Van Gaal and Van der Lem have been criticised for stifling creative players. Sjaak Swart snorts with derision at the memory of wingers Finidi George and Marc Overmars being obliged to pass the ball back when faced with two or more defenders: 'I *never* gave the ball back to my defence. Never! If two players were about to hit me, maybe. But to pass back every time and then wait till the ball comes again? No! When I have the ball, I go! Making Overmars and Finidi pass back? It's unbelievable! But that was the system of Van Gaal. Many games you are sleeping! On television, they say "Ajax seventy per cent ball possession". So what? It's not football. The creativity is gone.'

Van der Lem insists this is a misunderstanding: 'Our way of thinking was that if there were two defenders marking one of our players in one position, it meant somewhere one of our players was free. So we tried to find that free player. If Finidi or Overmars were one against one, of course they could dribble. But at top-level nowadays, it is very hard to dribble past two. The defenders are faster and stronger and more ruthless every year. You dribble past one, but the second one will just bring you down. So we say it's better to play the ball out and find the free man. Maybe he is on the other side of the field. So we tried to reach him with one ball back, instant control and a pass: then the other winger can go.' He draws me a diagram (how I have grown to love them) to show how the ball was relayed at speed through the Ajax formation in much the same way as the Pony Express would use teams of fresh horses to deliver messages as fast as physically possible in the days before telegraphy. 'We skipped stations. Not going from the first to the second, to third, to fourth . . . No, we tried to skip stations very fast to get as fast as possible to the other side. The speed of the ball has to be high. Control has to be fast and perfect. Not a high ball: it has to be low and must be played too quick for the opposing defender to cover the situation. You need a lot of technical skills to play the ball fast and accurately over longer distances. The players at the edge of the field could all play that ball. You need to control the ball very fast in the direction you want to go. You must know in advance where space is and which player you want to reach.'

Ajax trained relentlessly in triangular formations to hone their rapid-fire passing and movement. 'We believed in repetition. Every day. Every day. The system needed passing over short distances inside the opposition half where space was limited. So we trained in triangles, passing and kicking in triangles, with very short control and a lot of movement between three players. From a fixed situation, this created a lot of possibilities. We trained endlessly, endlessly in small spaces.' An even more high-octane version of this unique routine involved trios of triangles. 'We had triangles of triangles with two groups of three and one of four if you include the goalkeeper, which we did. We always started training with this. It was a part of warming up, to prepare the players for what was coming. The player receiving the ball would say where he wanted it with his eyes or by the way he moved. His control had to be short, but not too short because otherwise he couldn't play the next ball. He has to see what the next player needs. Part of the art was that the triangles got smaller all time because the space was already so small and everyone was testing each other. It started out with gaps of twelve metres. Then eleven metres. Then ten, and so on. At one point the triangles were only eight-by-eight metres, which was incredible with such a high speed of ball. Really incredible! But the ball-speed always had to be functional. There's no point if I'm four metres away from you and I hit a very hard ball which is impossible to control. That's too much. And a ball played in front of the striker must maintain the high speed of the game and it has to be just enough for the striker to be onside but not so safe that it slows him down. It must not be offside, but only just. It has to be perfect.'

The Ajax system is built on triangles, and so too has been Jan Benthem's life – literally. As a young architect in the mid-1980s, he entered and won a competition to design the simplest house imaginable. This turned out to be a steel and glass box without foundations, held up by a lattice of green steel triangles. The house still exists in Almere, outside Amsterdam. It become known as 'the simplest house in the world' and Benthem, arguably the most powerful and influential architect in the country, still lives in it. It still gives him enormous pleasure. He shows me a floor-plan of four tiny box-rooms and a larger open space. 'This house was the smallest minimum I could think of. I sleep with my wife in the living room now because we don't have a bedroom for ourselves. The house was a simple box of eight by eight metres. I started with the bedroom. I asked: what do we need? To sleep, you need about two metres. That's all. But you don't need windows because normally it's night when you're there. So the room is two-by-two metres with a bed on one side, a door and some cupboards to put things in. What do you need for the kitchen and bathroom? Again, not more than two-by-two metres for each. And you don't need windows because you don't need windows in the bathroom and you don't spend much time in the kitchen, either. If you want children, you'll need another bed-room. So this also is two-by-two metres and, again, no windows. So, on one side I made four closed boxes. Then we wanted a living room. Let's make that square, too. But in the living room you do need windows because you want a view. So why not make a living room of glass only? How could it be simpler? Glass is a strong material, so maybe the glass can support the roof too. Then you can leave the frames out! I made a very thin, light roof, with some insulation. I made a super-light construction and I used cables to support the roof. The house was designed without foundations. The competition was to make a house without piles driven into the ground, so you need a very strong construction: steel triangles, something you can adjust if there is subsidence. A triangle is the strongest form you can think of in a building: the lightest form with the biggest strength.'

*   *   *

There is little room for sentiment in either top football or in running a major airport. Searching for perfection, Louis van Gaal pruned and shaped his squad as ruthlessly and as perceptively as Rinus Michels had done thirty years earlier. When a blunder against Auxerre by popular goalkeeper Stanley Menzo cost Ajax a place in the 1993 UEFA Cup semi-final, Van Gaal wielded the axe, bringing in Edwin van der Sar instead. (Menzo later sought counselling to get over the trauma of being dropped.) Fitfully brilliant winger Bryan Roy, a protégé of Cruyff, was also adored by the Ajax faithful. But Van Gaal sold him to Foggia in Italy when he concluded that Roy would never be a sufficiently reliable component for the system. His replacement was the then little-known Overmars. Yet in many ways Schiphol is a far tougher organisation than Ajax. The turnover of staff in senior management positions is terrifyingly high. Hardly any of its top fifty personnel have been there for the last fifteen years. Buildings and computer systems that outlive their usefulness or can be replaced by more efficient systems are discarded immediately.

In the late 1990s, as Ajax and Schiphol both faced a rapidly changing environment and problems generated by their success, there's no doubt which organisation coped better.

Jack the Ripper himself could scarcely have had a more destructive effective on Ajax than the Bosman ruling. Van Gaal's dream team was not so much damaged as disembowelled by the case, which granted players much greater freedom of movement. Thanks to Bosman, every one of the club's young stars who won the Champions' League in 1995 soon left for foreign clubs. Seedorf, Davids, Kluivert, Reiziger, Bogarde, Litmanen, Kanu, Overmars, Finidi, the De Boer twins, Van der Sar. The whole lot. Most went first to Italy but ended up at Barcelona with Van Gaal. The fans half-heartedly dubbed the resulting Catalan–Amsterdam hybrid 'Barc-Ajax' but derived little local satisfaction from it. Van Gaal – seen as fanatical and obsessive – is not loved as Cruyff is. 'BarcAjax' may be one of the most admired teams in Europe, but the guys in the actual white and red shirts are no longer counted among European football's big boys.

Off the pitch, Ajax's problems were more of their own creating as they gawkily attempted to make the transition from intimate club to mega-business. The high-tech Arena, conceived as a way of providing the revenues to enable Ajax to compete on more equal terms with the big clubs of Italy, Spain and England, is in fact deeply flawed. Grass refuses to grow properly there, so a new pitch has had to be laid at the rate of about three per season. Plenty of older fans think the Arena is the biggest mistake Ajax has ever made. They feel alienated by the stadium's oddly tinny acoustics and obviously commercial imperatives, and many simply refuse to go there any more. The 'multi-functional' stadium's brightly coloured plastic seats are, for the most part, filled now by people from outside the city. The club doesn't own the building; it merely has its offices in one section and rents the rest on match days. 'The old Ajax stadium was too small and it was not a beauty by any standard,' says landscape architect Dirk Sijmons. 'But it was nice and cosy. And it was built for football rather than for making money. You see now how vulnerable Ajax is. It is like one of those crabs who, when they grow, have to find a new shell. And while they are looking, they are very vulnerable. Ajax have to go through a period like that now because the Arena is not a home. They play there on a Sunday. But then there is a Rolling Stones concert. Then a big congress. Then the unveiling of the new Mitsubishi space-car. Then, after seven days, Ajax are allowed to go and play football again.

'This Dutch multi-functional obsession of making money with the same building in many ways, making the parking space available every day, that kind of thing . . . It is a very brilliant idea, of course, but it squeezes the life out of what a football stadium is. A stadium has to rest between matches too. It should wait empty for a week before the game, before the next flow of people arrives. A stadium somehow needs to meditate. That's what the Arena can never offer. It is an institution whose only purpose is to make money, and one of those ways to make money is Ajax. That's all there is to it. And everyone feels this. You have to sort of put out the lights when you leave, and then it's someone else's. We are just guests here.

[Feyenoord's] De Kuip is fantastic stadium. When it is empty the acoustics are beautiful; when a bird cries you hear it from everywhere. Empty stadiums are very special. And when it is completely full, it can be so intimate. It has to do with being completely perfect in its dimensions, the fact that there are two balconies, that the stands are close to the pitch but not claustrophobic. When the Japanese want to copy a stadium, that's the one they should choose.' Even Ajax's loyal Bobby Haarms, who has been at the club for nearly fifty years and worked in various capacities under Reynolds, Buckingham, Michels, Kovacs, Cruyff, Beenhakker and Van Gaal, cannot hide the fact that the Arena makes him miserable. The stadium's oppressive security system and endless series of locked corridors require him to carry a giant bunch of keys like a Newgate prison warder. 'De Meer was for football. Everything there was perfect. This place . . . well, it's for money.'

Schiphol, meanwhile, is grappling with barely less complex questions of identity and scale. As it grew from seventeen million passengers in 1989 to thirty-eight million a decade later Schiphol mutated into a small city, with burgeoning numbers of offices and cafés and a shopping centre. The airport has become so large – and its attendant congestion and pollution so irksome – that plans were even floated (before being rejected as too expensive) to relocate it to an artificial island twenty miles into the North Sea connected to land by a high-speed rail-link. The culture is changing, too. 'The whole airport environment has changed in the last ten years. From a functional machine for traffic it has become much more of an environment for spending time and money in,' says Benthem. 'Airports of the past were places where you basically didn't want to be, just a space to pass. It's nice to make spaces where people enjoy themselves and like to be.'

The authority that runs Schiphol has come up with a radical new problem. 'They always said to us: "We want sober and functional." ' Now, a new manager thinks the time for sober and functional is over. He says he likes the cosy atmosphere of the airport at

Christmas. It's very nice at Christmas. We have lights everywhere, trees every ten metres. The manager said: "We need to have the airport like Christmas all year round." Well, Holland is a completely artificial country. You want Christmas all year round? We can fix that, no problem. Personally, I think it's cluttering, but he is my boss. At the same time, someone will say: it will cost us money, so do you really need it? That is a controlling mechanism which is always there to keep things sane. You can have a meeting about it and you think about it some more. And then you have another meeting. You say: "Can we discuss it another time? Do you really mean this? Or do you really mean something else? You want it to be cosy like Christmas but maybe you really mean. . ." You discuss it out.'

The airport has fundamentally altered, though. It makes most of its income these days from shopping rather than anything related to flying. That means Benthem must juggle totally contradictory imperatives. 'In an airport you want the best flows, the most obvious route from one point to another. In a shopping centre you want people to get lost. You let them in and never let them go out again! So you have to combine that in the airport where it is changing from a machine for traffic into a machine to generate money. So you have to have a fine balance between finding your way and losing your way! You have to realise the problem and make the best of both worlds. What is the shortest way from your car to the airport but that makes it impossible to miss the shops? That's the clever solution.'

Solutions, solutions. Problems, problems.

In football, Johan Cruyff says, 'Simple play is also the most beautiful. How often do you see a pass of forty metres when twenty metres is enough? Or a one-two in the penalty area when there are seven people around you and a simple wide pass around the seven would be a solution? The solution that seems the simplest is in fact the most difficult one.' Benthem takes the idea a stage further: 'I think it is very Dutch to look for a simple solution. And the biggest thrill in our work is to find an even simpler solution. That is what we like. In the end the most satisfying solution is the one where you have cleared everything away and there is no solution at all any more but, at the same time, the problem has been solved. That's the nicest way of doing it.'

5 out of 6: frank, patrick, frank, jaap, patrick, paul . . . and gyuri

'The more I practice the luckier I get'

Ben Hogan

When at last it was over, when the Dutch had finished fumbling their spot-kicks and as the amazed Italians celebrated their good fortune, the vast Orange crowd poured quickly and in deathly silence from the Arena and flowed over the little bridge to the Metro station. Holland's month-long carnival suddenly resembled a scene from T.S. Eliot's *The Waste Land* – . . . *so many, I had not thought a penalty shoot-out had undone so many*. On the other side of Amsterdam, I had watched Holland–Italy on TV with friends. When the shoot-out came, I put my jacket on and moved to the door, ready for a speedy exit. There was no doubt in my mind as to what was about to happen and I just wanted to be alone after-wards. I watched the unequal contest from a strange angle. Then I left and slowly cycled through a city in shock. Largely silent groups of men and women wearing their no-longer-funny orange hats, T-shirts and face-paint stumbled dazed from bars and homes. They stood in numbed groups or walked very slowly through the streets. Some sat head in hands on the steps of their houses. On the banks of the Amstel, a tall blond man in an orange T-shirt shook his head and distilled into his mobile phone the question the entire nation was asking: 'How can we do it? It's unbelievable. Five penalties? How can we miss five penalties in one game? How is that possible?'

For Holland, it's the key football question of the age. The next day, after the almost unbearable pictures of Frank Rijkaard sitting in the team bus with tears streaming down his face, Louis van Gaal was installed as bondscoach. In his very first press conference he announced his intention to make Holland World Champions in Japan. Like your style, Louis! At last, one feels that here may be the man with the necessary combination of intensity, obsession and football wisdom to get the job done. But until Van Gaal – or anyone else – finds a way to solve Holland's penalty problems, there is no chance of that dream being realised.

Penalty expertise has, sadly, become an essential prerequisite for winning the world's major football tournaments. Over the last decade, roughly one in three matches in the knockout stages of the two main tournaments have gone to penalties. Nine of the last twelve semi-finals in World or European Championship have been decided by penalties. Meanwhile, Holland have firmly established themselves as the world's worst penalty takers. 'Forget England and Germany,' said *Het Parool* after the Italy game. 'The Dutch are now the laughing stock of world football.' To rub the point in, on German TV the Sat 1 chat-show host Harald Schmidt declared he had a new way to insult Dutch drivers. Instead of showing a single finger he stuck his whole hand out of his car window – 'Get it? Five fingers for five penalties! Ha ha ha!' De Oranje have taken part in five shoot-outs and lost them all (Fifa's seventy-fifth anniversary match against Argentina in 1979, the semi-final of Euro '92, the quarter final of '96 and the semi-finals of '98 and '00). In nearly thirty years of shoot-outs, Dutch club-teams have won just four against foreign opposition. Until now, opponents may not have calculated that a draw is enough to knock out Holland, but after the Euro 2000 fiasco they'd have to be stupid to reach any other conclusion.

The Dutch have always hated penalties and considered the shoot-out an abomination. But its merciless, made-for-TV melo-drama has its admirers. In his book *On Penalties* Andrew Anthony argues that, 'The shoot-out is as near perfect an allegory of the human condition as sport offers. Of course, the field is rich in experiential metaphors, with all the triumphs and disasters, winners and losers, and countless other stupefying clichés that make up the world of competitive games. The beauty of the penalty, though, is that it powerfully represents the fear and the hope, the regret or relief that are compressed into the meaningful junctures of life. The football penalty is unique in sport because of the emphasis it places on conscious choice. For a brief period, the game stops and the penalty taker enters his own chamber of truth, a place where actions have ineluctable consequences. The penalty shoot-out goes even further. In its combination of individual choice and collective responsibility it attains an almost moral significance.'

He's right about the 'ineluctable consequences', but wrong about the moral aspect. It is precisely the amoral consequences of the shoot-out that are the problem. The term 'shoot-out' comes from the Hollywood Western where, in the climactic final scene, the good guys in white hats invariably killed the bad guys in black hats. Even in Sergio Leone's cynical spaghetti variations on the genre, shoot-out victory went to the more morally deserving. The Good killed The Bad and let The Ugly live. Football shoot-outs disrupt and subvert this moral universe, for The Bad and The Ugly often kill The Good. Think of West Germany's scandalous victory over France in 1982, or Argentina's triumph against Italy in 1990. The Italy–Holland shoot-out produced a result that, whatever it revealed about the two countries' penalty skills, was a bizarre travesty of the game that preceded it. As an Italian journalist in the Arena joked: 'Zoff is a tactical genius: he pinned the Dutch into our half for two hours. Then they were cooked.'

The football shoot-out is really much closer in spirit to Russian roulette or that scene in *Spartacus* where sadistic Roman general Laurence Olivier forces Kirk Douglas and Tony Curtis to fight to the death for his own amusement. No ritual could be better designed for crushing individual players. After Clarence Seedorf's decisive miss in the Euro '96 quarter final, his friend the French midfielder Christian Karembeu, who finished on the winning side, observed of the shoot-out: 'It is loading a bullet into the chamber of a gun and asking everyone to pull the trigger. Someone will get the bullet; you know that. And it will reduce them to nothing. Fair? Fairness is not even an issue.' Michel Platini, a great penalty taker in his day and now a senior bureaucrat has said, 'The player who misses a decisive penalty suffers a lifelong trauma. He is branded as if he had killed his colleagues and parents.'

Even Fifa's President Sepp Blatter sees the problem. Just prior to Euro 2000 he said, 'Football is a team sport. But when you have penalties it becomes an individual sport and that is not good for the spirit of the game and it is not good for the individual.' Citing the 1994 World Cup Final penalty shoot-out misses of Roberto Baggio and Franco Baresi, he continued: 'Look at how it affected them. Thankfully, Baggio was able to go away and rebuild his career and put it behind him . . . but I don't think Baresi overcame his trauma so well. I think he is still suffering.'

The most worrying thing about the shoot-out, though, has been its corrosive tactical consequences. Fifa has spent the years since the cynical excesses of the 1990 World Cup trying to make the game a more attacking and goal-oriented spectacle. Most of the key rule-changes since then (three points for a win, no tackles from behind, no handling of back passes, and so on) have been designed to encourage fast, open attacking play. But the shoot-out has the opposite effect. It encourages fearful, ugly, defensive football. Thanks to the shoot-out, it has become a standard tournament tactic for inferior teams to play for a draw with a view to winning on penalties. The shoot-out makes it theoretically possible to win a World Cup by playing four successive 0–0 draws and being good at penalties. Because being good at penalties and being good at football are different things entirely.

After the Italy game, for the first time, the Dutch public seemed to react to a penalty failure with anger and derision rather than sympathy for the players. Yet the defeat will be far harder for those players to bear. When I asked Frank de Boer about the two penalties he missed more than a month later he said, 'Sorry, it's a subject that is too painful to talk about.' Patrick Kluivert, who scored with his shoot-out kick, but, much more significantly hit the post with Holland's second penalty in normal time, was more forthcoming, but no less upset. 'It is always difficult when you talk about penalties. You win or you lose. And we lost. It's very painful, a nightmare in fact. Afterwards, life goes on, but you'll always be remembered for that match. So it's not an easy thing to forget. The quarter final against Yugoslavia – when I scored three goals – was fantastic but there was so little time to remember it, because the next match was waiting for us. It was so painful, because we had the feeling we could win the tournament for sure. We should have won. We had to win. But you also have to have a little bit of luck along the way. That's important. If my first penalty had been a centimetre or two to the right, it would have gone in . . . But it didn't. We were playing very good football – and then we lost on penalties. It's very difficult for us. Some people say we need to practise more on penalties, but that wasn't the problem. We practised many times. We practised after every training session. In fact, I think we practised too much. And everyone is different when it comes to taking penalties.'

If the Dutch are ever to win the World Cup (or another Euro) something must therefore be done. But what? There seem to be just two options, both of them radical.

The first is risky, unprecedented and highly political. It means reviving the spirit of *nederland gidsland* and acting as a moral guiding light unto the footballing nations. It means committing symbolic suicide and taking a stand for the sake of the future integrity of the world game. Here's the plan. The Dutch will solve their penalty shoot-out problems by getting penalty shoot-outs abolished.

This is how it works. Before the next World Cup, Holland will announce they are no longer willing to support the institution of penalties on the grounds that it is disfiguring the world game. Therefore, if a match in which they are involved goes to a shoot-out, they will simply not partake. Instead of shooting at goal, Dutch penalty takers will pass the ball gently to the referee. The Dutch goalkeeper will stand to one side with his arms folded. Thus, Ghandian principles of non-violence would be applied to football. The action would also echo anti-penalty protests of the Corinthian Casuals a century ago. The Dutch announcement will be timed far enough in advance for Fifa to finally come up with an alternative method of resolving drawn matches. From a Dutch point of view, almost any other method – including coin tossing, which would give them at least a fifty–fifty chance – would be preferable. Many methods have been suggested. Personally, I'd leave it to a panel of judges to declare the winner on 'points', as is done in boxing. The Corinthians, who considered penalties 'un-gentlemanly', failed of course – but then their protests were not carried live to a global television audience of billions.

Holland would be throwing away a major World Cup match – perhaps even the Final. But, since they would almost certainly lose the shoot-out anyway, they would be losing no more than they already had by failing to win the game in 90 or 120 minutes. More importantly, the Dutch would be able to simultaneously claim the moral high-ground and fatally undermine the institution of the shoot-out, which has never been fully accepted as fair by fans, players or administrators. Playing the longer game – getting rid of penalties – would leave the Dutch in a much stronger position for all future tournaments.

This approach is fraught with dangers, though. It would require nerves of steel and be painful for the players to implement. The Dutch could legitimately be accused of resorting to such a strategy only because they can't take penalties (though Van Gaal could point out that he won a World Club Championship with Ajax on penalties). Fifa are unlikely to take kindly to such a blatant public challenge and may react with disciplinary threats (although, as the Dutch action would be hard to distinguish from their penalty performance against Italy, it's hard see how the players could be accused of breaking the rules or bringing the game into disrepute).

It would be as well to have an emergency back-up plan. But if anything Holland's seems even more outlandish. Plan B requires the Dutch to get good at penalties.

Gyuri Vergouw is a high-powered, half-Hungarian Dutch management consultant who loves football and is entirely fed up with Holland's 'beautiful losing'. Vergouw normally works with corporate clients, identifying business or structural problems and coming up with creative solutions. In the jargon of his trade, he sees penalties as the 'critical success factor' of international football. He yearns to see De Oranje win the World Cup 'just once before I die', and has therefore launched a one-man campaign to solve the country's penalty crisis. He believes the Dutch can teach themselves to be better at taking and saving penalties and has published a witty and persuasive book on the subject, *Strafschop: The Quest for the Ultimate Penalty*. He reinforces his message through websites and media appearances and by lobbying coaches. 'We can probably improve by more than ten per cent,' he says. 'But I guarantee at least ten per cent. If I had been able to coach the Dutch penalty takers we would have scored four out of six penalties rather than one.' If he is right, following his advice means the difference between the certainty of losing and having a chance.

People used to accuse the great American golfer Ben Hogan of being lucky when he won. Hogan was one of sport's legendary obsessives, a perfectionist who practised constantly and even managed to rebuild his career after a car crash had left him unable to walk. Some of his greatest golf was played when he was in agony and barely able to stand on his rebuilt legs. He was famed for his ability to sink important putts when his opponents buckled under pressure. 'Yes, I'm lucky,' he used to reply. 'And the more I practise, the luckier I get.'

Vergouw begs the Dutch to take a similar approach. 'Not only do we think penalties are dishonourable and not really part of the game. We also tell ourselves you can't train on them. The players think they are the best technically. They think they are so technically skilled that they will make it.' He blames Johan Cruyff for some of this attitude. 'Cruyff never liked to take penalties in a game, though he never missed one in training. But he had Neeskens or Muhren to do it for him. And when he was playing, there were no shoot-outs, so it was not an interesting subject for him. When Cruyff says you can't train on this, everyone believes him. But he's wrong.' After the Italy game, Cruyff repeated his view that the shoot-out is a lottery. National goalkeeping coach Pim Doesburg and Edwin van der Sar (a terrific goalkeeper in normal play, but poor at stopping penalties) said the same thing. 'They all say it's a lottery. Well, I'm sorry, but that's just nonsense! And it's time to say something completely different. I've said it in every newspaper and on television and I will go on saying it. On one thing Cruyff is right: penalties are not really part of football. But that does not mean there is no craft, skill, expertise or technique involved. Cruyff knows everything about soccer, but he is not a penalty specialist. I say: Cruyff doesn't understand anything about shoot-outs and penalties and we should stop listening to him on this subject.'

For his book, Vergouw talked to goalkeepers and penalty takers, coaches and former penalty geniuses like Robbie Rensenbrink and Gerrie Muhren. He also tracked down academic research in obscure psychological and management journals. These included such studies as 'Anticipation of Professional Soccer Goalkeepers when Facing Right- and Left-Footed Penalty Kicks' by T. McMorris and S. Colenso (published in the journal *Perceptual and Motor Skills*) and 'Anticipation and Movement Strategies in Elite Soccer Goalkeepers' by A. Morris and L. Burwits. Vergouw condensed his findings into his book, launched his websites and now urges coaches to ditch their traditional attitude to spot-kicks. During Euro 2000 he personally delivered twenty-five copies of *Strafschop* to Frank Rijkaard and the Dutch players in Hoenderloo ('I don't think they read it') and was struck by the response to an appearance on the *Villa Barend and Van Dorp* television show. 'I was only repeating information that is widely available in journals and books. But the audience and the panel went quiet while I was talking. I had the odd feeling that they were hearing it all for the first time.'

Vergouw insists that long-term, scientific-based training can transform Holland's players. Modern Dutch goalkeepers can learn from and emulate Italy's Toldo or Hans van Breukelen, the Dutchman who specialised in intimidating penalty takers, could read the direction of ninety per cent of kicks and saved a penalty for Holland in the final of Euro '88. 'Training on penalties means doing it properly. It doesn't mean just taking one or two, or even two hundred penalties. It means taking penalties and looking critically at what goes right and what goes wrong. It means looking at things like the angle of the run of the penalty taker. Where does he place his standing leg? Where in the goal does he aim? How much power does he use? How does he focus?'

There are a host of variables that can be studied to improve technique: the habits of opponents (for kickers as well as goalkeepers); picking the target area (low shots are always risky while shots to the top corner are harder to perfect but impossible to stop); the distance, speed and angle of run-up (a straight run is much harder to read whereas approaching the ball at an angle gives away information); the placement of the standing leg. Studies on the velocity of the ball, the distance it travels and the reaction times of goalkeepers show that using seventy-five per cent power is sufficient to score. There is a wealth of surprising but crucial data. Right-handed keepers, for example, are better at saving shots on their left side.

Cruyff insists that penalty training is a waste of time because it can never prepare a player for the enormous stress of taking a vital penalty in a big match. If the same logic was applied to flying, pilots and astronauts would never bother to train on flight simulators. Vergouw: 'People say you can't train psychologically.

But you can improve your technique and preparation to the point where the stress is lessened. It also helps if you put stress into the training. They should tell the goalkeeper where the ball is going, for example. And when a player misses in training he has to run an extra lap around the field, or has to buy his colleagues Cokes after the game. Players are competitive; money isn't important to them but they hate doing things like that.' He says Holland's leading club teams and the national side should practise for years rather than weeks or days ahead of a big game. He suggests each player hones three different types of penalty to perfection: one in each top corner, for example, and a 'speciality'. Crucially, they should also plan ahead by deciding where to put their penalties long before the game – ideally, the night before – and not to change their minds. Last-minute improvisation and mind-changing is invariably fatal. 'If a player prepares thoroughly, then the moment he walks up to take a vital penalty he is better able to control the stress because he has taken his penalty hundreds of times and knows exactly what to do. He knows how to place the shot, where to put his standing leg and so on.'

He insists that, whatever the players say, the men at the heart of the Italy disaster – Frank de Boer, Patrick Kluivert, Jaap Stam, Paul Bosvelt and the Dutch coaching staff – cannot have practised enough, or correctly, for Euro 2000. 'The Dutch players say now they trained a lot, but I heard they trained only by taking two or three penalties each and they did it at the closed training sessions – and there were only four of those. They just watched who took their penalties and said, "That's a goal. That's not a goal. That's a goal . . ." So Paul Bosvelt scored three times in training and suddenly he was in the top five penalty takers. That's what I understand happened. They say they trained properly on it, but I really disagree. On the night, you could see very clearly they were improvising. They had not practised enough.'

Vergouw stresses that penalties are the only football subject on which he wishes to be heard. 'I just want to help the nation avoid this kind of pain again. Every time it happens, the Dutch shy away

from the problem. They tell themselves: "It's a pity. We can't do anything about it. Let's just go on." And they never change at all. It's a crazy
attitude.' He hopes that with Van Gaal things will change. 'I'd like to
think Louis van Gaal will read my book and be open to suggestions. I
hope to discuss it with him and I've written to him telling him that
more information is available. If he doesn't respond then I'll just go on
fighting. I have the Internet. I have publicity. It seems I am the only
one speaking out about the subject. I have no attachment to Cruyff,
Rijkaard or Van Gaal so I can say what I like. I am not afraid to upset
anyone. Frankly, I don't give a damn because this is what I believe in.'

Gyuri Vergouw is the Cassandra of Dutch football. Cassandra, you
will recall, was one of the most tragic figures of Greek myth: simultaneously blessed with the gift of prophecy and cursed with never
being believed. Cassandra foresaw but was powerless to prevent the
sack of her city, Troy, the killing of Agamemnon, and her own rape
and murder. Vergouw wrote his book long before Euro 2000 and in
it he predicted hat Holland would reach the semi-final and then lose
on penalties. Frank de Boer was top of his list of Dutch players who
'absolutely must not take a penalty.' De Boer was 'a hopeless case, a
dreamer, one of hose people who, in the middle of something, suddenly notices little birds flying in the sky. He wants to do things extra
beautifully. When the ball is on the penalty spot, you need a simple
man who doesn't think so much." Vergouw reckons the only surprising thing about the three penalties De Boer took during Euro
2000 was than one of them actually went in. 'Everyone said the
penalty against the Czechs [in the last minute of Holland's first
match] was great because he scored. But it was a poor penalty
because everything about his run and body language and shot made
it obvious where the ball was going. The goalkeeper should have
saved it. De Boer didn't practise enough, or not in the right way. His
football technique is great, but his penalty technique is not.' On his
website, Vergouw rated the Dutch penalties against Italy on a scale of
nought to ten. De Boer's first penalty (in the first half) scored a five.
Patrick Kluivert's shot against the post was five and a half ('that can

happen, but why wasn't anyone following up?'). The penalty with which Kluivert's scored in the shout-out was a six ('too low but nice and hard'). De Boer's catastrophic penalty in the shoot-out was a zero ('a hopeless, terrible penalty; everything was wrong; a disgrace at any level of football'). He explains: 'The optimum angle of run-up for a penalty is not from right or left, which gives the goalkeeper clues about where the ball is going, but straight and from about five metres. This is long enough to generate speed into he ball but not so long that you waster your energy with he run. De Boer took much too short a run-up so there was not speed at all. At that moment you knew the goalkeeper had twenty-five per cent more chance of saving it. Then look at the angle of his run. His run-up and his body language showed where the ball would go. Another twenty per cent in Toldo's favour. Then look at the placement. He put the ball in a very comfortable position for the goalkeeper to make a save. Another twenty-five per cent for Toldo. So De Boer gives the goalkeeper seventy per cent more chance of saving than if he had delivered a well-practised, well-thought-out penalty.'

Vergouw not only predicted Holland's penalty defeat. He also anticipated the subsequent excuses, explanations and rationalisations. He even listed them all on page 68 of his book: 'It's a lottery . . . It has nothing to do with football . . . You've got to be lucky . . . We didn't train on it . . . In training they all went in . . . We expected to win in normal time . . . But that lad was sure to score . . . Who could have thought it would still be a draw after 120 minutes? . . . We still came second and for our little country that's still very nice.' As he goes through the list sadly on the sunny terrace of the Café Wildschut, he suddenly becomes angry: 'I never ever want to hear this crap ever again!' he says. 'Not from a fan, from a player or from a coach, or from anyone! Never!'

It may take a while. As we talked, a waiter – a keen amateur footballer – notice Gyuri's book and asked about it. Gyuri explained his theories passionately and persuasively. 'That's really interesting,' said the writer. 'But of course, when it comes to penalties, you can't train on them."

28: the calvinist carnival

"...Oh Orange
Thou ripe and juicy Orange
Thou sweet and luscious Orange..."

Johann Wolfgang von Goethe

I thought I'd made a decent effort to join in. I was wearing an orange T-shirt and a baseball cap with the word 'Holland' printed in black on the peak. But as soon as I took my seat among the massed Dutch fans for the group game against Denmark in Rotterdam, I realised I was embarrassingly, pathetically under-dressed. As with every other Netherlands match in Euro 2000, the entire Dutch nation seemed to have put on fancy dress. Packed together in the stands, the local fans transformed the curved bowl of De Kuip into a bay of glowing orange. *The Observer* noted 'the almost Van Goghian beauty of the massed shirts of the Dutch fans, stippled and shimmering beyond the pitch.' Up close, though, the word 'stippled' barely begins to convey the spectacle.

A middle aged couple had turned up in full evening dress: impeccably tailored tie and tails for him, elegant ball gown and feather boa for her, and all of it in luminous Day-Glo orange. Lots of men in orange lion suits. Blonde girls with fetching overbites wearing orange jumpsuits and a variety of elegant, inflatable, plastic orange headwear (footballs, windmills, crowns). Ridiculously tall Dutchmen with big beards (dyed orange) came dressed as traditional peasant girls complete with orange pigtails and painted-on freckles (guess what colour). In the seat in front of me was a man wearing an orange boiler suit. His face was painted orange, and on his head he wore a dreadlock wig, each strand woven from packets of orange condoms.

Holland's footballers ultimately failed on the pitch in Euro 2000. But if there were prizes for spectators, the host nation would have won the tournament at a canter. Not since the confetti-hurling Argentinians of the World Cup of 1978 has a football tournament's home fans made such an impression on the watching worldwide TV audience. But where the Argentinians got themselves noticed by the sheer scary intensity of their fanatical devotion, the party-loving Oranje Legioen, with their *toeters* (the oompah band which follows the team and leads the singing) inspired universal affection through the exuberance of their orange carnival.

And it wasn't just fans with tickets who entered into the spirit. The whole country went (to mix a suitably fruity metaphor) orange bananas. Fountains in the centre of Rotterdam spurted orange water. Orange mechanics' overalls became high fashion items. Pets, including dogs, cats, hamsters and parakeets were coloured orange. One farmer dyed his whole herd of dairy cows. Dutch TV carried pictures of a wedding where the bride wore an orange dress and the groom had orange hair. Near the Dutch team's training camp at Hoenderloo, the local townspeople were even sillier. In the style of Clint Eastwood in *High Plains Drifter*, where he paints the entire town red and renames it Hell, so Hoenderloo's residents daubed all their homes with orange paint, festooned their gardens with orange bunting and balloons, bought orange garden gnomes and renamed their village 'Oranjeloo'.

During Holland's matches, the streets emptied as the nation watched on TV. The atmosphere in pubs, bars and town squares was much the same as in the stadiums. I saw Holland beat France 3-2 in a heaving pub near the Leidseplein with my friend Neil, a Brit who's lived in Amsterdam for four years. Beside us stood beautiful dark-haired twin sisters, students who claimed never to have watched football before, yet knew everything about the team, its tactics and philosophy. Across the street, as the goals rattled in, a man evidently related to Ugly Naked Man from the TV show *Friends* stripped to his patriotic underwear and pranced in the window. After the game, a joyous street party erupted in the square. French fans in blue, passing tourists of all colours nationalities and allegiances were swept up in the celebration and made to feel welcome and wholly included. These were the days, you'll recall, when, elsewhere in the low countries, belligerent all-male groups of English fans were seen on TV squaring up to riot police, singing 'No Surrender to the IRA' and insulting foreigners. The Dutch fans celebrated as sweetly and joyfully as their team played pretty football. As the party throbbed and swirled around us, beaming, bemused Neil seemed ecstatic. "Brilliant!.. just brilliant!" he kept saying. His eyes shone. He marvelled at the lack of hidden malice. But at one point something in the delirious, gentle happiness around us reminded him of its total absence in relation to the English national team. He turned to me with anguish in his heart and sadness in his soul to ask 'Why can't we ever be like this in England?'

Why indeed. Can English fans learn to throw a football party like the Dutch? Probably not. The Orange Carnival – a relatively recent phenomenon, historically speaking – seems to spring from deeply and specifically Dutch sources. For it is not only in relation to football that Holland dyes and tries to go to heaven. Almost any excuse will do.

Each year on April 30, the country celebrates Queen's Day, a curious festival marked by selling things on the street and drinking to excess. Again, everyone puts on orange clothes (often the national football shirt). Queen's Day is the only day in the year people are permitted to sell things in the street without a license. The fact that the junk from one's neighbour's attic suddenly becomes available at a very reasonable price causes great excitement. For a couple of guilders you can pick up a rusty wok, old records by crooner Andre Hazes or a video recorder from the early eighties which almost works. Meanwhile, hundreds of thousands of orange-clad revellers descend on the centre of Amsterdam to party on the canals and get festive on an epic scale in the narrow streets. Queen's Day is increasingly marketed as one of the country's top tourist attractions and, from all the hype, I imagined it to be a tradition going back centuries at least and possibly even pre-dating

the pyramids. In fact, the festival is an invented tradition. It was
inaugurated by Queen Juliana in 1948 but was initially a stiff and
formal affair. At the royal palace there were modest military parades
and, elsewhere, until the seventies, children would be lined up in
town squares to sing the praises of the monarch. Only in the last
20 years or so, in the wake of the social and cultural revolution of
the sixties, did Queen's Day acquire its present character.

Perhaps the key word in all this is 'orange'. With the possible exception of the Irish green, no nation is now so identified with a single
colour as the Dutch. The colour orange is, of course, the symbol of
the Dutch royal family, deriving from the town of Orange in
Provence, a possession acquired by the (originally German) royal
house of Nassau. But where the symbol has been around for centuries, the phenomenon of the whole country painting itself orange
is very recent. The colour was in evidence during the great celebrations which marked the country's liberation from Nazi occupation
in 1945, but not on remotely the same scale as today's impromptu
orange festivals. The current extraordinary, excessive Dutch use of
orange surely carries some separate potent charge of its own. What,
as old semioticians would say, does all this orange signify?

It must mean something. 'Colour is a means of exerting a direct
influence on the soul' said the painter Wassily Kandinsky, who
claimed to be able to hear colours as well as see them. 'Colour is a
keyboard, the eyes, the hammers and the soul is the piano with
many strings,' he declared. 'The artist is the hand which plays,
touching one key or another purposively to cause vibrations in the
soul'. Orange, said Kandinsky, 'is like a man, convinced of his own
powers. Its note is that of the Angelus, or of an old violin.'

Two hundred years before Ruud Gullit, one of the greatest stars of
Oranje, as the national team is known, coined the phrase 'sexy football', orange inspired Goethe to write an erotic poem: 'Seest thou
yon smiling Orange? / Upon the tree still hangs it; / Already
March hath vanish'd, / And new-born flow'rs are shooting. / I

draw nigh to the tree then, / And there I say: Oh Orange, / Thou ripe and juicy Orange, / Thou sweet and luscious Orange, / I shake the tree, I shake it, / Oh fall into my lap!'

'Lying between celestial gold and cthonian red, the primary symbolism of [orange] is that of the point of balance between the spirit and the libido', explains the *Penguin Dictionary of Symbols*. 'Acccording to traditions going back to worship of the Earth Mother, this balance was sought in the ritualistic orgy, regarded as bringing with it initiatory sublimation and revelation.' Dionysos, the Greek god of wine, madness and theatre, was said to dress in orange. So too did the followers of Baghwan Shree Rajneesh, a guru best known for his teachings on sex and spirituality. Vietnamese brides traditionally wear orange as a sign of fertility. Orange is the colour of robes worn by Buddhist monks, of Masai warriors, of the Australian desert and aboriginal paintings.

But what on earth is it doing in such vivid abundance in a cold flat land beside the North Sea?

I turned for guidance to Ann Lloyd, a colour consultant in London, who advises individual and corporate clients. Lloyd cheerfully admits to knowing little about Dutch footballers or their fans. ('I've heard they're quite good, aren't they?') Yet, when I ask her about their colour, she describes things that only someone with intimate knowledge of *het nederlands voetbal* could know. Colours, she says, have identifiable psychological and spiritual characteristics which are related to their physical properties. Red, for example, has the longest wavelength and is the colour of primal urges. At the other end of the spectrum, violet, which has a short, rapid wavelength, is the most 'spiritual' of colours. Orange, in this scheme of things, is the colour of 'consciousness in the physical,' the first stage of human awareness. Where red represents unthinking blind instinct, orange is more social and elevated. In relation, say, to hunting, red is merely about killing and eating. But add a little orange and you get the idea that hunting is better when it's done by people as a group. With sex, red is merely for procreation. But with orange comes the idea of sex for pleasure and feeling. Hence Ruud Gullit's sexy football? 'Well, orange is a very sexual, sensuous colour. It likes to express itself through its body. But if it's an unhappy orange, it will be rather sleazy. One night stands and that sort of thing.'

Lloyd says orange is 'a very creative colour, the colour of artisan creativity. There's a dextrousness with the hands and feet, a very physical statement.' It is also a colour of insight. 'Like Buddhism, it goes deep within to find the "being" reason for things. It doesn't think about things philosophically; it just knows. Orange's base is in the belly, so it's about gut feelings, deciding from emotions, a gut knowing, and trusting that.' Moreover it is 'the colour of bliss, of true ecstasy. It's about the sheer joy of being, very fun-loving, humorous, playful, party-going, sometimes endless party-going. When orange feels good about itself, its qualities make them sociable, friendly and gregarious. They like doing things communally. I would think orange players are more likely to pass the ball than play as individuals. They'll enjoy taking risks, being spontaneous and revelling in their sense of adventure.'

But Lloyd warns that things can go wrong when orange is not 'centred'. Much of the drama of orange turns on the tension between the individual and the group. Thus the Orange Carnival has a dark side, as when Holland plays Germany. Queen's Day has also been known to turn nasty. In 2001, riots involving tear gas and much damage erupted near Amsterdam's Central Station after the sheer weight of numbers persuaded panicked railway officials to stop running trains. Lloyd explains: 'Orange is very into groups. If it's an unhappy, un-centred orange, they'll want to escape from themselves, into drugs, perhaps, or parties or team jollity. Dependency and co-dependency issues come up a lot. Phobias and obsessions can also arise, both of which are dependencies on things or people outside their own selves. In extremis, this could be a tendency towards fascism also. Orange can be manic depressive, either utterly happy with themselves or catastrophically down and depressed. If they're depressed, it's because they feel unworthy and unhappy in themselves. They get stuck and can't see a way out, can't see how to make changes. There's fear too: fear about survival, about not making it.'

A lot of baffling things about Dutch football — the amazing technique and passing; the weird patterns of self-destruction — suddenly make more sense. As we noted earlier, Uri Geller, the paranormalist and football fan, senses a lack of real spirit among Dutch fans. 'The Dutch supporters make a lot of noise, but there is something dead in them.'

This was apparent in Rotterdam in the game against Denmark. Despite their terrific costumes, the Dutch fans were, to my English eyes, oddly passive. Before the game and for the first hour, as Bergkamp, Kluivert and Co. struggled to break the determined Danish defence, it was the relatively tiny group of Danish fans in the stadium who were making almost all the noise. Apart from a smattering of Father Christmases, the Danish outfits were relatively unimaginative. But with their mass swaying, relentless singing and chanting they generated an emotional energy which completely eclipsed the orange hordes. Only when the Dutch scored the first of three quick goals did the balance shift.

Cultural commentator Paul Scheffer, one of Holland's most stimulating writers on questions of national identity, suggests this may be because most of the Dutch spectators are not really fans in the sense that we in Britain understand the concept: 'There's a rather placid atmosphere around the game for many. Bill Shankly said football was more important than life and death. Here football is a matter of beer and laughing.'

When Scheffer went to the World Cups in Italy in 1990 and France in 1998 he formed the impression that many of the army of Dutch fans simply weren't too bothered about the football. 'You might think it's strange to go all that way and not care about the game, but the truth is that in the stadiums they sometimes hardly watched the match. They were busy drinking and singing and showing their costumes and having their carnival. In fact, when you ask the people in the most outrageous orange costumes if they go to league games in Holland, they say: "no, never!". It's just a big party for them. They combine the World Cup with a holiday, take the whole family. They enjoy it, but it has more to do with the surroundings than with the game itself. It's just an occasion to have a nice collective experience.'

Of course, there are also plenty in Holland who care passionately about the game, people who, for example, cannot bear to watch images of Holland's Euro 2000 failure against Italy. Scheffer is one of these. But, he says, such people are simply not in a majority, especially when it comes to the national team. 'Football is so important these days that a lot of people want to be associated with it. But in the really passionate football countries like England, Italy and Germany, you see how fans get behind their team. You have hopeful singing – "come on England" and that sort of thing. But here, if the Dutch team is 0-1 down, total silence. Even when they're 1-0 up sometimes it's quiet. I think people who really love football would never come up with the idea of dressing up the way we do. You don't see this kind of carnival in Italy because Italians are much too nervous about the game to dress up in silly costumes. It takes a lot of energy to dress up like that. No. The Italians will put on a shirt, or carry a flag or a scarf, but not more until the game is won. Then maybe you can have a carnival. But when the Dutch do it, I'm sure it's for the occasion, not the game.'

Gawi Keijser, a South Africa-born writer who lives in Holland, argues the Orange Carnival nevertheless has some very positive effects. 'There is something magical about sport. Even in America, a sporting arena is where, even if only for a short time, all social and economic differences are put aside, even if it's only for the duration of the game.' He compares the 'oranging' of the Netherlands to the healing, multicultural 'Rainbow Nation' idea which, relatively briefly, swept Mandela's post-apartheid South Africa during and after the country's 1995 Rugby World Cup triumph. 'Euro 2000 was like that for the Dutch. The Netherlands is going though a big identity crisis, partly because it is becoming a multicultural society and also because of the EU. But Euro 2000 was one of the few moments when one can talk of national identity. In Euro 2000 the orange was everywhere. It hurt your eyes to look at it. It was a symbol of national identity, an abstract symbol for unifying people.'

But he agrees with Scheffer's diagnosis of lack of passion. 'Supporters here are much more docile than in England. The Dutch aren't passionate. In Euro 2000, they had their nice orange costumes. They sang their songs, but when Holland loses it's not a national crisis. Losing to Italy was forgotten the next day. When South Africa loses in any sport, the nation is in shock for weeks. In England, people are much more passionate about football than people are here. You have a tradition of boys going to matches with their fathers, of caring passionately about their clubs. We don't have that in the same way.'

So just why do the Dutch need their Orange Carnival?

The noted historian and expert of Dutch medieval literature Professor Herman Pleij of the University of Amsterdam, argues that it fills a deep emotional and cultural need which has nothing to do with football. 'The Dutch are very self-centred,' he says. 'They live in their house and their house is their castle. It is a very difficult, complicated thing to be allowed to enter the home of a Dutch family. People from other countries often complain about this. We need this orange to compensate. We need to be able to come together, to feel together because we are also human. We need this kind of statement, this ritual statement of being members of the same family. And that's what we do with orange in sport and other festivals. It's an excuse for a party, for dressing up, for wearing funny clothes.'

In the affluent, secularised, post-Calvinist, apres-60s Dutch cultural landscape the old ideologies have died and older traditions and rituals have been discarded. 'In the Netherlands, every group in society – the Catholics, the Protestants, the socialists, and so on – all used to have their own rituals. But this all disappeared in the 60s and 70s. There are no rituals left. But a society needs rituals to express feelings. There is a general lack in the Netherlands of feelings of togetherness. So we compensate for this with sport.'

In Amsterdam it became popular to refer to the Ajax stars as *goden-*

zonen (sons of God). Only a generation or two ago, such talk would probably have been considered blasphemous by most in the Netherlands. And this adoration of sportsmen is all the more strange in a country where almost no other kind of hero worship is considered acceptable. But times have changed. 'We laugh at traditions in the Netherlands, and we do not look very much to the past,' says Pleij. 'In fact, we laugh at heroes, so we have no national heroes. Sports heroes are the only heroes we are prepared to like because we think of them as normal boys and girls from next door. We like them to be simple. We pat them on the back, we praise them. But their careers are very short and, when they come back, they seem just like us. These are our only heroes and we worship them in a very exaggerated way. It is a compensation for the lack of these kind of rituals elsewhere in our lives.'

Although orange is notionally a royal symbol and Queen Beatrix is strikingly popular compared to her British counterpart, Pleij points out that current 'orangism' has little to do with the House of Orange. 'It's certainly not a worshipping of the royal house. We use the Queen and the royal family for something far more important.' Festive orangism, which started slowly in the seventies and eighties with football and seems to grow in intensity each year has spread to other sports and has simply re-attached itself to royalty. 'Queen's Day is not a monarchist feast, not about loving the queen. We use the monarchy as an excuse. The orange carnival allows us to behave as if we are one big family, shouting, having fun, feeling that we share many things. There is a growing need to express these feelings of togetherness.'

Meanwhile, Paul Scheffer is amused and slightly baffled that the Dutch have managed to convince the world – and themselves – that they are a perpetually fun-loving, tolerant people with a Mediterranean carnival sensibility. 'It's like the rather astonishing way Amsterdam is called the Venice of the North. Perhaps we are the Venice of the North, but we are certainly not the Brazilians of the North, although many people seem to think that we are, because we indulge in carnavalesque behavior once in a while.' Contrary to popular myth, he insists Holland actually has a 'rather boring, Swiss kind of society' as well as a prodigiously efficient work-force. 'Of course we are not completely Swiss or Swedish. But we do have rather disciplined and organised aspects.' He also challenges the popular image of Holland as a uniquely tolerant and relaxed society. 'I find that people much prefer to stick to looking at the surface. The image and message we convey to the outside world is that we are com-pletely easy-going. When people think of Amsterdam, they think of our downtrodden "coffee shops" where you can buy many things but not coffee. They think we are very tolerant and multicultural. But Dutch tol-erance was developed in order to keep the peace, to avoid trouble. It has never been a laissez-faire tolerance. The Netherlands I know is a rather disciplined, conformist, society where everything tends towards the cen-tre. Our tolerance is always in the context of something highly organ-ised and on the theme of conflict avoidance. Tolerance is always in the name of consensus-building. Dutch culture is about being separate from each other. We created cultural difference and separation where physical separation was not available. We should not confuse this tradition with the image of a free-floating, carnivalesque, open-minded society. Of course, the image is part of the reality too. But it's only a small part.'

Meanwhile, the very extremity of the Orange Carnival reveals that it is more likely to be a way for the Dutch to let off steam than be evidence of an essentially freewheeling, fun-loving lifestyle. 'We live a rather orderly, nine to five life. Why are our roads completely full of cars between 7.30 and 9am and between 4.30 and 6pm? Perhaps the carnival is an escape from our society rather than a symbol of it. Isn't carnival always like that? In Catholic countries, everything is very proper and serious, but for two days of carnival, everything explodes…and then things go back to how it was before. In Holland, we have our Calvinist Carnival. And it is more of an interruption of the flow of daily life than a continuous flowing thing which has deep roots in the way we live. The truth is that many aspects of Dutch life are more grey than orange.'

-14: Body Snatchers

Watching Holland's football team over the last few years has been a bit like seeing a loved one slowly succumbing to Alzheimer's. The body remains strong but the personality is cruelly altered. Memory fails, former beauty is ravaged. Heartbreakingly brief lucid moments are followed by long periods of rambling incoherence, anger and – most chilling of all – simple blankness. We pray for recovery but know deep inside that the long-term prognosis is unlikely to be good. Actually, there's too much running around for the problem to be Alzheimer's. It's more like *Invasion of the Body Snatchers*. Outwardly, everything appears normal, but something unimaginably sinister has happened. It's not so much a change of personality, more like they've all been… taken over. (*"My wife – she not my wife!"*) You think I'm crazy? Gunter Netzer has noticed it too. To explain: The famous shirts are the same shade of orange. Jolly-looking Dutch fans still flock to games in silly costumes. It's only when the team starts to play that it hits you. Instead of the old, familiar, enchanting, stylish, clever football, the Dutch now play ugly, inept, boring football. Instead of beautiful losing, they care only about the result. It's alien. You feel like screaming: "They're all pods, all of them!"

"You're right. It's horrible," says sports-writer turned political columnist Bert Wagendorp. "Holland are not Holland any more. I can hardly remember the last time they played well. Maybe the 6-0 against Scotland. That was four years ago. Before then, you have to go back to Euro 2000. OK, we lost to Italy but it was still football. Now all the coaches and players talk about is discipline and winning and we struggle against teams like Luxembourg and Albania. Away to Albania! Oh, what a horrible game! No combinations, no imagination, and a lucky win with a goal in injury time. I thought to myself: two more games like this and I will stop watching football." The verdict of Netzer, a great admirer of the old brilliant orange style, is calmer but no less damning: "The Dutch School of Johan Cruyff was the best I've ever seen in football. Always dominating, always based on their own strength and never adapting to the opponent. You can do that only if you have the best players. I really love the Dutch football culture, but it's gone. The old style has been replaced by this new realism and you can only hope that the Dutch will have some success with it. But the beauty has faded. I only see a team with very good players, but very result-oriented. I compare them with Bayern Munich of some years back. Good results, but the fans thought they were boring. And if you play great football, people will forgive failure. If you play boring people won't."

The era of Dennis Bergkamp and the De Boers suddenly seems as irrecoverable as that of Rembrandt and Hals. Stripped by the richer European clubs, the Eredivisie is something of a Mickey Mouse League. The nickname of *bondscoach* Marco van Basten – 'San Marco' – is now used only with heavy irony. He has many angry critics and few defenders in the press. Meanwhile, the big clubs in Holland are as weak as anyone can remember. Ajax, birthplace, heart and soul of the Dutch style, lies eviscerated by bad management and unwise coaching. Having fallen to the second or third rank, they are humiliated in Europe by the likes of FC Copenhagen and Slavia Prague. Departing coach Henk ten Cate recently delivered a damning verdict on the club. Ajax, he said, "still think it's 1995. But times have changed. The goals haven't, and that is not realistic. It's hard to attract top players to Amsterdam, and the youth development of Ajax isn't the best in the country anymore." Feyenoord may be less dire than they were a couple of years back. But PSV openly embrace "results football" and their unsentimental coach Ronald Koeman approaches big Champions League matches with the tactics and spirit of Otto Rehhagel's Greece. With the exception of Louis van Gaal at little AZ, no one seems much interested in playing with style and adventure any more. On TV, commentators even sneer across the North Sea at Arsene Wenger's dazzling Arsenal version of Total Football. "Yeah it's nice to watch," said Wim Kieft ". . . but it's not efficient enough."

The harsher, less lovable new spirit in football seems to fit quite well with the harsher, less lovable new spirit in the Netherlands. Nevertheless, great cultures don't die overnight, and a furious battle now rages over the soul of the Dutch game, and thereby the nation. Notionally, the dispute centres on tactics. Should the national team stick with wingers and 4-3-3 or adopt mainstream European practice and switch to a more defensive 4-4-2? But the argument is almost theological in nature

The key figure, inevitably, is Johan Cruyff. Critics say he talks like an ayatollah; supporters claim he is defending a metaphysical truth. Either way, his role in the Netherlands is unique: he is simultaneously guru and godfather, provocateur and prophet, defender of the faith. In April 2007, he turned 60. He devotes most of his time now to his charitable foundations. But while he has no formal post in football, he wields influence behind the scenes. He advised the group around Joan Laporta that took control of Barcelona in 2003 – and persuaded them to hire Frank Rijkaard as coach. Cruyff also advised the KNVB to pick Van Basten as *bondscoach* and has influenced appointments at Ajax, most notably getting his old pal Piet Keizer a job as technical advisor. Cruyff also speaks to the nation regularly through his newspaper column and appearances as a TV match pundit. From these pulpits he denounces the drift in Dutch football and urges a return to the principles of the seventies. He also makes odd attacks on individuals, such as a recent claim that Real Madrid's prolific goalscorer Van Nistelrooy is a "weak player." What is new is that for the first time Cruyff is ridiculed. He faces contempt from people who were once among his greatest admirers.

Van Basten arrived in office in 2004 promising to play traditional Dutch attacking football. But he soon fell out with Van

Nistelrooy, banished the powerful Mark van Bommel and, until recently, froze out the rejuvenated, newly-mature Clarence Seedorf. Seedorf is terrific and central for AC Milan, but on the rare occasions he is permitted to play for Holland, Van Basten orders him to hug the touchline. That's like having Von Karajan to conduct your orchestra and asking him to play the banjo. Holland has talent in midfield and attack: when fit, Robin van Persie, Wesley Sneijder, Rafael van der Vaart and Arjen Robben are a tasty quartet. But the defence is weak and, crucially, there's no one like Krol, Koeman or De Boer any more to launch attacks from the back. That Van Basten's only previous coaching experience was with the Ajax youth team didn't bother anyone at first. He seemed a breath of fresh air after the much-maligned Dick Advocaat. Van Basten's replacement of nineties stars with energetic unknowns like Landzaat and Kuyt was greeted with wild acclaim. Qualification for the 2006 World Cup went swimmingly and a book published before the tournament captured the public mood: *Marco Alles Kan* (Marco Can Do Everything).

But Holland's poor showing in Germany changed many minds. No one expected to see a Dutch team having trouble passing the ball, or spending so much of a game against Ivory Coast frantically defending a one goal lead. Indeed, at the World Cup, the teams that looked most like old Holland were Germany, Argentina and France. Roughed up and knocked out by Portugal, the guys in orange looked naïve and out of their depth. Van Basten claimed he was building for Euro 2008, but the qualification process for that tournament also proved distressing. Van Basten scrambled most of the results he needed, but failed to create a coherent team. Most controversially, he stuck to Cruyff's belief – now hardened into dogma – that Holland must play with old-fashioned wingers. This has been a problem for two reasons. First, apart from Robben, Holland doesn't have good wingers any more (non-specialists like Van Persie or Van der Vaart are used wide). Second, the system is widely regarded as obsolete.

In summer 2007 the issue exploded into a public scrap between Cruyff and Foppe de Haan, coach of the national under-21 team.

Just before the European youth championship, Foppe announced he was ditching wingers and switching to 4-4-2 because 4-3-3 was "old-fashioned and hard to play". Furious, Cruyff accused him of jeopardising Holland's national heritage: "These kind of remarks can damage Dutch football. Because people might doubt our heritage. Our way of playing football, with which we aim to differentiate ourselves from the rest. This way of playing has been damaged through the years by coaches and youth development trainers. If you don't teach kids to play this in the right way, how can you expect them to play it right?" According to Cruyff 4-4-2 lacked sophistication and was "a lazy way of playing." "Let's put it this way," he said. "4-4-2 is a great system for mediocre players. . . . A lot of bodies at the back to stop the opponent from penetrating, strong muscle men in midfield and two fast and opportunistic strikers up front. A bit like [Mourinho's] Chelsea. And PSV Eindhoven. Successful teams, for sure, but not the teams that will be remembered for their great play."

In typical Cruyff style (but only for a few lines) he then got highly technical: "The big difference between 4-4-2 and 4-3-3 is the variety between the 3 lines (defense, midfield, offense). If you play 4-4-2 you have the back four and the four in the middle. And two strikers. In total, three lines. With 4-3-3 and if it is well executed, you can create extra lines every 5 to 6 meters. But, you need to know how. The central defender can come up and join the middle midfielder. That's an extra line right in front of the three remaining defenders. The wide playing midfielders can move forward a bit. So you create an extra line. If the central striker steps back a bit in to midfield, like I used to do, you have a fortified line with three players and two strikers/wingers up front that can use the free space the central striker left open. And that's just one combination of many! But, to do this, you need a coach who has the ability and the guts to implement it."

In response, Foppe agreed that young players should play 4-3-3 to learn the game. Otherwise, he stuck to his guns, adding, "learning and getting results are different things." Having thus pointedly

ignored Cruyff's advice, Foppe proceeded to win the youth tournament for the second year running, and most of the press took his
side. Since then, even Louis van Gaal's AZ – the last of the hold-
outs – has gone over to 4-4-2. Demands for Van Basten to follow
suit in the flagship national team have become cacophonous.

"Everybody in Holland is now convinced the 4-3-3 system as
advocated by Cruyff cannot be played anymore," says Henk Spaan
columnist in *Het Parool* and editor of *Hard Gras*. "The game is
so physical now and the midfield is so overcrowded you cannot
play with wingers in front of the ball. In the seventies, a midfield
player ran between four and four and a half kilometres per match.
Now it is between ten and 12 kilometres per match. And winger
in front of the ball runs only four or five kilometres. So any team
using old-fashioned wingers loses about 10 kilometres running in
their game. Cruyff and Van Basten are the only two people now
who advocate this system. Everyone else watching international
developments knows it is impossible. And we do not have the
coaches to do it anymore. Only Louis van Gaal is able to have his
teams play in this way. But not Van Basten or ten Cate. They are
not up to this task." Are the old ideals dead? "Yes. It is more concrete now. People say winning is more important than the beauty
of the game."

Spaan insists Cruyff's credibility is shot: "Johan Cruyff used to
be an *eminence grise*. Now he's like the angry old men on the
Muppet Show. Really he doesn't have a clue, though he used to. He
has become a bad influence on Dutch football. Cruyff is unhappy
with everything and everything he says and does has a hidden
agenda. I don't take him seriously anymore. Everyone used to
respect him. They even respected his lack of verbal intelligence. But
people don't respect him now. He is always meddling and never
takes responsibility. He has 'advisorships' everywhere, but no official relationship with Ajax, the KNVB or Barcelona. It's never official because he hates responsibility. It's all politics with Cruyff and
it overshadows his football wisdom. When Ronaldinho went to
Barcelona Cruyff intrigued against him. He speaks against Van

Nistelrooy to support Van Basten. When he described Van Nistelrooy as a weak player, the public thought: 'is Cruyff still up to it?'"

The verdict of Simon Kuper is even harsher. "When people retire in any profession they stop thinking – and Cruyff stopped coaching and thinking innovatively in 1996. He's a control freak. Everything he says has to be right, and has to be proved to be right all the time. It's like Islam: no development is possible. Cruyff says: 'You must play dominant football ... play your own game and don't adjust to your opponent. . . . Never adjust.' But that's not a rule of football. That's just his personality. He has become rigid and dogmatic, as if Dutch football has to be a tribute band to the seventies and observe every single oddity of the seventies style. In the seventies, Cruyff was young and revolutionary and sexy. But all revolutionaries get old and reactionary eventually. In ageing hippy terms what he's doing now is like refusing to accept that 1968 is over."

Kuper insists effective football is not only a matter of technique and tactics; it also depends on physical strength. "If you field a bunch of dwarves in midfield you'll never have the ball." Cruyff also misreads his own past, Kuper claims. "1974 is now seen as almost purely spiritual. But Krol, Neeskens, Suurbier and the rest were tough guys. At Euro 2000, Rijkaard was a realist and Stam, Davids, Cocu and Kluivert were chunky boys too. They could look after themselves. But look at the players now: Van der Vaart . . . Robben . . . Sneijder! Van Persie is the only one with a body." Aligning himself with Guus Hiddink and Foppe, he says nice football is perfectly possible without 4-3-3. "4-4-2 cannot be as stupid as Cruyff says it is. Holland won in 1988 with 4-4-2. In any case, players' capacity to move between lines means formations are increasingly fluid and less relevant than they were. It is sensible to make adjustments. Even Louis van Gaal has abandoned 4-3-3. Cruyff can sit in his living room announcing 'truths'. But Van Gaal has to work in the real world." Why, Kuper asks, do Ajax now fare worse in Europe than PSV, or even Groningen, Twente and AZ? "The answer must have something to do with 4-3-3. Ajax is also a tribute band, a ridiculous attempt to recreate 1973. They would do much better if they accepted they are a mid-ranking European team, and adopted tactics and expectations accordingly. If they want to win matches at home, yes, they can also play 4-4-2 and be defensive. But any Ajax coach who did that would be slaughtered by *Voetbal International*, the *Telegraaf* and Cruyff."

Kuper admires Koeman and sees a 'PSV-adjusted' future. "AZ are the tinpot heroes. They reached the semifinal of the UEFA Cup and they nearly won the Dutch league. It's very sweet. But the only Dutch team that does anything is actually PSV. Some see Koeman as betrayer of old values. I think there's a clarity and honesty to what he does. He plays in a Dutch way, but modified by reality. There's no shame in using defensive tactics to beat Arsenal [in the Champions League]. To win against them was a real triumph. In any case, the Hiddinkites are now winning the argument."

Making the case for the defence – or rather, the attack – is one of Cruyff's oldest media friends, Frits Barend. "Johan Cruyff still thinks and talks very well about soccer," he insists. "Of course there are more physical abilities but the game didn't change so much. It is still 11 players and one ball. Sometimes I watch matches on television with him, and it's incredible how much he sees. A player plays the ball to the right, and he'll say: 'He should have played it to the left' because he sees the whole field even when you can't see it on the screen. Then the camera moves and you see there was in fact a player on the left totally free who didn't get the ball."

He rejects the suggestion that Cruyff is a manipulative, vengeful control freak. "He's not like that. Not at all! He's happy with his grandchildren, and when people ask him something he gives his opinions like everyone else gives opinions. They're just opinions. He doesn't choose the players. He doesn't manipulate and control people. It's true that he and Van Basten think a lot the same, and I think it's a pity. Van Basten needs someone like Tonny Bruins Slot who'll give him a different view. But that's Van Basten's problem, not Cruyff's problem. Actually, I thought it was a little strange what

Cruyff said about Van Nistelrooy, but then he likes to provoke a little bit. And why is he not allowed to give his opinion?"

One of Holland's most talented and philosophical sports writers, Arthur van den Boogaard, defends the old master with passion. "The problems we have are not because Cruyff is or is not like a muppet but because there are not enough good players in Holland. Cruyff has always had this idea of how soccer is supposed to be played, and he still has it, and it still works. It comes close to being the 'solution of soccer' almost in a metaphysical way: a vision of harmonies on the field. Cruyff just happens to know it because he is a genius. So when Cruyff says Van Nistelrooy is not a good player, he doesn't mean Van Nistelrooy is not a good player. He means only that Van Nistelrooy does not fit his ideal, perfect, metaphysical way of playing. And I agree with him about that." He likens Cruyff's comments to a grand master analysing chess. "If you see someone make a wrong move, you cannot say it is a good move, even if it wins the game. Objectively, logically, it's still a bad move. So, yes, Van Nistelrooy scores a lot of goals, but, yes, he also has his limitations. We can make a system to feed him, to let him score goals, but it would be more like an Italian or German system, and it cannot work because we don't have the players for it. In Euro 2004 Holland reached the semifinal, but played very badly. And who was the man in front? Ruud van Nistelrooy."

The only problem with Van Basten, he suggests, is that while Van Basten admires Cruyff and even resembles Cruyff, he is not Cruyff. Meanwhile, Cruyff has a problem of his own: the problem of being Cruyff. "He sees things in football that other people cannot see. He just has this gift. He can't help it. He's the genius. It's also his biggest problem. He is a genius in a team sport so he needs these other people. It's very difficult for him. Of course, Cruyff lost a lot of games also. But that is not interesting about what he says. He is still very consistent. He still follows his ideas, and he will until the end because he knows it works. It *is* the solution. It doesn't mean you always win, but it means you're always striving for perfection."

Where, then, does Dutch football go from here? Can the old

brilliance be sustained or recreated in a new form? Can the flow of great players be maintained? Or will Holland's football be globalised into mush? In other words, will the culture described elsewhere in this book live or die? The truth is that no one knows.

Henk Spaan: "Actually I'm quite optimistic. As soon as the influence of Cruyff can be banished there is a chance for a good national team. Dutch players will still be clever, technical and intuitive like Van der Vaart and Van Persie will be the new Bergkamp, only he's more of a killer than Bergkamp." While Ajax are in decline, he says, new power centres have sprung up to supply talent: AZ, Feyenoord, PSV, and the youth system Van Gaal set up for the KNVB. "It is still amazing that a player like Van Persie can break through from a small country like Holland into the world. The Dutch team needs a good coach like Hiddink or Van Gaal. Martin Jol and Foppe de Haan are also good. There's plenty of talent."

Simon Kuper: "Holland must lay the ghosts because at the moment it is ghost football. The Scots and the English reinvented themselves. The Dutch must do the same. It will have to be something different. The best elements of the old style can be retained. Holland will still have players who think, who pass in one, who aren't in love with the ball. They will never have big, clumsy defenders. But at club level no one believes you'll ever see a team like Ajax '95 again. It's impossible. And it's never going to be '74 ever again either. It's not a question of tactics but of football economy. Holland's tradition will enable them to be better than average. They will never decline to the level of Greece, Hungary or Austria. But we're not going to see the historical oddity of the last 30 years carry on either."

Frits Barend: "Is it dying? Of course not. Even when Holland and the clubs play horribly, they still play in a Dutch style: ball possession, trying to attack. And this will not change. It's in our nature. Some of our players are not quite as good as we think they are. But at the same time, we do have good players, especially in attack. Holland could even be a sleeping giant. You talk about the death of the old style, but Foppe de Haan's team also played attractive offensive football, and last week I saw PSV play with four strikers. If Holland were to beat a poor team by seven or eight goals – and it could happen – it would be back. It could be back in a single match. Just one match."

The most elegiac answer was Arthur van den Boogaard's, putting me in mind me of the Arthurian legend of the Fisher King: when the king is well, his land thrives, as he sickens the land also becomes sick: "In Holland, there is before Cruyff and after Cruyff. You see it obviously in the history of our soccer, but also in other aspects. I think we are coming to the after. Not yet. For now, it continues. But it's logical in historical terms that the power of Cruyff should become less as he gets old. It will be like the passing of the age of Rembrandt. We still love all the paintings he made, and the older we get the more we appreciate them. That's how it will be with Cruyff. Not because he is nice. He's not so nice. Or sensitive. Or well balanced. He's just this world figure. You know, there was always a tension between Cruyff's vision and normal pragmatic football. He made what he did seem so normal that others thought they could do it too. But they can't do it. So, how long will it last? For as long as Cruyff has clarity in his mind. He is 60 now. I think of him still being clear when he's 75. Then it will change. His legacy and his vision are indestructible, but they will become part of our history. Did you ever see the beautiful little haiku-like poem Xander van der Drift wrote for *Johan* magazine? [a football magazine of the late 90s and early 2000s named after Cruyff] He wrote it in 1999, and I agree with it very much. He meant Cruyff is our giant, and it will hit us one day. It goes: "Question of the 21st Century: where were you when Johan Cruyff died?"

epilogue: plonkers

Call me soccer's Nostradamus if you like. But, writing in December 2001, I feel confident in making a few bold predictions about Holland and the 2002 World Cup. Here's what's going to happen. Holland will not miss a single penalty. In fact, they will be unbeatable. None of the tournament's big teams (France, Argentina, Brazil) will even get near them. But the Dutch will not triumph. They will not entertain. The skills of Kluivert and Van Nistelrooy will leave the billion-strong worldwide TV audience cold. Dutch fans will be quiet as the grave. At the world's greatest sporting feast, there will be no orange carnival. All this shall come to pass. How do I know? Because the Dutch presence at the World Cup will be like that of the Bruce Willis character in *The Sixth Sense*. Holland will be there in spirit only. In the movie, Willis gets shot by one of his patients. With the Dutch, as per bloody usual, the wound is entirely self-inflicted.

In July 2000, Louis van Gaal, arguably the most influential coach of the 1990s, succeeded to his birthright. The ebullient former Ajax boss became coach of the national team and vowed to win the 2002 World Cup. His simple first step was to guide his team through the obligatory qualifying tournament. Holland faced three fall-guys (Andorra, Estonia and Cyprus) one potentially tricky team, Ireland (who hadn't reached a major tournament in six years), and one obviously dangerous side, Portugal (semi-finalists at Euro 2000). In order to advance, the Dutch only had to finish second out of six. They beat the fall guys easily enough, as did their rivals. But in the four matches that mattered, against the Irish and Portugese, Holland proved themselves once again to be willfully, irredeemably, perversely Dutch.

First, unfashionable Ireland came to the Amsterdam Arena. The Dutch started the game like dilettantes; elegant as always, but patently bored by the whole affair. As they made pretty patterns, the Irish ran and tackled. Then Ireland took the lead. Then they scored again. Two goals down, the Dutch realised they had a game on their hands and rallied. In the last twenty minutes, they evened the score at 2-2. Exciting stuff, but a draw meant Holland had dropped two points in their first game. Ooops!

Next up: Portugal, in Rotterdam. This time the Dutch suffered hearing difficulties. For Portugal's crucial first goal, goalkeeper Edwin van der Sar was distracted by a whistle blown in the crowd. As he and his defenders hesitated, thinking the referee had stopped the game, Sergio Conceição nipped in to score. Portugal's second goal followed a blunder by Michael Reiziger playing on the left side of defense instead of his usual right. Van Gaal was unapologetic: 'Reiziger makes mistakes when he plays on the right too,' he explained later. Portugal won 2-0.

Having blown two vital matches, Holland was now in trouble. But they'd been in worse scrapes before, and if they could win the return match against the Portugese in March, all would be well. When the big night came in Porto, Holland rose to the occasion thrillingly. Properly motivated at last, orange waves surged and overwhelmed the hosts. Early on, the Dutch got a penalty. Jerrel Hasselbaink volunteered, stepped off a ridiculously short run and crabbed a terrible shot onto the post. Astoundingly, the ball squirmed across the line. Hasselbaink celebrated by running into the goal, burying his face in the netting, his entire body quivering with joy, and screaming. In the second half, Kluivert scored a second goal and the Dutch started to coast. Late in the match, Van Gaal made his move. Most coaches in this situation would put on extra defenders or midfielders to close the game, but Van Gaal did the opposite. Looking for another goal, he sent on forwards. First, striker Roy Makaay replaced winger Boudewijn Zenden, then Pierre van Hooijdoink came on for Hasselbaink. This was not an act of madness. If the Dutch won by three goals instead of two, they would be ahead if the teams finished the group even on points. Van Gaal was taking a big risk, though. With seven minutes left, the Dutch failed to clear and Pauleta seized on the defensive error to score. Like a boxer losing on points who lands a lucky punch to swing the fight, the Portugese suddenly came storming back for the equaliser. Holland, with too many forwards on the field, were ill-equipped to hold out. Two minutes into injury time, Portugal won a penalty. With the last kick of the match, Luis Figo, a protégé of Cruyff at Barcelona, but certainly no Dutchman when it comes to taking penalties, converted with aplomb. The draw would take Portugal to the World Cup. From the jaws of magnificent victory, the Dutch had snatched absurd disaster.

Nevertheless things could still turn out right. If Holland won their next match, in Dublin, they could finish second in the group and reach the World Cup via a playoff against Iran. I mentioned to Patrick Kluivert, whose website I'd been ghosting, that I was getting a bit worried. 'Don't worry,' he said. 'We have to win, that's all there is to it. We're not thinking about anything else. Everything will be OK.' Two weeks before the match Holland warmed up with a friendly against England in London. The Dutch easily won the match, 2-0, and played with such style that the English drooled with admiration. It seemed like 1977 all over again: the Dutch played a game of such poise and power that the English could barely understand them, let alone hope to compete. How, the English wondered, could such a team possibly fail to reach the World Cup?

D-Day. Dublin, September 1, 2001. Holland must win to qualify for the World Cup. Ireland needs a draw. The Dutch approach the match with total confidence. Despite all previous disappointments, they expect to win comfortably, a view shared by almost everyone in Ireland. Apart from Roy Keane and Robbie Keane (who, not being Dutch, are not brothers), the Irish squad consists mainly of unglamorous players from the English league. No one gives them a prayer.

In the second minute of the match, Kluivert robs an Irish defender and bursts through on goal. His shot, though, slides narrowly wide. More chances come and go as Van Bommel, Zenden and Van Nistelrooy miss when they should score. But Ireland, famous in football for their big hearts and noisy, sweet-natured fans, refuse to follow the script. Inspired by Roy Keane, snarling epitome of English-style aggression, they tackle, chase and harry. Holland has more skill, but they can't match Ireland's energy.

The Dutch begin to lose momentum, and the longer the score stays 0-0, the edgier they become. With thirty-five minutes to go, Van Gaal surprisingly takes off Zenden and sends on Hasselbaink, normally a centre-forward, but now asked to play an unfamiliar role as a winger. At his best, Hasselbaink is an explosive performer and Holland desperately needs a big bang just now.

Almost immediately, they get a potentially match-winning lucky break. Gary Kelly is sent off for a silly foul, so now it's eleven Dutchmen against ten Irishmen. As long as Holland sticks to passing and movement, Ireland can't hope to plug all the gaps. The pressure mounts. A goal is surely imminent. In a desperate scramble, the Irish goalkeeper knocks down Van Nistelrooy, but the referee fails to award a penalty. Then Van Gaal sends on yet another centre-forward, Van Hooijdonk, in place of defender Arthur Numan.

Two minutes later, a goal finally arrives—for Ireland. Jason McAteer, a thirty-year-old member of Blackburn Rovers's reserve team, races into a gap in the Dutch defence the size of Zeeland to gleefully ping a volley past Van der Sar. Lansdowne Road goes nuts. Holland still has twenty-five minutes and some of the supposedly best players in the world to save the game, but they start to panic. Van Gaal, a repressed emotional presence on the touchline at the best of times, but now agitated beyond control, makes one final, disastrous substitution. He withdraws his second and most dangerous winger, Marc Overmars, who's been playing well, and sends on midfielder Giovanni van Bronckhorst. Van Bronckhorst is not quick like Overmars, and he isn't famous for his crosses. Holland now has four centre-forwards on the field: Van Nistelrooy, Kluivert, Van Hooijdonk (all getting in each other's way in the centre) and Hasselbaink (who seems to have no idea what to do on the wing and keeps cutting in for hopeless long-range shots). With their balance broken and their composure in tatters the Dutch – the sophisticated, ever-thoughtful Dutch – begin to play perhaps the most idiotic football in their history. Instead of trying to work the ball forward or find gaps, they resort to long, diagonal crosses to the crowded edge of the Irish penalty area. The ball, of course, keeps rebounding harmlessly. For decades, the Dutch have mocked the English for playing this way, but at least the English know how to do it effectively. Van Gaal has by now lost all control and is rushing up and down, gesticulating wildly and screaming at his players, who ignore him. In the bedlam, a few chances still come, but the Dutch forwards snatch at them and miss. In the end, the Irish are able to hang on quite easily.

Thus died the World Cup dreams of the 'generation without a backbone,' as the Dutch team was quickly dubbed. It also signalled the end of the wildly hubristic notion that Dutch footballers, especially those from Ajax, are *godenzonen*. Those whom the Gods destroy, they first make madly successful. Van Gaal, who was forced to resign three months later, made tactical mistakes. But it's hard not to sympathise with his complaint that his players let him down. In the mid-nineties, with essentially the same group, Van Gaal took similar chances and won. But his hungry tyros of 1995 have changed. At Ajax, Van Gaal motivated his players in training by yelling at them: 'You'll have to work harder than *that* if you want to get rich!' The tactic worked not wisely but too well. By 2001, most of the Dutch national team played for the biggest clubs of Europe, some earning more in a couple of months than most *totaalvoetballers* made in their whole careers in the seventies. The stars no longer liked to be lectured and scolded. They grumbled that Van Gaal would be better suited to work as an army instructor. If there was any way to motivate the Dutch players to exert themselves – just a little bit – to qualify for the World Cup, Van Gaal couldn't find it. But then he should never have had to.

Through their grotesque complacency, the Dutch stars betrayed their own talent. Many of the side will still be young enough to try to redeem themselves at Euro 2004. But the heart of the team – Edgar Davids, Philip Cocu, the De Boer brothers – will all be too old for the next World Cup in Germany in 2006. Even the relative youngsters Kluivert and Van Nistelrooy will be thirty.

Financial experts calculate that failure to reach the World Cup will cost the Dutch economy zillions of guilders. It will also dent Holland's international profile. Few outside the country have heard of the queen or prime minister, but almost everyone (apart from North Americans) has a soft spot for the men in orange.

The consequences for Dutch football itself are harder to gauge, but they could be dire. In the immediate wake of Dublin, there was much talk of the need for 'pragmatism' and a more 'realistic' approach. At Ajax, who are in as bad shape as at any time in the club's post-war history, coach Co Adriaanse (disciple of Van Gaal) promptly dispensed with double wingers and adopted a more defensive, Italian-style 3-5-2 system. Much good it did him. The team, a feeble parody of the great Ajax sides of the past, fell to a lowly Danish club in the Uefa Cup and Adriaanse was fired.

The Dutch have been down this road before. In the early eighties, at the end of *totaalvoetbal*, Dutch coaches followed a world-wide trend towards defensive football and Holland failed to reach the finals of three tournaments in a row. The big difference between then and now is that at that time Cruyff returned to Ajax, first as player, then as coach, and almost single-handedly guided the new generation to the sublime. Cruyff, who had major heart surgery in 1991, has influenced all the truly great Dutch footballers of the last forty years. But he is now semi-detached from football. He hasn't coached in five years and is increasingly devoted to his myriad educational and health charities, among them the Johan Cruyff Foundation and the Johan Cruyff University. Having discovered the richness of a world outside football, it seems unlikely his fertile mind can be lured back. He speaks now through media interviews and on his website rather than in the dressing room or on the training pitch.

More alarming is the lack of obvious emerging world-class talent in Holland. There are plenty of skillful youngsters about. But where are the truly exceptional, the Cruyffs, Van Hanegems, Van Bastens and Bergkamps? No one seems to know. Ajax's eighteen-year old midfielder Rafael van der Vaart, who lives in a caravan, tops the list of Dutch teenagers considered potential Next Big Things. But there is a gulf between potential and the real thing. Johan Cruyff, for one, takes a provocatively bleak view. For years, Cruyff has berated Holland's coaching establishment for failing to nurture genius. Not even Van der Vaart impresses him yet. Cruyff was recently asked if he wanted to be national coach. He said he didn't see any point as there was so little promising material to work with: 'There is no potential, no mentality. There is nothing.'

Most other observers are more optimistic, arguing that talent exists in sufficient quantities to ensure future generations of Dutch delight. Some even claim that losing to Ireland may prove a blessing in disguise, a stimulus to take future qualification tournament seriously. Whatever the future holds, though, don't expect the Dutch to rush to change their values.

Other important football countries may see failure in terms of humiliation and national disgrace, but not the Dutch. When Italy lost a World Cup match to North Korea in 1966, their players were pelted with rotten fruit and hysterical abuse. For Andres Escobar, the Colombian who scored an own-goal for the USA in 1994, it was worse. Escobar was shot dead a few days later by an angry fan. One England World Cup defeat was famously greeted by a tabloid headline screaming: 'The End of the World.' And when England failed to reach the 1994 tournament the BBC cleared its TV schedules for a two-hour special on the crisis facing the nation and its football.

By contrast, the reaction in the Netherlands to defeat by Ireland seemed almost eerily reasonable. There was no rending of garments. No one spoke of national decline. Newspapers, for the most part, treated the calamity as a sports story and kept it off the news and op-ed pages. Soon after the final whistle in Dublin, Henk Kessler, the KNVB's director of professional football, was asked by reporters if he considered the defeat a disaster for the Netherlands. The very idea seemed to appall him. 'Remember,' he said, 'this is still just a game.'

index

acknowledgements

My heartfelt thanks to all the people quoted in the book who so generously gave me their time, insights and knowledge. My equal gratitude to all the other people who helped in big and small ways at various stages of the project and without whom this book would not exist: Max Arian, Robert Aspeslagh, Frits Barend, Aaron Betsky, Fred Blankemeyer, Hugo Borst, Joram ten Brink, Carissa Bub, Edith van Campen, Egmont Children's Books, Ingrid Coltart, Lex van Dam, Tamar Dromi, David Endt, Annie Fisher, Oscar van Gelderen, Brian Glanville, Loes Gompes, Harke Groenevelt, Jeroen Henneman, Engeline Henny, Herman Hertzberger, Egbert van Hes, Jan van der Hoef, Bernard Hulsman, Cor Jaring, Mike Jones, Milika de Jonge, Jane Judd, Sean Kelly, James Kennedy, Chris Keulemans, Frank van Kolfschooten, Momo Kovacevic, Simon Kuper, Jan Leerkes, Eric van Leeuwen, George Lewith, Monica Macdonald, Virginie Mamadouh, Chris Maume, Hans van der Meer, Jan Michael, Matthijs van Nieuwkerk, Bouke Oldenhof, Hans Oldewarris, Guy Oliver, Aart Oxenaar, Jos de Putter, Gerhard Rein, Hans Righart, Jennifer Rupp, Francien Schoonens, Ineke Schwartz, Santiago Segurola, Henk Spaan, Peter Spier, John Thackara, Tjebbe van Tijen, Dalia Ventura, Isabel Verdurme, Evert Vermeer, Lucas Verweij, Jurryt van de Vooren, Lilian Widder- shoven, Faas Wilkes, Alexis Winner, Theun de Winter, Andy Woodcock.

David Winner, Amsterdam 2000